How to Complain:

The Essential Consumer Guide to Getting Refunds, Redress and Results!

Helen Dewdney
The Complaining Cow

www.thecomplainingcow.co.uk

Third Edition 2nd Revision 2019 published by The Complaining Cow

Although the author and publisher have made every effort to ensure that the information in this book was correct at going to press, the author and publisher do not assume and hereby disclaim any liability to any party for any loss, damage, or disruption caused by errors or omissions, whether such errors or omissions result from negligence, accident, or any other cause. If professional advice or other expert assistance is required, the services of a competent professional should be sought.

ISBN 978-0-9930704-2-6

The Complaining Cow
Trademark of Helen Dewdney
www.thecomplainingcow.co.uk

CONTENTS

This book is dedicated to my father John Dewdney who along with my mother brought me up to be principled. Without this grounding I would never have developed such a passion for complaining for the principle of the thing. He never quite finished his book on philosophy. I hope he would have been proud of mine.

Also to my son Oliver, the Complaining Calf who appears to be a chip off the old block!

The Complaining Cow

1 INTRODUCTION

I am The Complaining Cow and I complain effectively. I've been complaining effectively for over 30 years. When I was about 12 years old, I started a school magazine. I got a couple of friends together and we sold each copy for 10p. Then something annoyed me. The boys and girls were put together for P.E. and we only did "boys' games". I had no problem with playing what were considered then to be "boys' games" (aside from hating all sports of course!) My issue was that we never played netball - the only game I was actually good at. I played Goal Attack – I'm sure I liked that position because it had the word "Attack" in it! Anyway I digress... I mentioned this to my father who casually said "I wonder what the Sex Discrimination Act would say about that…" So did I and through the magazine I decided to ask the whole school if they did. The result? I got stopped from producing the magazine. Staff it appeared did not want the pupils or perhaps their parents to wonder about this question. However, the following week the discrimination (as I perceived it) stopped and we played netball.

Now of course, I would write an article about equality, varied curriculum, anti discriminatory practice, etc. etc. But of course it wouldn't be happening, the equivalent now might be not letting the girls play football? Back in the 80's I think it was poor planning and laziness – perhaps the head teacher wasn't aware that the staff were putting everyone together every week? Who knows? But what I do know, is that though most of the pupils were moaning about it at the time no-one did anything about it. So I did. That was the difference. It was the principle of the thing. It gave me my first lesson in censorship, stopped my tiny earnings, got me into trouble and was probably the first of the many times that my name came up in the staff room. But most importantly it made a change. Remember that this was long before the concept of School Councils where such issues would now easily be discussed by pupils with staff. That was the start of my passion for effecting change.

As a teenager I wrote to Jackie magazine talking about an organisation that raised funds for alternatives to experimenting on animals and got my letter printed. They didn't pay up so I had to write and complain. At college I wrote to Nursery World informing them that "100's of jobs" was grammatically incorrect twice over. No-one responded but they did change the fortnightly cover.

So, I pinpoint my censorship episode as the time I decided that if I was going to complain I was going to be effective. Principle of the thing, if it was wrong it should be brought to the Powers That Be's attention regardless of the names I got/get called for doing it. This has probably been the driving force in my life, fighting for the rights of children and young people, fighting the systems in local government (as employee and resident) and fighting for better customer service. All boils down to the same thing, sometimes changes have to be made, it is the "Principle of the Thing".

As I grew out of childhood and spent my own money I applied my "Principle of the Thing" mantra to goods and services when things weren't up to scratch.

I will complain about any amount. Not because I'm a serial or extreme complainer. 40p? Really you ask? Yes really. Wrongly charged. Principle! I complained about 40p. Yes I did, and here's why. I completed an online shopping order. All seemed fine. When I received my order with receipt, I checked it against the items. Oddly there was an additional item. This item was called "Department Sale". What sort of vegetable is that you ask as well you might and so did I! I asked what this item was and apparently I had had two of them! Two lots of 20ps totalling 40p. So I was curious and as you know if you read my blog regularly, it's a matter of principle! After asking about these charges this is how the email exchange panned out:

Supermarket: If you order an item that isn't on the online product database, we're unable to scan the item through the home shopping system at your local store. So, to make sure that we don't overcharge you for the product, we charge it at a heavily reduced price. This will show on your delivery paperwork as a 10p charge for example. I hope this has explained why we do this and thank you for taking the time to ask us about this.

Me: But what is the item?!!

Supermarket: I am sorry that there has been such confusion over this issue and for the inconvenience being caused. Could you advise me of where this charge is shown on your order, and how much it is? I may be able to trace the product for you.

Me: You have had this information in the initial complaint. See attached please.

Supermarket: I am sorry but I have been unable to trace the exact goods that the charge relates to. However I have refunded the 40p back to your account and this will appear in 3 to 5 days. Thank you for your patience in this matter.

Me: So what you are saying is that there was no reason for this charge? I wonder how many other orders you put this charge on?

Supermarket: Not at all! There was a reason for the charge as has been explained in previous emails. The problem is that without seeing what goods were physically delivered and then going through the delivery document to deduce which goods the charge was used for, it is impossible to say exactly what the charge was applied to.

Me: How can you order something online for an online order that isn't on the database?

Supermarket: Very easily when you start to understand that the online business and the store are different. An example would be where you might order apples online, but the store offer a regional variety of that apple which is not stored on our database. So to enable us to pick apples for you, we would have to mark it as a Department Sale to add it onto the order.

Me: I didn't order anything that I've not ordered before and I've never had that remark on a receipt and I had nothing additional delivered. Very dubious.

So for me, I wonder how many people are charged 40p and don't complain? It drives up fat cat profits and if more people complained these things would happen less often.

I often shared my complaints with friends and family on Facebook and from there people encouraged me to write a blog and from there I've provided help and advice through Facebook, Twitter and YouTube as well as the blog at www.thecomplainingcow.co.uk. And then there was great cry for a book! So here it is – the ultimate guide to complaining effectively and gaining redress.

I often get asked what I do to ensure that I gain redress each time I complain. It isn't always with the first email and sometimes not even the second. But one thing is for sure, I've certainly gained redress by the time I've finished!

Complaining effectively isn't rocket science and you do not need to be a lawyer but nor is it simple. Many factors come into play. Through this guide I will provide tips, examples or real cases where I have complained for myself or on behalf of someone else. I offer templates and advice on what to do when you need to take further action.

2 HOW TO USE THIS BOOK

In the following chapters you will find out about the different types of complainers, tips on how to complain effectively, common ways that consumers are fobbed off, the use of social media in complaining and an outline of the consumer laws that you may need.

I recommend emailing your complaints for speed, reliability and to keep a record of what has been said. Should you not be satisfied with the response you receive to your complaint I also include details on how you can take the matter further (to the relevant ombudsman for example).

This book is a guide to complaining to a variety of sectors. These sectors are in chapters and each chapter covers which laws protect you for particular goods and services and provides templates. In these templates I have used "xx" or a few more "xxx"s and/or bold for those parts which you will need to fill in relating to your particular case.

If you use the templates then you will need to add the person's/company's name and address to the left and yours and the date to the right. Templates end with "sincerely/ faithfully so delete as appropriate. (Sincerely when you know the person's name and faithfully when using Sir/Madam). Then sign your name and type your name underneath. If you email just put your name with a scanned signature if you have one. "Attachments" for email but "enclosures" for letters and list the enclosures after your name at the bottom of the letter.

Templates usually end in a standard format. "Should I not be fully satisfied with your response I will not hesitate in taking the matter further. This will include but not be limited to...."You may want to add relevant social media, Internet forums, review sites and consumer programmes. Please be aware that many of these templates use the

Consumer Rights Act 2015. If you are using this book to complain about a purchase/ service before this date a template may have the line "For services prior to 1st October 2015 quote "Supply of Goods and Services Act 1982"" – use this to replace the words "Consumer Rights Act 2015". If a template has the line "For purchases prior to 1st October 2015 then quote "Sale and Supply of Goods Act 1994""

I always state that I expect a reply within 7 days unless there are specific codes to follow. However, many consumer advice people will advise 14. I don't think there is any hard and fast rule, I'm just harsh and impatient. I've never had anyone come back and say I should have said 14, I just don't see the point in giving them more time. Traders may come back within 7 days and say that they are investigating the matter and will be in contact in x number of days. That is acceptable to me. If they don't get back in contact when they say they will or don't give me a date then that is not acceptable. In the latter case they will be given a maximum of 10 days and so far it has worked for me.

In some sections I have also provided stories and/or breakdowns of correspondence where I have complained in similar circumstances. These won't necessarily work as templates but do show you how effective complaints work. They also serve to show how much time is sometimes required.

There is also a section on the Small Claims Court process should your complaint need to reach this stage.

This book is for reference, it isn't a novel! So an index has been provided at the end for ease of finding out about the complaint you want. Also at the back of the book is a list of useful addresses including website addresses for taking the matter further.

3 WHAT TYPE OF COMPLAINER ARE YOU?

I believe that there are many types of complainers. Whatever type you are, this book will help you become more effective in your complaining.

The Professional Complainer

This title annoys me. A lot. I often get asked if I am a professional complainer. It is an utterly ridiculous term. I haven't trained to be a complainer. I haven't got any qualifications in complaining and I don't do it as a job – although I do now take up people's complaints for them when all else has failed and they need some help. I see this as providing consultancy advice and not what people mean when they ask "Are you a Professional Complainer?" No-one is a professional complainer. It is insulting to those with a profession.

The Serial Complainer

I often get asked if I am this kind of a complainer too. I think this term is best suited to people who complain continually to the same company. Frequently they have been offered some redress but they keep on spending a disproportionate amount of time on complaints. They 'phone the company, send emails, send letters and never give up – often over trivial matters.

The Extreme Complainer

Similar to the Serial Complainer, this person complains when the time spent is not comparable with the possible redress gained. S/he will complain about anything and everything sometimes with an end in mind but usually just for the sake of it and not because they feel genuinely aggrieved. There's a difference between complaining about the principle of some rotten apples for £1 and complaining about the assistant who annoyingly asks "Can I help you?" and hangs around when you just want to browse. That's subjective and annoys the heck out of me and I'll moan about it but I won't complain to anyone to gain redress!

The Dishonest Complainer

Serial and extreme complainers probably give a bad name to people who complain effectively and regularly with good reason. In addition to wasting their own time they often waste customer services' staff time which could be better spent with reasonable complainers. But the Dishonest Complainers are in a league of their own. They make up stories and complaints, putting hairs in meals for example, just to gain freebies.

The Opportunist Complainer

Similarities with The Dishonest Complainer. The Opportunist Complainers look for opportunities to complain and gain something to which they are usually not entitled, often keeping on at customer services until they are paid to "go away".

The Rude Complainer

This type of complainer can often be ineffective, serial and/or extreme. Swearing and shouting at staff and/or writing abusive letters/emails rightly rarely gains redress.

The Amusing Complainer

These complainers are a little bit different. Really good Amusing Complainers have gained media coverage for their complaints, such as the Sons of Maxwell's "United Breaks Guitars" song that went viral. (See it on YouTube) and the hilarious letter written to Richard Branson regarding the food on a Virgin flight. Amusing Complainers don't always need to know their legal rights if their correspondence is entertaining enough and the receiver has a sense of humour. This complaining style is usually effective but sometimes humour doesn't gain redress and to ensure that, they will need to become an effective complainer.

The Innovative Complainer

These are to be admired I have to say. Being innovative will usually work. Often the

Amusing Complainer falls into this category but to be truly innovative the quality needs to be more than just enough to make friends and family smile. My cousin 'phoned up a toy manufacturer's CEO's secretary and pretended to be from the BBC in order to gain access to the CEO. She was put through to him directly and went through her complaint. It can't be done with every complaint but when a complainer is innovative the response is usually good.

The Ineffective Complainer

This person tries. Not assertive, not knowing their legal rights, ineffective complainers try to get refunds but rarely get them. They get fobbed off when they try and complain. The Ineffective Complainer may vent a tweet or a post on a Facebook page but not follow it up to gain redress.

The Effective Complainer

In order always to gain redress one needs to be an effective complainer. The Effective Complainers know their legal rights, assert them politely and will not be fobbed off – when the company they paid tries to blame the manufacturer or delivery company for example.

4 ENSURING YOUR COMPLAINTS ARE EFFECTIVE

Follow these guidelines and you'll never be palmed off again with excuses, contravention of laws and no refunds. Feel empowered and get complaining effectively.

Act quickly

Don't waste weeks moaning, complain that day but remember to ensure you are calm if complaining in person or on the 'phone! So, although I say act quickly, don't act immediately if you are still really annoyed with someone, or something, that has happened and the company is at fault. Wait to write or 'phone until you are calmer but don't leave it so long you forget the facts.

What do you want?

Before you make contact, work out what you are entitled to and what you want. These may be two different things too! Say what you expect as recompense. Is it an apology, a refund, something for inconvenience or compensation? Be reasonable but assertive. Be prepared to come to an agreement. Generally speaking if you accept an offer of compensation it will mean that you cannot ask for more later on.

Telephoning

Use the telephone if you are comfortable doing this. Some people prefer this, finding it easier. But I rarely ring and always refuse if a 'phone call is offered. This is because I get heated (raise your voice and you've lost!), there is no record for future use, no proof of what was said and you'll forget something. Emails/letters provide time to reflect, ensure you don't forget anything and provide you with a record of correspondence which cannot be denied. If you do 'phone ensure that you get the full name of the person with whom you are talking, making a note of date, time and details of the conversation during the call. Always follow up in writing unless the 'phone call resolves the problem. Get the name of the person to whom you should address the complaint to reduce the likelihood of your letter being passed around.

Validity

Ensure your grievance is valid. Don't waste your time sending pointless correspondence with little weight – it won't get you anywhere. They need to know that you are serious. You don't want to be seen as an Extreme, Serial or Opportunist Complainer.

Company procedures

Be mindful of company procedures regarding complaints such as insurance claims, to ensure that you remain entitled to compensation. Certain companies such as suppliers of energy have their own procedures and you must follow these or risk delays in dealing with your complaint. Following two stages of internal complaint procedures for example before writing to the ombudsman. The ombudsman is likely to see in the company's favour if you have not followed procedure for correctly notifying it of your issues.

Initial complaint

Try to sort things out through Customer Services/the Manager first. If you are still not happy, then go to the CEO. You have more reason to go to the top if you have a complaint which has already been poorly dealt with than if you go straight there. Look up www.ceoemail.com for contact details for CEOs.

Correspondence

The easiest way to complain is by email and you can select "send a delivery receipt". However, if you write a letter, particularly if you need to post evidence which can't be emailed, ensure that you send the letter recorded delivery.

Good English

Use good English! PLEASE! Poor grammar and spelling show you in as negative a light as the company to which you are complaining. You also won't be taken seriously and anything you have to say will be taken with a pinch of salt if you can't get your own house in order!

The complaint handler may also make judgments about you, if you can't write well then you are unlikely to be able to take the matter further, to court for example. Ask for help from friends or family if necessary to help compose a letter.

Be formal. Use "Yours sincerely" when you know the person's name and "Yours faithfully" when Dear Sir or Madam. No "love from"s – I've seen it!

Don't write all in capitals. This is the equivalent of shouting which will not get you anywhere. Also it makes it very difficult to read so you will not be allowing the reader to see your complaint in the best light or get them in the mood to want to help!

Be polite

Remember that the people you are dealing with are usually not the people who have annoyed you and they are more likely to respond positively if you are polite. I am tempted to be sarcastic in nearly every letter I send but rarely does the complaint warrant it. Only use it after careful consideration and if it adds some humour. Never ever swear! Be rude and they can understandably refuse to deal with you. When the 'phone goes dead and you think the call centre person has hung up on you they probably have if you were shouting at them. If you ask for the recording of the call to be listened to by a senior member of staff and expect the call centre member of staff to be reprimanded think again. (Unless of course you weren't rude and they were in the wrong!)

Be objective

Don't accuse and insult with phrases such as "…she was stupid," use words and phrases like "…it appeared to me that…" Do however state facts. Don't make personal remarks about staff, they serve only to distract attention from the actual complaint.

Describe events

Bullet points are useful and make it very clear, especially when dates are involved. The easier you make it for the reader the easier it will be for them to resolve the matter for you. Be succinct.

If the complaint is long, summarise the points (e.g. 10 phone calls, 2 visits, 2 letters, wrong information etc.) Stick to the facts.

Deadline

Set a deadline for when you expect to hear back and let them know what you will be doing if you don't receive a satisfactory response. For letters/emails I believe 7 working days to be adequate. A longer deadline is needed sometimes. For instance if you are seeking repairs to your house. Keep to those deadlines yourself in any follow up. Be aware of deadlines in some companies' complaints procedures.

Terms and Conditions

Make sure you read through the terms and conditions of your contract carefully before complaining about a service. Look at what you signed up for and whether anything has been breached. Remember that even if you think that the contract frees the provider from any blame that it is still possible that it could be in breach of unfair contract terms.

Legal rights

Exercise your legal rights and use the relevant laws and legal jargon wherever possible. Showing that you know and use your legal rights appropriately means that you will always be taken seriously. Make sure you use the correct years and phrases. All the ones you may need are in this book. Quote them.

Reference numbers

Use reference numbers where appropriate. Make it easy for them to find your case by quoting booking references for example.

Evidence

Collect all the evidence you might need, such as invoices, receipts, adverts, witness statements etc. Keep copies of everything; you may need them if you have to take the matter further (Senior Management, Small Claims Court etc.)

Send copies where appropriate. For example, if a faulty washing machine has destroyed some clothes, send pictures of the clothes. As well as the refund on the washing machine you are entitled to compensation for the clothes.

Always try and obtain the name(s) of anyone you are complaining about, who gave you advice, wrote to you etc. and use these names in any correspondence.

Loyalty

Point out what a good customer you are and how, for example, you have always found the company to be really good in the past. This shows that you are a frequent customer so they are less likely to risk losing you.

Amounts

Some people advise suggesting a suitable amount for compensation/redress if you feel confident in doing this – and can back up your reasoning. However, I personally hate doing this because I always feel that I'll go in for the wrong amount. Usually a company offers more than I think and if a company offers much less than I think the complaint warrants then I will respond with my reasoning. A safer option I feel.

Don't apologise

Never ever apologise for complaining! If your complaint is valid then you are owed something and the company should thank you for bringing it to their attention so that they can improve service for all customers.

Taking things further

Inform them that if you are not happy you will take the matter further using the relevant people and organisations e.g. Financial Ombudsman, Trading Standards, Small Claims Court, the company's own complaints procedure, the media, review sites - even The Complaining Cow's Blog! You really only want to threaten if you are sure that it will have the desired effect and you are prepared to spend the time and effort taking it further (Small Claims Court for example).

If in your first correspondence to customer services you have indicated that you will take the matter further and you do remain dissatisfied, be persistent and go back and complain again, explaining why you remain unhappy. Go to the CEO explaining why and that you trust s/he will agree and resolve the matter speedily. If they don't, carry out the threat to go to the ombudsman, Small Claims Court etc. and don't be afraid of doing so.

Negotiating

When negotiating amounts write "Without prejudice" on your correspondence, this means that the amounts cannot be used in court. Ensure that you don't put this on your other correspondence. Whilst you have legal rights, you also have a legal obligation to keep your claim reasonable.

Agreements

Ensure you keep to your end of any agreement. After agreeing to post an item back for example, and being paid to do so, do not then say at a later point that you think it would be better just to dispose of it.

Accepting repairs

If you accept a repair ensure that you state that you are reserving your rights under the Sale of Goods Act 1979 (prior to 1st October 2015, thereafter the Consumer Rights Act 2015). This means that you can still claim full redress if the repair does not work or you are charged for it.

Returns

You are not obliged to take faulty items back to the retailer. However, your contract can require you to return goods to the place where you took possession of them, such as the retail shop. In this case the cost of return is your responsibility. Likewise, if you choose to return the goods to the original shop even though the contract does not require you to do so, then you have to bear that cost.

Why People Fail in Gaining Redress

You get poor service at the restaurant and don't complain. In my *How, When and Why Do You Complain?* survey in July 2014 (see *www.thecomplainingcow.co.uk* for full results) I posed the question "If you usually don't complain is it because..." 59% of respondents gave reasons for not complaining and only 41% said that they always complained.)

But what if you do complain but you don't gain redress? You buy an item that's faulty but you don't get a refund. Why? What's going wrong? The most likely reasons are detailed below:

1) Your expectations are too low. You think that the item was cheap so what do you expect? You think the meal you had at that place last time was bad so you aren't surprised when it is again. If a kettle was bought to boil water it should boil water. Simple! If you buy a meal it should be made with reasonable skill and care. If you had a bad meal there last time you should have complained and maybe things would have improved!

2) You don't know your legal rights. The main ones you need to know are The Sale of Goods Act 1979 (amended to the Sale and Supply of Goods Act 1994) and The Supply of Goods and Services Act 1982. Items should be of satisfactory quality, be fit for purpose, be as described and last a reasonable length of time. Your contract is always with the company that sold you the item. Services should be undertaken with reasonable skill and care and within a reasonable length of time. This is the same under the Consumer Rights Act 2015 from 1st October 2015. See chapter 5, *Consumer Rights*, for further details.

   In the survey mentioned above, only 7% said they knew their legal rights well and used them regularly. 5% know the basics of the Sale of Goods Act and Supply of Goods and Services Act 1982. A further 33% say that they check out their rights before complaining – but they may not of course always do so. In short, these percentages indicate that less than half of people complaining know and use their legal rights.

3) You think it will take too much time and effort. In the survey mentioned above, 46% of respondents said that when they don't complain it is because it takes too much effort or going back to the shop arguing about refunds takes too much time. Well, if you know your legal rights you won't be arguing, you'll be assertive. And if you still don't gain redress you can take the matter further, by which time you will be asking for more than a refund.

4) You shout at people on the 'phone or in person. Would you give me what I wanted if I yelled at you? Think, be polite, particularly as the person or people at fault aren't usually the people to whom you complain.

5) You've gone back to the wrong shop or rung your home 'phone provider instead of the mobile 'phone provider. Yes I have heard examples from both consumers and retailers. Check your facts first.

6) You think that because you have lost the receipt you can't get your money back.

Wrong. You just need proof of purchase such as a credit card bill.

7) You don't like complaining and aren't assertive. Fair enough, but seriously? You'd rather be out of pocket? If you are in the right you have nothing to worry about!

8) You are complaining about something trivial or you aren't out of pocket. There is a difference between complaining about 99p for a foul cup of coffee because it is the principle of the thing and complaining that you don't like the colour of the carpet in the cafe.

9) You are being dishonest and seriously exaggerating the fault or the inconvenience. Do this and you will usually be seen through and get less than if you had just been honest in the first place.

Common Fob Offs!

Many companies and individuals will try and fob you off in order not to give you a refund or redress. With 46% of consumers saying that they think it is too much effort to complain it isn't difficult for companies to put many people off as soon as they start to complain. Below are some common fob offs of which you should be aware and know how to deal with.

"We do not give refunds" Signs like this are illegal and you can report them to Trading Standards. Traders do not have to give you a refund if you have simply changed your mind about a purchase or the jumper didn't fit, for example. But if the item is faulty you are legally entitled to a full refund, (unless the fault was pointed out at time of purchase). This right is in place (until the time that you are deemed to have "accepted" the goods. "Accepted" is generally thought to be up to 4 weeks until 1st October 2015. Thereafter the Consumer Rights Act 2015 states that the right to reject goods lasts for 30 days unless the expected life of the goods is shorter, as with highly perishable goods.

"You/we will send it back to the manufacturer" Your contract is always with whoever received your money. If you buy a kettle from store A which was made by company B and that kettle stops working you are entitled to the repair, refund or replacement from company A.

"You will need to contact the delivery firm" That kettle you bought from store A was delivered to your house and the delivery driver dropped it, or left it on the doorstep and it was stolen. Store A is wrong to tell you to contact the delivery firm. Your contract is with store A and you claim your refund from it. It can claim from the delivery firm!

"You should have taken out a warranty" Warranties are rarely worth the paper they are written on in my opinion! Items should last a reasonable length of time, a washing machine should last more than 6 months so it is wholly irrelevant whether you have taken out a warranty.

"We don't take back items bought in the sale" Unless the fault was pointed out at time of purchase (and therefore contributed to the sale price) your legal rights remain the same as if the item was sold at full price.

"You caused the fault" As a general rule of thumb, if an item breaks up to 6 months from purchase then it is up to the trader to prove that the fault was caused by you and was not there at time of purchase and therefore you are legally entitled to the full refund, repair or replacement. From 1st October 2015 this 6 months rule is set in the Consumer Rights Act 2015.

"You don't have the receipt so we can't give a refund" The law states proof of purchase so this could be a credit card bill, easier to find online now than an old receipt.

"It is over 6 months so we do not need to give a refund" As a general rule this is actually correct but if you can still prove that the fault was there at point of purchase and/or the item has not lasted 'a reasonable length of time' then you are entitled to a replacement or repair.

Call Centres

I asked on my Facebook page what people hated about call centres and without doubt the top hates were:

- speaking to people in different countries where communication was difficult and English was not their first language
- call centre staff just reading from a script
- call centre staff hanging up on calls
- music playing
- refusal to give names
- being passed from one department to another

- call centre staff not knowing the answer to questions
- refusal to pass you to someone senior
- having to go through all the keypad options before you get to speak to someone....

It would appear most of us don't have a good word to say about call centres.

The inside information from call centre staff

Interestingly, people who had worked in call centres gave some insight into why we get some of the problems. Here are some reasons:

Some of this information came from a member of staff from a very big well-known company as well as from call centres!

- The call queues waiting times are specifically designed to be long enough to encourage you to 'give up'. You will wait a designated 'minimum time' even if agents are available.
- Queue messages are designed to discourage you – "you are 457th in the queue" or plainly tell you to go away "many common issues can be resolved by visiting our web site at xxx.com" – and they will become increasingly discouraging as time passes.
- Response scripts are specifically designed to restrict what call handlers can do and, ideally, convert a call into a new sale. 'Escalation' paths for calls are specifically designed to delay or avoid resolution.
- Staff are given average call times.
- Passing the call on to another employee counts as a conclusion to the call (even when the caller is placed in another long queue elsewhere in the organisation).
- The computer systems used are terrible – not all data is available since the call centre is sometimes not run by the company you are calling.
- The call centre staff are not trained to give you satisfaction but to simply get close to the required percentage success rates.

What can you do?

I tend not to use call centres because they are generally so diabolical. I write. Where the matter is not urgent and this is a possibility, I always advise writing. Be clear, concise and polite. Make sure you have all the details and list the issues. Ensure you include all your account details. If you do not get a satisfactory response write to the CEO. You can find email contact details at www.ceoemail.com. For most companies you can consider taking the matter to the relevant ombudsman, e.g. Energy Ombudsman, CISAS,

Financial Ombudsman etc. You need to wait until 8 weeks after you start the complaint or request a "deadlock letter". This is a letter from the company stating that they will not communicate further on the matter.

If you have to ring, be polite, get the name of the person you are speaking to as soon into the conversation as you can. Make a note of the start and finish times of calls, including the length of time you were on the phone. If the person keeps repeating what they are saying and it is of no help ask to speak to a supervisor. You may or may not get this but note everything down. Ask them to send you confirmation on anything they have agreed, if possible whilst you are still on the 'phone. Be clear and assertive (but not aggressive) in what you want and provide deadlines for this. Under the Supply of Goods and Services Act 1982 (Consumer Rights Act 2015 from 1st October 2015) you are entitled to services to be carried out with reasonable skill and care. Leaving you on the 'phone and not answering queries or providing you with the service you are paying for is a breach and you can tell them so. Asserting your legal rights often gets you taken more seriously and you are more likely to get the call escalated. Follow up all bad experiences with a call centre with a letter/email of complaint detailing the problems and the issues with the call (as well as your original complaint!) and assert your legal rights. You should find you get some redress!

Helplines

A key point to note is that there is now a prohibition on not providing basic rate numbers for post-contract customer helplines. (Consumer Contracts (Information, Cancellation and Additional Charges) Regulations 2013). Where traders offer telephone helplines for consumers to contact them about something they have bought, there should be a number available for the consumer to call for this purpose at no more than the basic rate. This includes Financial institutions.

Comparison websites

These are a must for finding the cheapest deal. Try to use more than one comparison site as they do not all list every company. It may seem like tedious work but it can save you hundreds of pounds. You can use these for insurance, broadband, TV, energy and banking.

Check the terms and conditions of the site and tick the box that says you don't want to be contacted by anyone! It could be considered an Unfair Contract if the site states that it is not responsible for the information it provides. Check how the results are presented from one site to another and that the actual service provided is the same.

The Ofgem voluntary code of practice for price comparison websites now prevents them from displaying products on which they earn commission more prominently than those on which they don't.

Comparison websites 'accredited' by Ofgem must prominently list the energy companies from which they receive commission on sales, as well as clearly stating that they earn commission on certain tariffs. The websites will no longer be allowed to limit by default the tariffs that a consumer sees when making a search. Websites need to display all tariffs available to a consumer regardless of supplier. Sites that comply with the code are listed as 'accredited' by Ofgem and can display related logos on their sites.

Ofcom also has an accreditation scheme and members of this are listed on their website (and included in chapter 27 *Useful Contacts*). The key requirements of the Ofcom Price Accreditation Scheme are that information presented to consumers must be comprehensive, accurate and transparent. Accredited price comparison websites must show a good selection of providers (covering at least 90% of the market) and enable consumers to rank according to price. There isn't a requirement to show absolutely all deals in the market. Given the large number of small providers in some markets, it may not be practical for a price comparison website to list all providers and options.

The guidance states that commercial arrangements must be transparent. Ofcom accredited price comparison websites must not discriminate against particular providers and, where a selection of packages is included, this should not result in an unfair or unbiased representation of an operator. Accredited price comparison websites are prevented from filtering results by commission payments.

The FCA (Financial Conduct Authority) authorises and regulates some price comparison websites but it does not make recommendations. It undertook a review of comparison websites earlier this year and followed them up to ensure that they had addressed the specific issues identified. It will use the full range of regulatory tools available as appropriate if any of them have not done so. The FCA uses a wide range of enforcement powers – criminal, civil and regulatory – to protect consumers and to take action against firms or individuals that do not meet its standards. You can search for companies regulated by the FCA on the register on its website.

Using social media

There have been some great complaints on social media. David Caroll's United Airlines video and the man who paid for tweets to complain about BA losing his luggage (that worked out at a penny a tweet though, so why would you?) But these go viral because they provide something different not because the company has responded well to a complaint.

Remember February 2018 when KFC didn't have any chicken? Their Twitter feed was brilliant and they interacted with consumers hilariously. They even interacted with Iceland and people on Twitter loved it. KFC making jokes about the whole situation turned a potential PR disaster into a positive one, showing how they constructively deal with complaints. Most companies still have a long way to go in dealing with complaints generally as well as on social media.

So, complaining on social media – does it work? Paul Lewis (the freelance financial journalist who often appears on the BBC Money Box programme amongst others) in early 2014 asked how effective Twitter was for complaining. The responses to Paul's tweet were interesting. Many people said it was quicker than 'phoning though they were still having to email the issues in many cases. Others said that it was good for shaming. Others said it was good for getting a response but once into DMs (direct message) and emails it dropped off again. (This is one of the reasons I ended up taking Tesco to court. My last shot was to engage the social media team but they were still unable to help.) No-one had had any really complicated problem sorted but a few did get their issues addressed once the social media team got involved. It has been known for people to copy me into a tweet and have their issues resolved! That makes me laugh but people really shouldn't have to do that.

I tweet to the likes of Tesco, Marks and Spencer and Sainsbury's and gain redress. Now that's where I love Twitter for complaining. A quick picture of damaged or faulty goods and a tweet and bingo, done. Tweet back asking for order details, exchange a direct message (DM) and refund made. Perfect, and it probably takes slightly less time to do than an email and emails can take a long time to get a response. It also saves going to the shop to take something back.

So that's an example of social media working well. Basically where it is quick and simple it works really well. However for anything more than something that can be sorted quickly, how can limited characters possibly work? When I had a problem ordering stuff from The Body Shop, I tweeted the problem and their delay in responding to it. They were overwhelmed by emails tweets and FB messages with the same complaint and it didn't make any difference to the standard responses they were giving people. Nor did any issues get resolved. My detailed complaint to the CEO did get results though....!

In the How, When and Why Do You Complain? survey respondents were asked about using social media when complaining.

Remember the line "Receive good service tell 1, receive poor service tell 10"? Not anymore.

Fewer than 2% of people tell no-one.
49% tell 1 - 10 people
11% tell 10 - 20 and now
38% tell hundreds and sometimes thousands of people due to social media.

So companies should be warned! It is wholly irrelevant how many complaints they actually receive! 60% say they don't always complain but look how many people they are telling:

68% of respondents use social media to complain and 37% of those find it effective sometimes
16% find it always effective
12% find it is never effective
Clearly social media is on the rise.

Generally speaking, (and obviously I see a lot of complaining!) the responses to Paul's tweet confirmed what I see, get told and advise on as well as my own experience. Social media is another tool, nothing more and nothing less. It is another means by which you can complain. It has a place and I use it. It is quick but some companies are better than others at dealing with the complaints. This usually comes down to training in communication, processes etc. and whether staff have been adequately equipped with knowledge and are empowered. But it is still a mixed bag out there as to who is good and who isn't.

Alternative Dispute Resolution

ADR is a process that enables disputes between a consumer and a business to be settled via an independent mechanism outside the court system and can provide a quicker resolution. There are different forms of ADR:

- Arbitration – an impartial and independent third party will decide how to resolve your dispute. In most cases, the arbitrator's decision is binding and cannot be challenged in court. Costs vary and sometimes arbitration is free as with IDRS and ACAS services.
- Adjudication – by ombudsmen and free to the consumer. This is binding on the trader but not on you should you not agree and want to take the matter to court. For details of ombudsmen see the relevant sector chapter.
- Mediation/conciliation – remains confidential and cannot be used in a later court hearing. The cost varies: in some instances it's free; in others, it can get expensive (See chapter 27 *Useful Contacts*).
- Negotiation – which is used most commonly in employment situations. You can choose to have a union representative or someone else present while you negotiate.

Generally, arbitration is binding on both parties to the dispute; mediation/conciliation and negotiation are non-binding; and adjudication and ombudsmen schemes do not bind the complainant, but will be binding on the other side.

5   CONSUMER RIGHTS

Knowing your consumer rights undoubtedly puts you in an extremely strong position when you are complaining. It is hard for a company to argue with you if you clearly know your rights and ultimately can threaten to take it to the Small Claims Court!

There have been many changes to consumer law in the last ten years, some of them reflecting the digital age in which we live.

BREXIT

At the time of going to print, Brexit is still a mess. No final decisions have been made about anything.

EU law continues to apply until the UK leaves the EU. When the UK does leave, the European Union (Withdrawal) Act 2018 comes into force which is the repealing of the European Communities Act 1972. It allows for the Parliamentary approval of the withdrawal agreement being negotiated between the Government and the European Union.

The UK will retain existing EU law. The laws made over the last 40 years whilst the UK was an EU member will remain in place. (Unless the Government decides to change any of them).

Many of the EU directives regarding consumer rights are actually enshrined in UK law. So, most will remain the same unless/until they are updated, repealed or changed by Parliament.

The various possible changes have been included in the relevant chapters.

Cheques Act 1992

Very few people write cheques these days! However, just in case you do write/receive cheques you should be aware that most are crossed a/c payee. This Act gives statutory power to the "a/c payee" crossing when it is used. A cheque which bears the "a/c payee" crossing can only be paid into an account in the name of the beneficiary exactly as it appears on the cheque. Similarly, a cheque payable to two beneficiaries can only be paid into an account in the name of the two beneficiaries exactly as it appears on the cheque.

A cheque is valid for as long as the debt between the two parties (i.e. issuer and payee) exists. In other words, cheques do not have an expiry date.

Notwithstanding the above, it is common banking practice to reject a cheque presented for payment bearing a date more than six months earlier to protect the payer - on the basis that payment may already have been made by some other means or the cheque may have been lost or stolen. However this is at the discretion of individual banks.

Where there is a dispute, a cheque remains legally valid in order to prove a debt for a period of six years, which is the Statute of Limitations.

The Consumer Rights Act 2015

This Act came into force from 1st October 2015, when the following Acts were repealed/amended:

- *Supply of Goods (Implied Terms) Act 1973* now covers business to business contracts and consumer to consumer contracts only.
- *Sale of Goods Act 1979/ Sale and Supply of Goods Act 1994* applies to business to business contracts and to consumer to consumer contracts.
- *Supply of Goods and Services Act 1982* now covers business to business contracts and consumer to consumer contracts only.
- *Sale and Supply of Goods to Consumers Regulations 2002* is replaced
- *Unfair Contract Terms Act 1977* now covers business to business and consumer to consumer contracts only.
- *Unfair Terms in Consumer Contracts Regulations 1999* is replaced.

The sale and supply of goods

The person transferring or selling the goods must have the right to do so and the goods must be of a satisfactory quality. Goods must be of a standard that a reasonable person would regard as satisfactory. Quality is a general term, which covers a number of matters including:

- fitness for all the purposes for which goods of that kind are usually supplied
- appearance and finish
- freedom from minor defects
- safety
- durability.

In assessing quality, all relevant circumstances must be considered by the retailer, including price, description, and their own or the manufacturer's advertising. Goods must:

- be fit for a particular purpose. When you indicate that goods are required for a particular purpose, or where it is obvious that goods are intended for a particular purpose and a trader supplies them to meet that requirement, the goods should be fit for that specified purpose;
- match the description, sample or model. When you rely on a description, sample or display model the goods supplied must conform;
- be installed correctly, where installation has been agreed as part of the contract.

The consumer can reject the goods within 30 days unless the expected life of the goods is shorter e.g. highly perishable goods. You can also choose repair or replacement in this time and up to 6 months after purchase as it is assumed that the fault was there at the time of delivery unless the trader can prove otherwise or unless this assumption is inconsistent with the circumstances (for example, obvious signs of misuse).

If more than six months have passed, you have to prove the defect was there at the time of delivery. You must also prove the defect was there at the time of delivery if you exercise the short-term right to reject goods. Some defects do not become apparent until some time after delivery, and in these cases it is enough to prove that there was an underlying or hidden defect at that time.

All these rules also apply for distance selling and digital goods.

Digital goods

The Act defines 'digital content' as meaning 'data which are produced and supplied in digital form'. Therefore a huge array of digital-format products fall within this definition such as:

- computer games
- virtual items purchased within computer games
- television programmes
- films
- books
- computer software
- mobile phone apps
- systems software for operating goods – for example, domestic appliances, toys, motor vehicles, etc.

These digital goods are covered by the Act and therefore must be of satisfactory quality, as described, be fit for a particular purpose, match the description and be installed correctly when this has been agreed as part of the contract.

You can reject the goods within 30 days and insist on a full refund up to this time and a repair or replacement anytime up to 6 months. After 6 months you will need to prove that the fault was there at point of purchase and you have up to 6 years to claim.

In many cases digital content is supplied in a format that can be physically touched such as a Blu-ray disc containing a film. Increasingly, however, digital content does not have a tangible form – for example, a film downloaded to a computer or a virtual car purchased when playing a computer game.

Digital content non-physical form

OK, now this is where it gets complicated and the potential for challenges in court is high!

- Non-physical form such as downloads are not covered by the 30 day rule. You can see why, you could download something and use it and then try and get your money back.
- The right to reject applies only to goods and digital content sold as part of the goods (often referred to as being on a tangible medium, such as a disc, but this also includes digital content that is within the goods, e.g. the program on a washing machine). Digital content that is downloaded is not subject to the right to reject as

the consumer is not in a position to return the digital content.

- If the download has corrupted other apps on a device this may not be apparent for some time. A consumer may not discover this for some days, perhaps even after 30 days. If a washing machine damaged goods three months after purchase you should expect the retailer to reimburse costs of goods damaged by the washing machine so this would be the same with software.
- If software or computer games are unopened they are considered tangible form and once opened and put on a machine/in a toy etc. the 30 day rule still applies.
- Replacement or repair is, generally, a first stage that must be gone through before any refund is payable. If someone downloads an ebook, for example, and then insists on refund for any reason. The repair or replacement must be within a reasonable time and without significant inconvenience to the consumer, unless it is impossible or disproportionately expensive. Failing successful repair or replacement, the consumer could be entitled to a price reduction which can be up to the full price.
- If a trader advertised that an ebook would work on a particular device but it was actually incompatible with that device, the consumer would be entitled to a repair or more likely a replacement in the form of a version that is compatible with the device. If that is not possible, then the consumer would be entitled to a reduction in the purchase price, up to a full refund.
- There are no statutory provisions putting an obligation on the consumer to prove that the trader has breached the relevant consumer right. Replacement or repair is, generally, a first stage that must be gone through before any refund is payable, and this goes some way towards protecting traders against opportunistic claims. Traders will no doubt establish customs and practices to guard against abuses of the right in relation to digital goods.
- If the consumer made a mistake and downloaded the wrong item, then this is not covered by the Consumer Rights Act. Depending on the specifics of the case, the consumer may have rights under the Consumer Contract Regulations (which provide the 14 day cooling off period for distance purchases) but many websites stipulate that by downloading the content the consumer loses that 14 day right as they have consumed the digital content.

The contract for the supply of services

A contract is an agreement consisting of an offer and acceptance. When a consumer buys services from a trader, both parties enter into a contract which is legally binding. In order for a term to be binding it must clearly be part of the contract and be legal. Terms given to a consumer after the contract is made are not part of the contract and they have no effect. A contract can be verbal but it is advisable to detail important terms in writing so there can be no dispute later on.

All services:

- should be carried out with reasonable care and skill;
- should be carried out with information given verbally or in writing to the consumer which is binding where the consumer relies on it;
- must be done for a reasonable price (if no fixed price was set in advance);
- must be carried out within a reasonable time (if no specific time was agreed).

Unfair contracts

The Consumer Rights Act 2015 contains equivalent rights and protections to the Unfair Contract Terms Act 1977 and the Unfair Terms in Consumer Contracts Regulations 1999. This means that, although there may be some technical differences in the way these aspects are implemented, from a consumer's point of view there would be no difference – under the Consumer Rights Act 2015 the consumer may argue that a term is "unfair" in the same way as they would have under the aforementioned Acts.

The law creates a 'fairness test' to stop consumers being put at unfair disadvantage. A term is unfair if it tilts the rights and responsibilities between the consumer and the trader too much in favour of the trader. The test is applied by looking at what words are used and how they could be interpreted. It takes into consideration what is being sold, what the other terms of the contract say and all the circumstances at the time the term was agreed. There is an exemption for the essential obligations of contracts – setting the price and describing the main subject matter – provided the wording used is clear and prominent. There is also an exemption for wording that has to be used by law.

The Consumer Rights Act 2015

Lettings

- lettings agents are required to include a description of each fee which explains the service that is covered by the cost or the purpose for which it is imposed.
- as the list of fees covers charges to both landlords and tenants this improved transparency will highlight where agents are charging both parties for the same service.
- these requirements will prevent an agent drip feeding fees to tenants meaning consumers will be more confident about the charges they will be expected to pay when renting a property and it should also encourage more competitive letting agents' fees.

Ticketing

- requirement for additional information to be provided to the consumer by the seller, including seat number (if applicable), the face value and any restrictions that apply to who may use the ticket.
- requirement for operators of secondary ticketing platforms to report illegal activity relating to the secondary sale of tickets if they become aware of it.

The Government introduced extra new rules for secondary ticket sellers on 06 April 2018

- identify the location to which the ticket provides access e.g. the particular seat or standing area of the venue
- disclose any restrictions around who can use the ticket or how it must be used (e.g. alongside ID of the original buyer)
- disclose the original price of the ticket
- reveal the details of connections they have with either the online facility on which they are selling, or the organiser of the event for which the ticket is being sold
- supply the unique ticket number (UTN) to a buyer if the event organiser specifies one.

Consumer Credit Act 1974

In January 2013 changes were made to this Act following a European Directive on Additional Assumptions for the Calculation of the Annual Percentage Rate of Charge on Credit Agreements (EC Directive 2011/90/EU).

This is a wide ranging Act regulating consumer credit and covers the following areas:

Content and form of credit agreements
Method of calculating annual percentage rate (APR)
Procedures relating to events of default, termination or early settlement
Credit Advertising – must show true rates of interest without hidden extras

Section 75 provides that certain conditions must be met. Most credit card purchases will be covered, but the cash price of the goods or services must be more than £100 and not more than £30,000. If the item or service you are buying costs more than £30,000, you may have protection under Section 75A. For this section to apply the price of the item or service must be more than £30,000 and the amount of credit arranged less than £60,260. The credit provider could be in breach of contract if you can't trace the seller, you've contacted the seller but they've failed to respond, the seller has become insolvent or you've taken reasonable steps to pursue the seller but you haven't obtained satisfaction.

Consumers have rights to pay off the debt before the time stipulated.

A creditor must assess a customer's creditworthiness, (including from information from the consumer and a credit reference agency) before agreeing or increasing credit. (The consumer, if denied credit can ask for contact details of the agency and request a report). The customer must be informed of the nature and parties to the agreement. Key financial information must be provided separately to the credit agreement, including; the amount of credit or the credit limit; the duration of the agreement; the APR; the total amount payable; the amounts and timings of repayments.

You are covered by the cooling off period of 14 days if you sign a credit agreement off trade premises - signing an agreement in your home, or an energy agreement outside a supermarket for example.

Consumers Estate Agents and Redress Act 2007 and Estate Agents Act 1979

Anyone with a complaint about an estate agent relating to residential property now has access to a free redress scheme. Estate agents are required to have commissioned a Home Information Pack (HIP) prior to marketing any property.

Consumer Insurance (Disclosure and Representations) Act 2012

This Act came into force on the 6th April 2013. It removed the duty on consumers to disclose any facts that a prudent underwriter would consider material and replaces this with a duty to take reasonable care not to make a misrepresentation. So a consumer must not give false information but the insurer must ask relevant, clear and specific questions.

The Consumer Protection Act 1987

This Act (a European directive) prohibits the manufacture and supply of unsafe goods making the manufacturer or seller of a defective product responsible for any damage it causes. So for example if a kettle burns you or sets fire to something in your house then you can claim from the manufacturer. The Act states that in the instance where a manufacturer has made a defective product which has caused a personal injury or damage to your property, it, not the trader is responsible. The value of the damage must be more than £275.

Claims under the Act must be made within 3 years of the date of damage or when it came to the knowledge of the claimant. However, no claim can be brought more than 10 years after the date the product was last put into circulation.

This Act allows local councils to seize unsafe goods and suspend the sale of suspected unsafe goods and also prohibits misleading price indications.

Section 10 originally imposed a general safety requirement on consumer products but this was repealed when its effect was superseded by the broader requirements of the General Product Safety Regulations 2005.

The Consumer Protection from Unfair Trading Regulations 2008

The Consumer Protection from Unfair Trading Regulations 2008 implemented the European Union-wide Directive 2005/29/EC concerning unfair commercial practices in the internal market. The Regulations replace much consumer protection legislation, including Part III of the Consumer Protection Act 1987 (which dealt with misleading prices), the majority of the Trade Descriptions Act 1968 (which it mainly repeals), and the Control of Misleading Advertising Regulations 1988.

For a practice to be unfair under these regulations it must harm, or be likely to harm, the economic interests of the average consumer. For example, when a shopper makes a purchasing decision he or she would not have made had he or she been given accurate information or not put under unfair pressure to do so.

Detailed list of prohibitions

The regulations prohibit trading practices that are unfair to consumers. There are four different types of practices covered:

A general ban – on conduct below a level which may be expected towards consumers (honest market practice/good faith).

Misleading practices – through the information the practice contains or its deceptive presentation, it causes, or is likely to cause, the average consumer to take a different transactional decision. Examples include general misleading information, creating confusion with competitors' products or failing to honour commitments made in a code of conduct.

Aggressive sales techniques using harassment, coercion or undue influence – significantly impairing, or likely to significantly impair, the average consumer's freedom of choice or conduct in relation to the product through the use of harassment, coercion or undue influence, thereby causing him to take a different transactional decision.

31 specific practices – 1) Falsely claiming accreditation, (claiming to be a signatory to a code of conduct when the trader is not, for example), 2) A trader not being who they say they are (displaying a trust mark, quality mark or equivalent without having obtained required authorisation), 3) Claiming fabricated endorsements 4) Not being true to the terms of an endorsement, 5) Bait advertising such as not disclosing existence of grounds for a special offer not being available, 6) Falsely stating "Limited time only" or particular terms to elicit an immediate decision by the customer, 7) Illegally selling goods, 8) Presenting rights given to consumers in law as a distinctive feature of the trader's offer, 9) Over promise, under deliver (falsely claiming that a product is able to cure illnesses, dysfunction or malformations), 10) Promoting a product a trader doesn't wish to sell (making an invite to purchase at a specified price and then (a) refusing to show the advertised item to consumers; (b) refusing to take orders for it or deliver it within a reasonable time; or (c) demonstrating a defective sample of it, with the intention of promoting a different product (known as bait and switch), 11) Scare tactics (making a materially inaccurate claim concerning the nature and extent of the risk to the personal security of the consumer or his or her family if the consumer does not purchase the product), 12) Creating extra paperwork (requiring a consumer who wishes to claim on an insurance policy to produce documents which could not reasonably be considered relevant or failing systematically to respond to pertinent correspondence, in order to dissuade a consumer from exercising his/her contractual rights, 13) Being dishonest about advertorials, 14) Faking goods, including making a product look a competitor's 15) Claiming a closing down sale when this is untrue, 16) Passing on materially inaccurate information on market conditions or on the possibility of finding the product with the intention of inducing the consumer to acquire the product at conditions less favourable than normal market conditions, 17) Forcing the deal (seeking payment which gives the consumer the impression that he/she has already ordered the marketed product), 18) Falsely claiming or creating the impression that the trader is not acting for purposes relating to his/her trade, business, craft or profession, or the trader falsely representing itself as a consumer, 19) Advertising to children (including in an advertisement a direct exhortation to children to buy advertised products or persuade their parents or other adults to buy advertised products for them. 20) Pyramid schemes (establishing, operating or promoting a pyramid promotional scheme), 21) Claiming that products are able to facilitate winning in games of chance, 22) Claiming in a commercial practice to offer a competition or prize promotion without awarding the prizes described or a reasonable equivalent, 23) Describing a product as 'gratis', 'free', 'without charge' or similar if the consumer has to pay anything other than the unavoidable cost of responding to the commercial practice and collecting or paying for delivery of the item, 24) Creating the false impression that the consumer has already won, will win, or will on doing a particular act win, a prize or other equivalent benefit, when in fact either: a) there is no prize or other equivalent benefit, or b) taking any action in relation to claiming the prize or other equivalent benefit is subject to the consumer paying money or incurring a cost., 25) Forcing the sale (creating the impression that the consumer cannot leave the premises until a contract is formed), 26) Conducting personal visits to the consumer's home and ignoring the consumer's request to leave or not to return, except in circumstances and to the extent justified under national law, to enforce a contractual obligation, 27) Pestering the consumer (making persistent and unwanted solicitations by telephone, fax, e-mail or other remote media), 28) Using guilt to make sales (explicitly informing a consumer that if he or she does not buy the product or service, the trader's job or livelihood will be in jeopardy), 29) Asking for payment from someone when they didn't ask for the product, 30) Providing after-sales service to a consumer in a language which is not an official one of the European Member States where the trader is located without disclosing this prior to transaction, 31) Misleading after-sales information (creating the false impression that after-sales service in relation to a product is available in a European Member State other than the one in which the product is sold).

Amendment remedies to Consumer Protection (Amendment) Regulations 2014
The law is complex and consumers were left with no remedy, or having to rely on complex civil law. Amendments were made to the regulations to apply from October 2014. New rights only apply if the trader has committed a misleading or aggressive practice under the 2008 Regulations. They provide simple standardised remedies against traders who have breached the requirements and if a consumer is misled or intimidated into entering a contract or making a payment, consumers have three types of remedies available:

Unwind a contract and get money back:
Consumers can undo the transaction into which they entered restoring them to the position they were in before entering the contract or making the payment.

Discount on the price paid:
For goods or services that cost £5,000 or less, consumers have a right to a fixed percentage discount on the price. There are four pre-set bands of discount which can apply, depending on the severity of the misleading or aggressive practice:

(1) 25% if it is more than minor;
(2) 50% if it is significant;
(3) 75% if it is serious; and
(4) 100% (full price) if it is very serious.

Damages for detriment caused:
Can be secured when losses exceed price paid and can also be applied when the consumer has incurred distress and inconvenience. Damages are unlikely to exceed £1,000

Consumer Rights (Payment Surcharges) Regulations 2012

The aim for this European Directive was to ensure that consumers felt safe buying from anywhere in Europe. It also takes into account that we now shop more online and it covers the digital age.

The implementation has a significant effect in modernising consumer law, much of which was written 20-30 years ago. Digital content was of course not covered then. The new laws have introduced a distinct category to deal with digital content, which will sit along-side existing categories dealing with the provision of goods and services. From the 13th January 2018 companies were no longer able to charge any fees for the use of credit or debit cards. This includes payment methods such as Apple Pay and PayPal, too. The change also applies to Government departments and local councils.

The surcharge ban was written into UK law so will remain after Brexit whether there is a deal or no-deal arrangement. However, you may not be protected purchasing goods or services from the EU or from EU-based companies. This is because cross-border payments will no longer be covered by the surcharge ban. Charges for UK consumers could be reintroduced by European companies, including those providing travel services.

The Government has said that in the case of a no-deal Brexit the cost of card payments for transactions between the UK and EU are likely to increase.

Consumer Contracts (Information, Cancellation and Additional Charges) Regulations 2013

Information which a trader must give to a consumer before and after making a sale
This is the need to ensure the customer understands what goods and services are being provided and ensuring there are no hidden costs. If the paperwork does not comply

with the new requirements the consumer may not have to pay. When retailers send you email confirmation of the purchase this must now include a full description of the goods and services purchased including their characteristics and the full price including tax and any additional charges or delivery prices.

How that information should be given
The purpose of the 'durable medium' requirement is to ensure that, should a dispute arise at some point after the contract has been concluded, both parties have a record of what was agreed. The burden of proof that the relevant information has been provided rests with the trader.

Consumers' right to change their mind when buying at a distance or off-premises
Consumers now have 14 days to inform the company from receiving delivery and then a further 14 days from then to return items because they change their mind. In addition, refunds on cancelled contracts can be delayed until goods are returned. However, if the company has not provided the right information to the consumer then the length of the cooling off period can be extended. Although there are some exemptions:

- Fresh food and flowers
- Personalised or perishable goods
- Accommodation/transport/leisure services purchased for a particular timeframe
- Newspapers and magazines (unless they are part of a subscription)
- Sealed audio, video or computer software that has been opened
- Buying or building property or paying rent
- Medical products and services
- Hiring a taxi, boat or plane
- Goods that fluctuate in price (such as foreign exchange)
- Emergency repairs and maintenance
- Financial products, package holidays or timeshares (different rights apply)

Delivery times and passing of risk
Unless agreed with the trader, goods should be delivered without undue delay and within 30 days. If a particular date or period for delivery has been agreed then delivery should be within that time.

Prohibition on any additional payments which appear as a default option
Traders will need the active consent of the consumer for all payments – e.g. pre-ticked boxes for additional payments, will no longer be permitted. Consumers will not be liable for costs which they have not been told, pre-contract, that they must bear.

Prohibition on not providing basic rate numbers for post-contract customer helplines
Where traders offer telephone helplines for consumers to contact them about something they have bought, there should be a number available on which the consumer can call for this purpose at no more than the basic rate. This includes financial institutions.

Currently there is no requirement for package holiday and timeshare companies either. Some technical helplines may be exempt as well. This is as long as they're not using lines that customers are also expected to call to discuss problems with something that they've already bought. There are exclusions such as financial services, the property sector and government department helplines.

Contracts (Rights of Third Parties) Act 1999

This legislation gives rights to anyone who was intended to benefit from the transaction. For example, if someone buys a service as a gift for a friend and the service is not undertaken with reasonable skill and care either the recipient or the buyer of the gift can take action for breach of contract. (It must have been made clear that the service was a gift). Traders can use contract terms to exclude the rights of third parties so check terms and conditions.

The Defective Premises Act 1972

Where a person takes on work for or in connection with the provision of a dwelling, they owe a statutory duty to see that the work which is undertaken is done in a workmanlike or professional manner, with proper materials, so that the dwelling will be fit for habitation when completed. The Act is limited to defects in the home caused as a result of failures in design, workmanship or materials.

The Distance Selling Regulations 2000

The Directive has been repealed. For purchases prior to 13th June 2014 these regulations still apply. However, after this date the Consumer Contracts Regulations apply which provide more protection.

The Doorstop Selling Regulations 2008

The Directive has been repealed. For contracts signed after 13th June 2014 the Consumer Contracts Regulations apply which provide more protection.

Energy Act 2013

Limit on the number of energy tariffs offered to domestic consumers; requires the automatic migration of customers from poor value closed tariffs to cheaper deals and requires the provision of information by suppliers to consumers on the best alternative deals available to them from them.

Ofgem extends its licence regime to third-party intermediaries, such as switching websites.

Enforcement power for Ofgem to require energy businesses that breach gas or electricity licence conditions, or other relevant regulatory requirements to provide redress to consumers who suffer detriment as a result of the breach.

Amends the Warm Homes and Energy Conservation Act and proposes a new target for fuel poverty that would be set through secondary legislation by the Fuel Poverty (England) Regulations 2014. This set of regulations, which became law on 5 December 2014, gives effect to the new fuel poverty target.

EU directive 1999/44/EC

Whether you bought the goods in a shop or online, under EU rules you always have the right to a minimum two-year guarantee period at no cost. This 2-year guarantee is only your minimum right. Other UK laws included here give you more cover but you may want to use the minimum right to add more fire to your complaint. To use this directive the goods must have been purchased within two years and you need to report the fault within two months of discovering it. The goods should show no signs of damage through your actions or misuse.

The Financial Services Regulations 2004

Financial products are covered by The Consumer Rights Directive 2013. The Financial Services Regulations cover the sale of most financial services that take place at a distance (such as online or over the 'phone), directly, or through an intermediary such as an insurance broker. Generally, you have 14 days to cancel starting from the day of purchase. There are some products where you don't have the right to cancel, such as where the price of the service depends on fluctuations in the financial markets.

For pension products, you get 30 days from when you enter into the contract, and for life insurance you have 30 days from when you're told that the provider has agreed to accept you for cover. The refund should be received within 30 days.

The Food Safety Act 1990

Food and drink intended for human consumption must be treated in a controlled and managed way. Wherever food is manufactured, prepared or sold it must comply with food safety requirements and be "of the nature, substance and quality demanded", and must be correctly described (labelled).

General Product Safety Regulations 2005

They apply to all products (new and second-hand) used by consumers. Product-specific legislation takes precedence in areas where the provisions have similar objectives to the Regulations. (e.g. Cosmetic Products (Safety) Regulations 2008)

A general duty is placed on producers and distributors to place on the market (or supply) only products that are safe in normal or reasonably foreseeable use. The principal responsibility for day-to-day enforcement lies with local authorities.

It is recognised that certain technical standards carry a presumption of conformity with the general safety requirement, meaning that products that comply with them are deemed to be safe.

The Misrepresentation Act 1967

(It doesn't cover Scotland but Scottish law is broadly similar). It protects the consumer from being mis-led or mis-sold goods or services. If you enter into a contract and purchase an item or service because you believed a statement (not an opinion) regarding it, then you can end the contract, get a refund and claim compensation. There are three types of misrepresentation where a false statement could be deemed to have been made:

Fraudulently – statement made by someone that they know is untrue, believe is untrue or is made recklessly

Negligently – statement made carelessly or without reasonable grounds for believing its truth.

Innocently – statement made without fault.

Fraudulent/negligent statements
If you entered a contract as a result of a fraudulent or negligent statement you can cancel the contract. You can also claim damages in most cases. These claims are on the basis of negligence or fraud. The person who made the misrepresentation has to disprove the negligence. So for example, if you book a holiday on the basis that it is a holiday where children are not allowed and find that when you arrive the place is overrun with children then this is a clear breach.

Innocent statements
This is considered to be when either party enters into a contract having reasonable grounds for believing that a false statement was true. The contract is usually just cancelled in this situation.

Under Section 2(2) of the Misrepresentation Act 1967 the court has the discretion to award damages instead of allowing you to end the contract if it deems it appropriate. It cannot award both and the matter is judged on the nature of misrepresentation and actual losses suffered.

Limitations
If you chose to continue with the contract although you were aware of the misrepresentation you will not be able to end the contract or claim damages. For example, if you booked a holiday knowing that the hotel described in the brochure was family-friendly but you knew this was a mis-print due to other factors in the brochure or had had it pointed out to you and you proceeded with the booking you will have, in law, "affirmed" the contract.

You need to act quickly after discovering the misrepresentation. For example, if you have been sold a mobile 'phone contract on the basis of sending 500 free texts a month and you have continued to use the 'phone for a few months before complaining about being charged for them a court may say that you should have complained the first month in which you were charged. All cases are different however and are assessed as such.

Package Travel and Linked Travel Arrangements 2018

The new Package Travel and Linked Travel Arrangements 2018 have replaced and considerably modified the former 1992 Package Travel, Package Holidays and Package Tour Regulations 1992. The new regulations came into force on 01 July 2018. Holidays booked prior to this will be covered by the previous regulations.

A package holiday definition
A package holiday is one that has at least two components, all as part of a 'package' for which you pay an inclusive price: transport (such as flights, transfers etc.) accommodation and/or another tourist service which makes up a significant proportion of the package. It must last more than 24 hours.

If you submitted one set of payment details with a total price and didn't have to re-enter them and completed the transaction within 24 hours, this falls into the definition of a package.

The organiser (tour operator) is liable for the financial failures of hoteliers, suppliers and services within the terms of the contract.

Linked travel arrangements (LTA)
If you purchase a minimum of two different types of travel service from different providers this is not a package travel arrangement. However, if you buy two or more types of travel service together, put together by the travel organiser and you purchase both within a 24 hour period, this is a Linked Travel Arrangement.

For example, you buy a flight with a link to a hotel provided by a different company. If you buy an online flight and then have a link on the aircraft website to an accommodation website, where you purchase a hotel in a separate transaction.

The travel organiser must provide information to you in the same way as it does for a package. (See below).

An LTA does not give you the same protection that the package does. The organiser is not responsible for the service provided by the companies. However, it is responsible for providing financial protection for the refund when a travel service is not carried out due to insolvency. If it is responsible for the carriage of passengers – for example their airline flights – then it is also responsible for their repatriation.

Information
The Organiser must clearly state the details of the booking in a Standard Information Form, before you make any payment. The travel organiser also has to provide you strict details of the contract laid out in the Schedules to the Regulations, to accompany the confirmation invoice. This should include specifics of any arrangements, dates, times, costs, meals, excursions included/excluded, activities, transportation, cancellation fees, contact details for the package organiser, information on compulsory/voluntary

insurance regarding repatriation in the event of illness/death/accident, and/or the cost of termination of the contract by the traveller. Interestingly, it must also inform the traveller about visa and passport requirements.

Organiser makes changes
The Regulations state that an organiser must inform the traveller clearly and without undue delay. The organiser must provide the traveller with the option to terminate the contract without paying a termination fee if:

- it has no choice but to significantly alter the main characteristics of the package

or

- cannot fulfil any special requirements of the traveller which the organiser has previously accepted (paragraph 1 of Schedule 5)

or

- increases the price by more than 8%

You should be given a reasonable length of time to respond to the above. If you do not, the organiser must send you further communication with a deadline. If you still do not respond the organiser will terminate the contract and refund all payments within 14 days.

Traveller chooses to terminate a package
At any time before your package starts, you can terminate the contract. However, you may have to pay the organiser an appropriate fee which they can justify. The fee will take into account costs that the organiser no longer has to pay to a third party. It should also take into account "alternative deployment" of travel services. This is where the organiser has been able to sell a part of the package to someone else. There may be cases where the organiser has not been able to do this and decisions would be made on case-by-case basis.

For example, it would be justifiable to not reimburse the price of an air travel ticket if the organiser cannot cancel or sell it on.

Reasonable termination fees based on the above and the length of time between cancellation and the start of the package must be specified in the contract.

If there are unavoidable and extraordinary circumstances at the destination (or in the immediate vicinity which would affect the travel to the destination) of your package travel contract, such as war, security risks etc. you can terminate the contract without paying a termination fee. You should be fully refunded within 14 days.

Redress
The consumer is entitled to redress for a variety of things dependent on what regulation has been broken and when.

Loss of value – the difference between the cost paid for the holiday and the one received – e.g. the cost of a 4-star hotel which you paid for and the 2-star hotel to which you were moved.

Out-of-pocket expenses – incurred reasonable costs as a result of the breach of contract – e.g. having to pay for taxis when travel paid for was not provided.

Loss of enjoyment – compensation for the disappointment and distress caused by things going wrong – e.g. no children's activities which were advertised.

Personal injury, compensation for any personal injury incurred abroad – e.g. medical bills, consequential loss etc, but specialist legal advice is thoroughly recommended for personal injury claims).

Brexit
If there is a no deal Brexit, EU traders selling these arrangements in or to consumers in the UK will be required to comply with the insolvency protection requirements, as above, so you will still be financially protected if the company goes bust.

If the organiser is not based in the UK, or does not direct its business to the UK, this may not be the case. Request very clear information regarding insolvency protection before booking. You won't be covered by these regulations but you may be covered by insolvency protection arrangements in the EU member state.

Provision of Services Regulations 2009

Traders must respond to consumer complaints as quickly as possible, and make their best efforts to resolve those complaints. They must respond to emails and letters of complaint and they must return 'phone calls. Where a complaint appears to be valid, the trader should put things right promptly. If the trader disputes liability, they should give a clear explanation of their reasons.

Sale & Supply of Goods to Consumers regulations 2002

A set of common consumer rights on faulty goods in each EU country is provided for by Directive 1999/44/EC on the Sale of Consumer Goods ("the Directive"). A main aim of the Directive was to encourage people to shop across borders, knowing they have protection if anything is wrong with the products they buy. Existing UK law has been retained but slightly amended, mainly to give effect to specific remedies which, although they have been in use for many years, have not actually been part of the law. This extends consumers' rights under the Sale of Goods Act 1979. The main addition is that the consumer is entitled to a repair or replacement and that the goods are repaired or replaced within a reasonable period of time, without causing significant inconvenience to the consumer and with the seller bearing any necessary cost of repairing or replacing the goods.

If a repair or replacement is impossible or disproportionate (where the seller has to pay unreasonable costs) compared to the other remedies available, the seller can refuse the request. Factors that must be taken into consideration include the value of the goods if they had conformed to the contract, how significant it is that the goods are not as required and if there is an alternative to repair or replacement that will not inconvenience the consumer.

If the seller does not replace the goods within a reasonable period of time, without significant inconvenience to the consumer, or if the seller does not have to repair or replace the goods because to do so is impossible or disproportionate, then the consumer can require the seller to reduce the purchase price of the goods by an appropriate amount or treat the contract as at an end and have the purchase price refunded. Any refund can be reduced to take account of use already made of the goods.

The regulations also cover specific liability for public statements. The seller is liable for public statements made by him/her, the producer of the goods or his representative if the goods do not match up with the publicity. The seller can avoid liability if he can show that he did not know and could not have known about the statement, the statement had been withdrawn by the time the consumer purchased the goods or the statement could not have influenced the consumer's decision to purchase the goods.

Sale of Goods Act 1979 and updated Sale and Supply of Goods Act 1994

For purchases made prior to 1st October 2015. For purchases after this date see The Consumer Rights Act 2015

Your rights under this Act are with the retailer and not the manufacturer. (Unless you bought on Hire Purchase in which case the Supply of Goods Implied Terms Act 1973 applies, which makes the HP company responsible for the quality of the goods supplied and gives you slightly different rights.) Items must:
- be of satisfactory quality
- be fit for purpose
- be as described
- last a reasonable length of time

If not, the customer is entitled to a full refund, repair or replacement. For a definite full refund the item should be returned within a few weeks. After this time you may have to accept a repair or replacement. You can accept a repair but you do not have to do so and you maintain your rights if the repair is not satisfactory.

Items should last a reasonable length of time. It is generally considered that an item should be returned within a few weeks. However, if an item breaks in the first 6 months it is considered that the fault was there at time of purchase and it is down to the retailer to prove otherwise. After 6 months it is generally considered that the customer has to prove that the fault was there at time of purchase.

This Act was amended in 1994 and the word "merchantable quality" changed to "satisfactory quality".

You can use either the "amended Sale of Goods Act 1979" or the "Sale and Supply of Goods Act 1994" to quote your rights. I use both ways throughout this book.

The Supply of Extended Warranties on Domestic Electrical Goods Order 2005

If you purchase an extended warranty for domestic electrical goods (e.g. washing machines, televisions) you should have:

Seen that price of the extended warranty is displayed alongside the price of the electrical goods, both in store and in any printed adverts, catalogues etc.

Been given:

- details about the warranty, (there should be free information leaflets) including your statutory and cancellation rights.
- details on whether the warranty will be protected if the company goes out of business.
- 45 days to cancel it and you should have received a written reminder of this right. If you cancel it after that period you will receive a pro-rata refund.
- the right to buy an extended warranty at any point up to 30 days after buying the goods.

Any warranty discounts that are offered should also be available for that period.

These rules do not apply if:
- the warranty is provided for free
- the warranty does not cover repair or replacement of the goods

Supply of Goods and Services Act 1982

(Common law in Scotland). For purchases bought prior to 1st October 2015. For purchases after this date see The Consumer Rights Act 2015.

A service can include goods (e.g. fitting a bedroom including providing the furniture) or without goods (such as providing accountancy services).

All services should be carried out:
- with reasonable care and skill
- in a reasonable time (if there is no specific time agreed);
- and for a reasonable charge (if no fixed price was set in advance)

The Trade Descriptions Act 1968

Technically this remains in place but most of its specific provisions were repealed and superseded by the Consumer Protection from Unfair Trading Regulations 2008.

Unfair Contract Terms Act 1977

From 1st October 2015 this will cover business to business and consumer to consumer contracts only.

This Act covers nearly all forms of contract and it limits the applicability of disclaimers of liability, i.e. exemption clauses. The terms extend to both actual contract terms and notices that are seen to constitute a contractual obligation. So for example a very clear breach would be where you have paid a company for your car to be chauffeured to a car park and the driver damages the car. In the contract, in the small print it says that the company is not responsible for the cost of any damage caused by the driver. No conditions in the contract can restrict or exclude liability for financial loss or damage to property. They must be reasonable and fair.

Unfair Terms in Consumer Contracts Regulations 1999

Contracts formed on or after the 1st October 2015 will be replaced by the Consumer Rights Act 2015.

The EU (then EEC) Unfair Consumer Contract Terms Directive 93/13/EEC was transposed into domestic law and overlaps with the Unfair Contracts Act 1977. The regulations apply where a consumer has not been involved in the negotiation of terms and there is an imbalance in rights and obligations. The regulations don't apply where you and the trader have negotiated the terms. A contract term can be deemed unfair if it creates a 'significant imbalance' in the trader and consumer's positions. For example, a term that allows the trader to considerably change the goods or services to be supplied under the contract, whilst ensuring that the consumer is unable to cancel the contract if dissatisfied. Terms that take away a consumer's legal rights and/or permit a trader to keep an unreasonable amount of money as compensation if the customer does not keep to their end of the contract are also covered.

Contract terms must be in plain and intelligible language and if they aren't, then interpretation that favours the consumer applies.

Unsolicited Goods and Services Act 1971 / The Consumer Contracts (Information, Cancellation and Additional Charges) Regulations 2013

Most people are familiar with the Unsolicited Goods and Services Act 1971. Unsolicited goods are covered in the newer regulations which say you have a right to keep goods delivered to you that you didn't request.

You are under no legal obligation to contact the trader and can keep the goods. However, if you have been sent items by mistake, such as a duplicate order, additional items or things meant for someone else you should contact the company and request that they come and collect the goods. There should be no cost or

inconvenience to you and you should give the company a deadline within which
should collect the item(s).

Substitute goods are *not* unsolicited goods. However, substitute goods should be
agreed with the trader and you.

The Water Act 2014

Customers will have the freedom to switch water supplier from 2017. The Act will also
ensure affordable flood insurance for hundreds of thousands of households from 2015.
All water companies must follow the guaranteed standards scheme set out by Ofwat.
If a company doesn't meet these standards, you may be able to claim compensation.

The Act covers many issues. For the consumer the main measures are:
- *enabling all customers in England* to switch their water and sewerage supplier
- *establishing cross-border* arrangements with Scotland
- *enabling owners of small-scale water* storage to sell excess water into the public supply
- *improving the regulations* relating to merger of water sewage undertakers
- *giving Ofwat a new over-arching duty* to take greater account of long-term resilience
  and various other changes to improve Ofwat's regulation of the water industry
- *Guaranteed Standards Scheme* – water companies must abide by these standards or
  the consumer will be entitled to compensation in most cases.

The statutory basis for the Guaranteed Standards of Service are section 38 and section 95
of the Water Industry Act 1991. This gave the Secretary of State the authority to prescribe
regulations – Water Supply and Sewerage Services (Customer Service Standards)
Regulations 2008, SI 2008/594, otherwise known as Guaranteed Standards of Services,
which ensure the consumer receives a minimum standard or receives compensation.

Consumer laws covering purchases in the EU

EU legislation is intended to give consumers across the EU equivalent rights. Each
EU member state will use its own piece of law to implement an EU law, regulation or
directive as appropriate. If a consumer in the UK makes a purchase in France, then
French law would apply. This will give the same basic rights as UK law however there
may be some differences. For detailed differences you should contact the European
Consumer Centre (ECC) (See chapter 27 *Useful Contacts*). ECC will also be able to advise
on using Alternative Dispute Resolution or Small Claims Court action outside of the UK
and within the EU. If the EU retailer is actively marketing their goods to the UK, then you

... that UK law applies.

You *may* be able to use the Consumer Rights Act 2015, stating that this takes precedence over the law of the other EU country. This is based on the Brussels Regulation and you may be able to use this if the law in another country repairs or replaces but doesn't refund, for example. You would need to take further advice on this from the ECC. The Government has committed funding to the ECC for up to a year after Brexit.

Brexit

If there is a no deal Brexit you will still be able to return items purchased from an EU retailer. You will still be buying items under the law in the seller's country. However, it may be more difficult to return items and you may have to go that country if you want to take the matter to court.

If you incur problems after the exit date this will also apply.

If there is a deal there should be no change.

If there is a no-deal Brexit the UK will instantly stop being part of the EU agencies and regulatory bodies that are responsible for undertaking safety assessments, such as the European Food Safety Authority (EFSA). Therefore UK bodies would have to take on this responsibility to ensure consumer safety. UK consumers will still be able to monitor EU consumer product recalls via the Rapid Exchange of Information System (RAPEX) website. Alerts issued by RAPEX provide information about dangerous products and steps being taken to prevent or restrict marketing.

If there is a no-deal Brexit consumers will not be able to use the Online Dispute Resolution (ODR) platform run by the European Commission. You may not be able to use the UK-based alternative dispute resolution organisations for cross border disputes as they will no longer be required to act in cross-border disputes.

6 BUYING GOODS

Every time you buy goods or services from any kind of retailer be that a shop, garage, online or any other type of retailer, you have entered into a contract. That contract is covered by law to protect both retailer and consumer. For purchases made before 1st October 2015 the key law that consumers currently need to quote if something goes wrong is the Sale of Goods Act 1979, amended by the Sale and Supply of Goods Act 1994. Goods must be fit for purpose, of satisfactory quality and fit the description. "Does what it says on the tin" applies to all goods! If the item does not do these things then the retailer is in breach of contract and you are entitled to a full refund, repair or replacement. Items should last a reasonable length of time. From 1st October 2015 you need to quote the Consumer Rights Act 2015. Goods must be of a satisfactory quality, be fit for a particular purpose, match the description, sample or model and be installed correctly, where installation has been agreed as part of the contract.

For purchases made before 1st October 2015 it is generally assumed that for items less than 6 months old which are faulty, the consumer should receive a full refund, repair or replacement (minus any depreciation of value from use, e.g. car used for a couple of weeks has had some use and will have depreciated in value). After a few weeks it is considered that you have accepted the goods and the retailer can offer just a replacement or repair. After 6 months it is for the customer to prove that the fault was there at point of purchase. This is only a guideline. When my son said that we should complain and take something back to a pound shop, even I drew the line! However, I believe that a washing machine should last longer than six months before developing a fault and therefore I would expect redress if it went wrong after that time and I would take the matter to court if I didn't get it.

For purchases after 1st October 2015 things are more definite. The short-term right to

...s lasts specifically for 30 days unless the expected life of the goods is shorter, ... highly perishable goods. The right does not apply in cases where the only breach ...ates to an incorrect installation of goods.

A refund may be reduced to take account of any use you have had from the goods. However, no deduction can be made for you having the goods simply because the trader has delayed in collecting them. Nor can a deduction be made where goods are rejected within six months of supply, except where the goods are a motor vehicle.

The Consumer Rights Act 2015 and The Consumer Protection Act 1987 also mean that you can claim against the manufacturer if the faulty item damages other items or causes personal injury. Anyone can claim. So should a faulty washing machine damage clothes, the consumer can gain redress from the manufacturer. You can also claim for loss of earnings, pain and loss of amenity. So if you are a chef and the item has damaged your fingers so that you cannot cook, you would be entitled to more compensation than someone who is able to work not using all their fingers. I would advise seeking legal advice from a solicitor when claiming compensation for personal injury.

You can also take your case to the the Dispute Resolution Scheme if the retailer you bought the item from is a member.

When purchasing items in the EU, you are covered by EU legislation which is intended to give citizens across the EU equivalent rights. Each EU member state will use its own piece of law to implement an EU law, regulation or directive as appropriate. France will have an equivalent piece of law, as will Germany, Spain, etc. If you make a purchase in France, then French law will apply. This will give the same basic rights as UK law however there may be some differences. For advice on these differences you should contact the European Consumer Centre (ECC) details for which are in chapter 27 *Useful Contacts*.

A real example of gaining redress for a product causing damage to clothes

Laura purchased Lakeland "Blitz that Mould" mould and algae stain killer to tackle the mouldy patches around her house. After reading the label on the front and back she duly made sure the rooms were well ventilated and tested the product on an inconspicuous area as advised. Finding no adverse reactions she continued spraying the affected areas, returning 30 minutes later to see amazing results...

She decided to spray the damp patch inside her wardrobe (an alcove in the bedroom with a door on so not a standalone piece of furniture). The damp patch was on the sloping ceiling part so after checking the instructions again, she opened the windows and lightly sprayed the black area. She returned 30 minutes later to find that the spray had stained her clothing (which she did not remove prior to spraying as the label did not stipulate it was unsuitable for fabrics) – in total the spray ruined 4 jackets, 3 shirts, 1 cardigan and a top.

She re-read the label which merely stated it was not to be used on enamel, marble, aluminium, wood and granite - nowhere did it mention that it should be kept away from fabrics or that it contained bleach. The label read only "Contains: Less than 5% Anionic Surfactants, Sodium Hydroxide, Sodium Hypochlorite" – which means very little to the general public.

I wrote up the above into a complaint and added that under the Sale and Supply of Goods Act 1994 the product was not fit for purpose, not of satisfactory quality and misleading which also falls under the Consumer Regulations 2008 (Misleading omissions Part 2 Prohibitions). Photos were sent with the email with a breakdown of the costs of the damaged clothes totalling £365 (cost to replace was more).

Lakeland wanted her to 'phone them. It's important to put everything in writing, always, so we refused and Mary came back asking for Laura to return the bottle. Be careful in this type of scenario. What if it gets lost in the post? What if they test it and say it is OK when clearly it isn't? Ask them to pay postage and tell them that you are keeping some in case you need to do your own tests if you take the matter further.

She received an email saying that the product had actually been recalled and now has a warning about a bleaching action. Laura was offered £400. My guess was that their insurance kicks in at £500 so we requested a further £100 and got £50 for a total of £450.

TEMPLATE: **Rejecting an item not fit for specific purpose**

For purchases prior to 1st October 2015 quote "Sale and Supply of Goods Act 1994"

Dear [*xxx*]

Re: [*item*]

On the [*date*] I purchased [*item*]. I informed a member of your staff that I needed this item for [*insert the specific purpose*]. S/he recommended this product. However, it has proved unsuitable because [*describe problem*]. The Consumer Rights Act 2015 states that the retailer must supply goods that meet a specific purpose if that purpose is made clear at the point of purchase. You are therefore in breach of contract and I am rejecting the item and expect a full refund.

I look forward to hearing from you within seven days. Should I not be fully satisfied with your response I will not hesitate in taking the matter further which will include but not be limited to, informing Trading Standards and if necessary starting proceedings through the Small Claims Court.

Yours [*sincerely/faithfully*]

TEMPLATE: **Rejecting an item not as described**

For purchases prior to 1st October 2015 quote "Sale and Supply of Goods Act 1994"

Dear [*xxx*]

Re: [*item*]

On the [*date*] I purchased [*item*]. It was described as [*detail what is on packaging or what you were advised by a member of staff*]. It was due to this description that I purchased this item. Under the Consumer Rights Act 2015 I am entitled to items that match the description. Because I bought this item due to the information given to me, the Consumer Protection from Unfair Trading Regulations 2008 has also been breached and therefore I request a full refund.

I look forward to hearing from you within seven days. Should I not be fully satisfied with your response I will not hesitate in taking the matter further which will include but not be limited to, informing Trading Standards and if necessary starting proceedings through the Small Claims Court.

Yours [*sincerely/faithfully*]

TEMPLATE: **Rejecting faulty goods**

For purchases prior to 1st October 2015 quote "Sale and Supply of Goods Act 1994"

Dear [*xxx*]

Re: [*item*]

On the [*date*] I purchased [*item*] which has since developed a fault [*describe*]. Under the Consumer Rights Act 2015 I am entitled to items of a satisfactory quality that are fit for purpose, match the description and last a reasonable length of time [*delete the irrelevant entitlement to your case*]. This item is clearly in breach of this law and therefore I request a full refund.

I look forward to hearing from you within seven days. Should I not be fully satisfied with your response I will not hesitate in taking the matter further which will include but not be limited to, informing Trading Standards and if necessary starting proceedings through the Small Claims Court.

Yours [*sincerely/faithfully*]

Real example of rejecting an item over a year old

A friend had bought a sofa over a year ago from a mail order company, Studio. It was clearly faulty and she was having difficulty getting any response. I wrote an email for the CEO on her behalf. I stated that there were 2 really sharp metal rods (thin ones) poking through the fabric, so when hands were put down the middle bit of the sofa it really hurt, obviously. Karen had only done this once now knowing it was there but the item was clearly faulty and she has very young children to consider. Originally she was told that because she had had the bed more than a year there was nothing that could be done. However, once this was checked further (with one assumes, their legal department) she was told that it would have to go to quality control. Karen was promised a call back that never came and she had to chase it up, get a form to fill in and respond to a request to send photos of the issue which she did. The proof of postage for this was available. Again she had to chase and 'phone again to be told that her letter had not arrived. After that a leg on the sofa literally snapped off when she sat on the end causing her to fall. It was now not level.

The sofa was clearly faulty and under the Sale and Supply of Goods Act 1994 she was entitled to a full refund, repair or replacement. It was easily proven that the fault was there from the start and so the fact that she had had this item for over a year is irrelevant.

In addition to the full refund I expected them to arrange for removal of the sofa and provide redress for the inconvenience caused, not least the damage to Karen's hand, the time spent on the matter and the stress involved. Karen had not been able to use the sofa bed and so also expected redress for this particularly in light of Studio's delayed and non-existent responses prolonging the matter.

I added my usual "see you in court" line if we were not satisfied with the response. Karen received a replacement (which is what she wanted) plus £50.

Real example of complaining about a free gift

It was the principle of the thing! As every parent knows, that "free gift" on that comic is not free! We bought a Thomas the Tank Engine comic with a blow music thingy. It didn't work. So my then 3 year old and I wrote a letter. We pointed out that it was part of the sale of the comic and because the item didn't work they were in breach of the amended Sale of Goods Act 1979. My son received a response apologising and enclosing two Thomas books and asking him to tell his Mummy that they always quality check their gifts!

Real example of a shop refusing a refund for a faulty item

Andrea bought a Penguin Pocket Red T-shirt from Scotts, part of the JD Sports chain, paying £29.00. The shirt had been worn once and washed once and she returned it to the store two weeks later when she discovered a hole. She was told that the T-shirt would need to be sent off for inspection despite the notice in store saying that this would be when items were over 90 days old. She wrote and received a response saying that the fault was due to "contact damage". Utterly ridiculous, what contact damage and by whom? She believed that the hole was there at point of purchase and if it wasn't, that it developed within one day's wear and one wash and the hole was in the stitching which the photograph showed! Andrea then wrote and didn't receive a response. She emailed again and was told that they hadn't received the letter (despite it being signed for!) but would do another inspection. She then contacted me and I wrote this to send to the CEO:

Dear

I received a letter from *xxxx* department to which my complaint was passed. However, I have already written to this department and part of my complaint was the way they dealt with it. In fact the matter has now got worse. Scotts has rejected my claim regarding the faulty product. It has since said that my letter can't be found even though it was sent recorded delivery and was signed for, for which I obviously have proof. I am now being told to resend the t shirt. I am not going to do this. I have already sent it once and see no reason why I should be put to yet more inconvenience due to Scotts' appalling service. Under the amended Sales of Goods Act 1979 I am entitled to goods that are of satisfactory quality and fit for purpose. This t shirt clearly breaches that.

I expect a full refund and appropriate redress for the inconvenience caused. I look forward to hearing from you within seven days. Should I not be fully satisfied with your response I will start proceedings in the Small Claims Court against you with no further reference to you. I will be claiming for the cost of the t shirt, the cost of an independent report stating that the t shirt has only been washed once, cost of postage (recorded delivery etc.), redress for my time spent on the matter, the court fee and out of pocket expenses for attending court (e.g. work time, mileage, parking costs).

Yours sincerely

Andrea received a call from the manager of Customer Services saying that they said they didn't think they were in breach of consumer rights (I beg to differ) but as a goodwill gesture they would refund the full amount in a voucher (I had told Andrea not to accept this, cash refund only to which he then agreed) plus a £20 gift voucher on return of the t shirt. A good result in the end but the matter didn't end there.

Unfortunately, Andrea wrote to customer services to say that she had thought about the conversation and couldn't she just dispose of the garment? She received an email to say that if she did not return the garment she would not get a refund. As I say in my tips, you should keep to the agreements you make with customer services. They were paying the postage and providing a goodwill gesture so it was not unreasonable to return the item which they might want for quality control or tax purposes. It's a fair enough statement to say no return no refund and Andrea was receiving a goodwill gesture for the inconvenience.

As often is the case in customer services, the internal communication was appalling and Andrea received an email to say that they needed the t shirt for inspection and couldn't overturn the decision! Meanwhile, Andrea had tried to use the gift card in store and was told that there was no money on it and it would take some days for it to appear. This is obviously nonsense. She wasted more time in store trying to deal with the matter.

I wrote again outlining the embarrassment and poor service plus details of the ridiculous email she received. Andrea received a further £20 goodwill gesture receiving this time a card for £40 that worked.

This story outlines one of the classic fob offs – trying to say that the fault was not there at point of purchase. It also highlights the need to persevere sometimes and pursue your legal rights.

Real example of using Misrepresentation Act 1967

Laura's daughter Millie bought some Special K and wrote to the customer services. She used humour:

Dear Sir/Madam

I have been buying Special K for a few years now and especially enjoy the strawberry and chocolate flavour. You can imagine my disappointment upon opening the second box in a row to again find a measley amount of strawberries and chocolate – in fact I would say that if they were in the box then they were obviously wearing a Harry Potter invisibility cloak.

I don't expect the box to be crammed with strawberries and chocolate but the image on the front of the box clearly shows an abundance of both ingredients and I'm sure you didn't intend to be in breach of the Misrepresentation Act 1967.

As I am a penniless student thanks to our delightful government demanding extortionate tuition fees, I am not in a position to buy a punnet of strawberries and a bar of dark chocolate to sprinkle over the top of the remaining cereal that has been purchased. I also fear for my health as without the strawberries I am at risk of developing scurvy or some such deficiency without the strawberries contributing to my 5 a day. This will obviously have a knock on effect and disrupt not only my studies but my social life as my deteriorating skin condition will repel any admirers – in turn destroying any self confidence I may have.

I feel it is your duty to respond to my dilemma and explain the disappearance of the aforementioned ingredients.

Kind regards
Millie

You'd think that would bring a smile to someone's face wouldn't you? Poor student. Nope. She got back a really boring response. Millie was told that the equipment is electronically controlled and every effort is made to ensure there is a constant weight of fruit in every packet. The customer services woman was sorry that the packet was lacking in fruit (she didn't apologise for the lack of chocolate!) The Quality Assurance manager had addressed this with her staff and steps were being taken to stop it from happening again. Not even a Harry Potter reference in her reply. She provided a £5 voucher. Now, this was Millie's first complaint and I didn't want her to be put off by this poor response. So I reverted to type and wrote an email for her. I clarified the Misrepresentation Act 1967 for the CEO and I pointed out that a £5 voucher didn't cover two boxes of cereal and I may have made some reference to humourless staff… An apology and £15 voucher later I hope that Millie continues to complain when things aren't right.

Common fob offs

Too often a retailer will try and fob off consumers and not provide a full refund, repair or replacement. (See "Common fob offs"). In this case use one of the above templates and use the relevant line below for each fob off:

- We do not give refunds – "Under the Consumer Rights Act 2015 (Sale and Supply of Goods Act 1994 for purchases made before 1st October 2015) I am legally entitled to a refund, repair or replacement. It is illegal not to give refunds where items are faulty and I have only had the item two weeks – please ensure that that I receive a full refund within 7 days".
- You/we will send it back to the manufacturer – "Under the Consumer Rights Act 2015 (Sale and Supply of Goods Act 1994 for purchases made before 1st October 2015) my contract is with you and not the manufacturer".
- You will need to contact the delivery firm – "Under the Consumer Rights Act 2015 (Sale and Supply of Goods Act 1994 for purchases made before 1st October 2015) my contract is with you and not the delivery firm".
- You should have taken out a warranty – "A warranty is wholly irrelevant in this case. "Under the Consumer Rights Act 2015 (Sale and Supply of Goods Act 1994 for purchases made before 1st October 2015)" (fill in the relevant entitlement from above template).
- We don't take back items bought in the sale – "Under the Consumer Rights Act 2015 (Sale and Supply of Goods Act 1994 for purchases made before 1st October 2015) I am entitled to a full refund unless the fault was pointed out at point of purchase and therefore contributed to the reason for the discount. This fault was not pointed out at

point of purchase and therefore I am exercising my right under the aforementioned law to a full refund".

- You caused the fault – "Under the Consumer Rights Act 2015 (Sale and Supply of Goods Act 1994 for purchases made before 1st October 2015) I am entitled to items that are fit for purpose and are of satisfactory quality. I have had the item for (length of time) and therefore the onus is on the retailer to prove that I caused the fault or provide a full refund, repair or replacement".

- You don't have the receipt so we can't give a refund – "I have provided an alternative proof of purchase (detail, e.g. bank statement) which is sufficient evidence under the Consumer Rights Act 2015 (Sale and Supply of Goods Act 1994 for purchases made before 1st October 2015)".

- It is over 6 months so we do not need to give a refund – "Under the Consumer Rights Act 2015 (Sale and Supply of Goods Act 1994 for purchases made before 1st October 2015) I am entitled to goods that last a reasonable length of time and a xxx should last longer than xx months. The fault was clearly there at point of purchase/ or has developed due to a fault at point of purchase because (describe)".

TEMPLATE: **Requesting repair and retaining legal rights**
For purchases prior to 1st October 2015 quote "Sale and Supply of Goods Act 1994"

Dear [*xxx*]

Re: [*item*]

On the [*date*] I purchased [*item*] which has since developed a fault [*describe*]. Under the Consumer Rights Act 2015 I am entitled to items of a satisfactory quality, that are fit for purpose, match the description and last a reasonable length of time [*delete the irrelevant entitlement to your case*]. I have sent the item to the manufacturer under guarantee. However, I am retaining my rights under the aforementioned law to a full refund should the manufacturer not repair the item satisfactorily.

Yours [*sincerely/faithfully*]

Real example of using a guarantee

I have never requested a repair under guarantee as I always get a full refund. However, the nearest I got to it was with a cooker. Last year, we bought two new ovens. One of the oven's instructions (a display on the oven) was in German. I would say that was not fit for purpose, given that I don't speak German.

So I telephoned the company where we bought the ovens and started my spiel. At this point I just wanted to reset the display into English so I could turn the thing on! So no actual need for a full refund, just someone to tell me how to change it. So they just said they would contact the supplier to send out an engineer. But, I was pushed from pillar to post, customer services helpline, switchboard, AEG and one of them even advised "Can you use the other oven and follow the instructions on the one in English?" I kid you not, he expected me to use the other oven, counting the times I selected each electronic choice whenever I used the oven!

This was one of the very rare occasions I didn't keep on at the retailer, mainly because I didn't want a refund. Eventually I got an engineer out from Electrolux. Meanwhile I was trying to register the ovens on the AEG website. Now, on the site one can select the model number then put in the serial number. I did this with a couple of items and then tried the ovens. It wouldn't process. So I sent a complaint through the web form. I received an email stating that they needed the model numbers even though, there in front of them, was the model number! I pointed out that this had been sent. A week later I wrote again and received another response asking for the model number. So I emailed a screen shot with the model number in it! I didn't get a response.

Meanwhile! The clocks were out of sync so I tried to get this sorted too. I wrote to the CEO regarding the issues. I had a reply from the UK Head of Customer Care who wanted to 'phone me to discuss. I insisted on correspondence by email.

The "engineer" (a more correct title would be technician) arrived and said two new clocks were needed and left paperwork stating that he would be back the following week in the morning. I received a text a week later saying he was coming in the afternoon. I emailed the head chap again and told him what time the "engineer" would come in the morning! I was right. I got everything sorted and again was asked to telephone to discuss redress. I expected everything in writing and received £250.

Then, something happened to the lining – the oven was nearly a year old by this point, so they could possibly have argued a repair and changed the lining. I would argue that the lining should last and still fight for full refund/replacement. I got my new oven. A newer model too.

Mail order and online purchases

Your rights when purchasing items through an advert or catalogue are exactly the same as buying from any other retailer, so your correspondence about faulty items would be as above. In addition, under the Consumer Contracts (Information, Cancellation and Additional Charges) Regulations 2013, consumers have 14 days cooling off period for changing their minds. There are exceptions to this (see Consumer Rights earlier in the book for these). 14 days to inform the company from receiving delivery and then a further 14 days from then. Whether return postage has to be paid depends on the trader's terms and conditions.

If you paid extra for speedier delivery and it wasn't delivered within this time you are entitled to the charge back. If the item is faulty you do not pay return postage and you should receive the full cost of any postage paid for sending the item to you.

This Act provided specific coverage for digital content. Digital content must not be supplied by the retailer within the 14 day cooling off period unless the customer has agreed to it and once the download starts the cancellation right is lost. If the customer does not give consent then s/he will have to wait until after the 14 days before downloading. Having bought the wrong download and realising it before I actually downloaded but before this new law came in. I welcome this Act!

Should consumers order an item from an advertisement in a newspaper which is signed up to the Safe Home Ordering Scheme (previously known as the Mail Ordering Protection Scheme) they can get their money back if the trader goes into liquidation or stops trading. Keep a copy of the advert when ordering until the item has been received.

TEMPLATE: **Retailer refusing to pay return postage**
For purchases prior to 1st October 2015 quote "Sale and Supply of Goods Act 1994"

Dear [*xxx*]

On the [*date*] I purchased [*item*] from you. As you are aware it is faulty and I am returning it for a full refund. You have refused to pay for the postage. However, under the Consumer Rights Act 2015 I am entitled to goods of a satisfactory standard, fit for purpose and that are as described. I need only pay return postage where I have simply changed my mind.

Therefore, please advise whether you would like to collect the item or provide return postage costs/reimburse me.

I look forward to hearing from you within 7 days.

Yours [*sincerely/faithfully*]

Buying counterfeit items

Trading Standards departments differ across the country in what they can do to help. With budgets slashed in the last couple of years they will probably not be able to help you get your money back if you are unable to do so, but they may take action against the seller. Citizens Advice centres may also be able to help and they have an agreement with Trading Standards to help you report it. You can also report your problem directly to Citizens Advice via an online form and contact the Consumer helpline.

Report the issue to Action Fraud. It is the UK's national fraud and financially motivated internet crime reporting centre.

Brand-i works in partnership with the Trading Standards Institute. If you think a website may be selling counterfeit goods report it online on their website. This will be forwarded to the brand holder's protection department and the National Trading Standards eCrime team who should act accordingly.

See the chapter ebay regarding buying counterfeit items on eBay.

Bespoke items

You can still send items back even if you have had them specially made, such as clothes or furniture. Your rights under the Sale of Goods Act 1979/Consumer Rights Act 2015 are the same. If a service has formed part of the contract such as an installed bespoke piece of garden furniture then the trader should remove the goods for no cost. If the trader refuses to do this, arrange to have them removed and claim the costs back from the trader. This may have to be through the Small Claims Court.

Furniture

The Furniture Ombudsman is the independent scheme for furniture, home improvements and floor coverings. Its role is to raise standards and resolve disputes between consumers and businesses. Businesses who are members of The Furniture Ombudsman follow a Code of Practice, which covers all domestic furniture (including fitted kitchen bedroom and bathroom installations) and floor coverings. So you have this option if you have used the in house resolution process or 3 months has passed since you raised the complaint, whichever is the soonest.

TEMPLATE: **Item and service delay complaint**
For services prior to 1st October 2015 quote "Supply of Goods and Services Act 1982"

Dear [*xxx*]

On the [*date*] we agreed that you would provide [*detail item(s)*]. We agreed that this would be delivered on the [*date*]. It is now [*xx*] days after that date.

Under the Consumer Rights Act 2015 I am entitled to goods to be received within a reasonable length of time. Therefore you are in breach of contract. Please ensure that I receive the [*item(s)*] within seven days.

Should I not receive the item I will be cancelling the contract and seeking a full refund for the item and service and if this is not forthcoming will start proceedings though the Small Claims Court.

I look forward to hearing from you within seven days. Should I not be fully satisfied with your response I will not hesitate in taking the matter further as described above.

Yours [*faithfully/sincerely*]

Collection of items

If you have a contract with the trader, while you wait for the item(s) to be collected you should take care to ensure that the item(s) is (are) not lost, damaged or destroyed. If you don't have a contract then you should look after the items as if they were your own which is a slightly lower level of responsibility. The trader has up to 6 years to pick the item(s) up from you, so if it looks like there is not going to be a collection you should take legal advice about how to proceed.

Delivery

Goods must be delivered within the time frame agreed with the seller. If one hasn't been agreed (you have agreed a time frame if the listing supplies a time frame) the trader must deliver 'without undue delay' and at the very latest not more than 30 days from the day after the contract is made. After this time you are entitled to a full refund.

Of course, deliveries must also be carried out with reasonable skill and care. If you have not agreed for a neighbour to take in your parcel and s/he denies having it, then it is for the retailer to sort out and send a new one. This could get complicated if the neighbour has signed for it.

TEMPLATE: **Item not received**

Dear [*xxx*]

Re: [*Item*]

On the [*date*] I ordered and paid in advance for [*item(s)*]. It is now the [*date*] and I have not received [*it/them*].

The Consumer Contracts (Information, Cancellation and Additional Charges) Regulations 2013 part of the Consumer Rights Directive 2013 says that goods must be delivered within the time frame agreed with the seller. The listing for this item stated that I would receive the [*item(s)*] by [*date*]. You are therefore in breach of contract and I am requesting a full refund.

I look forward to hearing from you within seven days. Should I not be fully satisfied with your response I will not hesitate in taking the matter further which will include, but not be limited to, informing Trading Standards and if necessary starting proceedings through the Small Claims Court.

Yours [*sincerely/faithfully*]

Real example of delivery complaint

So, bargains. We all love them unless of course you are too rich or idiotic to care. In which case you wouldn't be reading this book on either count! Last Christmas I wanted some Body Shop stuff as presents using 16% off through Topcashback (that is the best cashback site which currently gives the most) plus a 50% discount code – so off I went to order the goodies.

Apparently though, it would appear that lots of other people had had the same thought and the site went down. Not completely. You could waste your time putting items in their basket only to fail at checkout. I and many other people took to Twitter and Facebook and I emailed. I was told that, due to all the problems of course, they were inundated and one had to wait days for a reply. I am The Complaining Cow, I don't do waiting.

I told the social media team on Twitter that I would get a response quicker than they said. They argued that I would not. I emailed the CEO of the Body Shop. I got a reply within five hours. Actually I got a 'phone call within hours but I don't do 'phone calls.

I wrote explaining that I had been inconvenienced, that the Topcashback percentage had gone down and that I doubted the legality of a site stating that one could purchase items online when one couldn't.

The CEO apologised, told me he had assigned the issue to someone else and would follow up. I thanked him and pointed out that I had deliberately finished my Christmas shopping in stores to continue on line and that the site had been down for many days. I put in a plea for everyone else too saying that I noted his remark that he too would be frustrated and annoyed in the same position. But I said that nothing was being done about everyone else in the same position and that having the website down for so many days was just ridiculous. So to anyone else who had problems with The Body Shop website Christmas 2013 I did try and sort it out for you too!

I agreed to a 'phone call to get my order in time and with all the discounts. Typically some of the items had gone out of stock in this time so I got a couple of upgrades for free, a gift and a £10 voucher.

It was then delivered. However, the lid was not put on properly on one of the oils and oil leaked over everything including my carpet. So I went back to Jeremy and Sonja who had been dealing with this. (The chappie she got to phone me each time was very good it has to be said). I pointed out their legal obligations and of course they offered to pay for the carpet to be cleaned.

I was gutted, the professional clean got the stain out. Could have done with a new hallway carpet! (Had the stain not come out then I would have been entitled to further redress - cost of a new carpet allowing for reduction for wear and tear of existing one).

But this does show that a) you can take a complaint further and get listened to b) even large companies don't always do well with social media and c) frequently when you go to the CEO the problem gets resolved and in this instance extremely well.

I was on the ITV news discussing this story. I spoke about rights when ordering purchases and said the same as Martin Lewis too but they cut that! You can see it on my YouTube channel.

7 FINANCE

The Financial Conduct Authority (FCA) regulates over 50,000 firms that offer credit, loans or debt services. Firms must be registered with the FCA in order to offer these. On its website, the FCA warns consumers of companies which are not registered with it and appear to be offering these services.

The Prudential Regulation Authority (PRA) is a part of the Bank of England and responsible for the prudential regulation and supervision of about 1,700 banks, building societies, credit unions, insurers and major investment firms.

Both work to ensure that companies meet standards set. It would be another book to detail all the standards and all the things that could go wrong. Below are the most common things people complain about.

The Money Advice Service is an independent service set up by government to help people manage their money, providing free and impartial advice. It also works in partnership with other organisations to help people make the most of their money.

Banks & building societies

Banks can charge you, should you go into the red. However it is worth complaining if you feel that it is unfair, for example if it was only for a couple of days and you transferred money as soon as you realised. I have done this a few times over the last 25 years. It has always worked. The only time it didn't work first time was a couple of years ago and I then wrote to the CEO outlining my loyalty as a customer and I then got the money refunded.

Remember that the bank does not have to refund correctly applied charges, I just feel they do not reflect anything like the extra administrative time the matter might take. The ease with which I have had the charge refunded in the past I believe shows that if you are seen to make the effort that will be acknowledged. My examples were all genuine mistakes where I had forgotten something leaving the account or, had miscalculated! Don't be afraid to admit to making a mistake as this also goes a long way to a friendly customer services representative being understanding.

Banks don't pay out refunds of charges as easily as they used to, but they are obliged to treat customers fairly so it is worth writing to complain. You can go back 6 years. Unlikely that you have the statements but you can look online at your account for information or you can request a list of transactions for the last 6 years. Don't ask for statements as the bank could charge you £10 per statement!

If you are in financial hardship, complain about more than one unfair charge over the years and threaten to take the matter to the Financial Ombudsman it is quite possible that you will receive a goodwill gesture. All cases where the Financial Ombudsman thinks treatment has been unfair will be looked at and the service is free so it is worth going further.

Generally speaking if the charge exceeds the amount you are overdrawn or you get stuck in debt because of the cycle of continuous charges you could take the matter to the Financial Ombudsman.

In response to your complaint banks could:

- *Refund in full.*

- *Refund in part.* Banks should deal with your case sympathetically so if you feel that the offer is not fair, contact the bank again with an amount that you think is more appropriate and negotiate.

- *Ask you to fill out a form.* The bank may want more information regarding your financial hardship. In this case fill out as fully as possible and return speedily as this shows that you are serious.

- *Require the refund be used to pay off debt.* If it was just the one charge it is likely that the bank will just refund the amount into the account. However, if you are claiming for the past 6 years it may be a figure into hundreds of pounds. If your account is in debt you should accept this offer. However, if you have other debts such as utility bills or mortgage arrears incurring higher charges contact the bank and explain the situation.

- *Reject but offer to help in other ways.* The bank may accept that you are in financial difficulties but not offer to refund the charges, choosing to do something else such as not making charges for the following 6 months or offering a repayment plan. You could accept this offer, but if you are not happy then write again.

- *Reject out of hand.* The bank may completely reject your request. Some banks may do this automatically for all claims as a matter of policy as many people will not pursue the matter. In this situation write again (I'd go to the CEO at this point) explaining your disappointment with the decision and threaten to take the matter to the Financial Ombudsman. If the claim is rejected again then proceed with the Financial Ombudsman. You have nothing to lose.

TEMPLATE: **Unfair charges**

Dear [*xxx*]

Re: [*Account no*]

I have been a [*bank name*] customer for [*xx* years. In that time I have never gone into the red/rarely gone into the red and when I have it was by mistake and for a very short time.

On [*date* I went into the red for [*xx*] days. As soon as I realised I rectified the situation. However, on [*date*] I was charged [£*xx*]. I believe this is not reflective of the error and trust that in light of my loyal custom you will waive this charge. I am also requesting interest on this charge/these charges at 8%.

I believe the fact that I have incurred these bank charges is contrary to the aims of the Lending Code (Section 9) and Banking Conduct of Business Sourcebook (section 5.1.4 'in particular, a firm should deal fairly with a banking customer whom it has reason to believe is in financial difficulty').

Should I not be happy with your response I will look at switching my bank account to one that is more accommodating of genuine mistakes and has offers for people switching. I will also take the matter to the Financial Ombudsman.

I look forward to hearing from you.

Yours [*faithfully/sincerely*]

TEMPLATE: **Unfair charges when in financial hardship**

Dear [*xxx*]

Re: [*Account no*]

I have been a [*bank name*] customer for [*xx*] years. On the [*date(s)*] I was charged [£*xx*] for going overdrawn. I believe that these charges are excessive.

I am in financial hardship due to: describe your personal situation

I believe the fact that I have been incurring bank charges is contrary to the aims of the Lending Code (Section 9) and Banking Conduct of Business Sourcebook (section 5.1.4 'in particular, a firm should deal fairly with a banking customer whom it has reason to believe is in financial difficulty').

Should I not be happy with your response I will look at switching my bank account. I will also take the matter to the Financial Ombudsman.

Yours [*faithfully/sincerely*]

Account administration

Sometimes, banks and building societies mess up your account. You change your name or contact details and they get it wrong. Or you don't get notified of changes to your account or a wrong payment is made. It is usually down to human error and we all make mistakes but you are entitled to services to be carried out with reasonable care and skill.

Real example of simple administration gone wrong

A few years ago I changed my name. The fact that I am now complaining to companies using a different name is an added bonus perhaps?! So, I got the certificate, paid for legal copies as some financial institutions needed that and others were happy with copies. Sent off the details to Halifax and asked a simple question about fees on their card.

I got a letter back addressed using my former name, not enclosing my document and not answering the question, but enclosing a new direct debit form! I complained pointing out the blatant rudeness, poor process, lack of reason given for sending me a direct debit form and not returning my deed poll certificate.

I got a letter back offering me £30. However, the letter was poorly written, did not explain all the issues and most importantly told me that they had destroyed my deed poll certificate! Unbelievable, it cost £12 and was my property! So I wrote again and sometimes one just has to be pedantic:

I pointed out the following to Ms R:

I expected to be reimbursed for the destruction of my property.

She had requested that I send my deed poll to the same address as before. Given that this was the address at which I had my property destroyed I refused to do that again. I enclosed another legal copy to her and trusted that she would at least not destroy it and return it!

I received no explanation as to why, when my property was destroyed, no-one wrote to me to ask for the (actually another) deed poll certificate. Had I not complained I could have continued to wait for both my certificate to be returned and to receive my new credit card!

She completely ignored my question about the card and I asked for a third time.

She had failed to explain or apologise for why I only received a direct debit form and covering letter which ignored two out of three points in my letter. I found this extremely rude and unacceptable.

Now here's the particularly pedantic part. I wrote "I quote from your letter "I can see that we've let you down with some of the points you've raised. However I hope I've explained that there are some instances where I believe our actions were necessary."" This would indicate that she believed, as she has written in the plural, that at least two of her actions were necessary and acceptable. I asked what she thought these were. The list was - destroying property which does not belong to Halifax and that I had paid for, not writing to me regarding this, ignoring my query about the credit card and writing to me in my former name. I do not believe that any of these actions (or rather non actions) were necessary, some were just downright rude. I asked her to explain which processes she thought were necessary so that I could inform the relevant authorities.

I also expected more than the £30 offered.

I got a response. In short, £12 reimbursement for the deed poll and £100 for the inconvenience. So that was that. Nope, I'm pedantic remember. So although satisfied with the amount, I did need to write again. I had specifically requested that the money was not put on my credit card and that a cheque was sent. However, she had put the money on the card! So I wrote again and hoped that the following would help her in the future:

1) The first page of her letter was a photocopy and not the original on letter headed notepaper.
2) Fifth bullet point, incorrect use of an apostrophe in the word "fees".
3) "are charges" not "is charges" would be grammatically correct (as in my letter which you could have copied).
4) "You have been advised there is…" No, I advised you on this point and the instances are plural and therefore "are" not "is" is appropriate.
5) No new paragraph on what should have been the first new paragraph on the second page.
6) "…should be made clear to your at the time" should have been "you" not "your".
7) "Halifax so not apply any loading.." doesn't make any sense, I assume that you mean "do".
8) "…and enclosed your Deed…""enclose" not "enclosed".

Real example of diabolical bank processes bordering on offensive

Halifax again. A close friend of mine, let's call her Vicky French, sadly lost her husband to cancer a couple of years ago. When she tried to make the necessary changes to their Halifax account, the treatment she received was nothing short of disgusting. So awful was it that I am going to simply reproduce the correspondence that I wrote for Vicky. This story is long but is a good demonstration of how you need to write a letter when so many things have gone wrong. The detail and clarity necessary means that it does often take a lot of time but it has to be done. I have actually changed the names of staff here because perhaps some of them have now been trained and are better at their jobs.

We wrote to the CEO on the 3rd March:

Dear Mr Horta-Osorio

I am incredulous at the treatment I have received from Halifax and have despaired and given up hope trying to sort out the matter with any customer service representative.

As a recent widow, the service I have received has been nothing short of unforgivable and shocking in the extreme. I therefore would like to bring the following to your attention:

I attach a copy of a letter to which I have not had a response. This is in keeping with the appalling service I have received from Halifax in the last couple of months.

On the 25th January 2012 I notified Halifax of my late husband's death. Since then I have received nothing but rudeness, ignorance and downright incompetent service. So many are the issues I will bullet point them for you.

1) On the 25th January 2012 I had an appointment at Halifax in xxxxxx with Dawn the bereavement advisor to notify her of the death of my husband. When I went to use my driving licence as ID a few days later I realised that I had not been given it back. I went into the branch and asked for it and was told that after an extensive search that they could not find it.

2) On the 6th February a letter was sent to my deceased husband and me. It was very upsetting to receive such a letter when staff had been informed of his death and yet could not even undertake what for Halifax staff would be a simple routine administrative task. Wholly unacceptable and wholly preventable.

3) I then received a letter dated the 8th February where I was informed that the documents would be sent to a dedicated bereavement team. In this letter it said "If Mr Michael French held an ISA with us..." is it really beyond the comprehension of a member of staff to look at the documents and see that one was clearly an ISA and change the language of the obvious standard paragraph?

4) I think attending a meeting on the 25th January and then receiving a letter dated 8th February is a poor delay in responding to matters particularly given the circumstances.

5) On Saturday 28th January 2012 I attempted to use my debit card in an ATM to withdraw cash from the joint account. The request was refused in spite of my being able to access the balance details. I had to withdraw cash on a credit card, thus incurring charges. On the 30th January – I spent 2 hours in the xxxxxx branch whilst staff attempted to find out why I was unable to withdraw funds from my joint account. They finally discovered that a block had been put on the account as one of the account holders was deceased but no-one knew why or how to remove it. A new card was ordered for me at this time to rule out the possibility that my card was damaged but my pin would remain the same. Later that day staff 'phoned me to say that the problem had been resolved and my card would be okay to use. I have incurred charges on my credit card and wasted over

two hours on this matter alone.

6) On the 9th February I was again unable to withdraw funds from the joint account and upon checking at the branch I discovered that my name had been removed from both joint accounts! How incredibly inefficient!

7) I later found that not only had my name been removed but so had all the direct debits, standing orders and payment details relating to our current account. I was unable to access past statements online or see any transactions on the account.

8) When I 'phoned the Bereavement Service Centre on the 9th February I was told that the Stage 1 team had removed the wrong name from the joint current account. Two names on one account and a member of staff cannot even take the care necessary to remove one name. Not difficult given that they had the copy of the death certificate there! Given that it is a dedicated team it is utterly incomprehensible and unforgiveable.

9) When I went to the branch following this, I was told that not only had the error been made on the current account but the same error had been made on the joint saver account. That was yet another 2 hours spent sorting out the matter.

10) That evening I checked my bank accounts online and discovered to my horror that all past history had been wiped from both accounts.

11) I 'phoned on the 13th February to ask for the complaint reference number in order to follow it up but was told by Kimberley that she had "voided the complaint" as she had spoken to the branch manager in xxxxxx on 10th February and assumed it had been sorted". It is MY decision and my right as to whether I wish to complain and a member of staff should not take it upon themselves to cancel a complaint just because they think the matter has been sorted. Even if it had (which it hadn't) that is wholly irrelevant. In fact the branch manager had spent the best part of the day notifying various companies that the direct debits had been cancelled in error trying to reinstate them.

12) The inconvenience of the incorrect cancelling of my direct debits has been immense. 12 direct debits were set up on this account. I spent many hours 'phoning the relevant companies, paying by credit card and some have ended up with double payments. This is time that I should not have had to spend on such matters at a deeply upsetting time.

13) I received a letter dated the 15th February. This letter was carelessly sent by Robert who could not even undertake a simple spell check on his letter and find that "Bereavement" was spelt incorrectly.

14) This letter enclosed a leaflet informing me of the Halifax complaint procedure even though I made my complaints clear on the telephone. I therefore spent yet more time on the matter writing the complaints.

15) On the 22nd February I wrote the attached letter to Halifax customer services. I have not even received an acknowledgement letter! I find this extremely ignorant.

16) Due to Halifax's mistakes I have had to wait for copies of statements in order to proceed with the Grant of Probate and tax returns for my late husband.

17) I have had to make numerous calls to Halifax at my expense. I am astounded by the service I have received from Halifax. Halifax has indulged in a catalogue of errors which have been deeply upsetting and added significantly to my already high stress levels. What should have been simple administrative procedures regularly undertaken by Halifax staff have included mistake after mistake with no due care and attention to anything. Not even who has died! Wholly reprehensible and unacceptable.

At no point has anyone properly apologised for the above errors.

I have not received services carried out with reasonable skill and care to which I am entitled under the Supply of Goods and Services Act 1982. Halifax is clearly in breach of this Act.

I trust that you will look into these matters at your earliest possible convenience. I expect to be fully compensated for the errors, my considerable time spent on the issues, the telephone calls, my costs, the inconvenience, the lack of appropriate understanding for my situation shown and the distress caused by having to deal with this over a time when I am grieving for my late husband.

Should I not be fully satisfied with your response I will not hesitate in taking the matter further. This will include, but not be limited to, informing the media, writing about my experience on various internet forums and of course the Financial Ombudsman.

I look forward to hearing from you

Yours sincerely

Vicky French

On the 8th March we wrote again saying that although Vicky expected a response within 7 days she did expect an acknowledgment. This provoked a response from Claire who said that the matter had been referred to a case handler.

Damon telephoned on the 8th March acknowledging the email and that he would 'phone again. Vicky as instructed by me told him that she only wanted a response in writing.

On the 12th March Damon wrote to Vicky. She received it on the 16th March. He listed her complaints and even made a mistake in doing so by saying that a complaint she had made was closed by xxxxxx branch when in fact it was the Bereavement Centre. He said that he did not propose to respond to each individual point as he didn't feel it would serve any purpose to examine them individually. (Amazing, all those complaints not examined to ensure they don't happen again to anyone else). He apologised for the inconvenience and distress caused and offered £500 plus costs of withdrawing funds from the credit card and replacement driving licence and provided a direct line number.

Meanwhile on the 13th March we had to write to Mr Horta-Osorio and Claire again:

Dear Mr Horta-Osorio

I did not think that the treatment afforded to me after the death of my husband on 6.1.12 by the Halifax Building Society could get any worse, but today I was once again reduced to tears by the incompetence or careless neglect of your staff.

As a widowed parent of a child receiving child benefit I am entitled to Widowed Parents Allowance from the date of my husband's demise. The bereavement payment was issued on 31.1.12 to our joint account and was returned as "not accepted" into that account.

Why was this the case? When I originally notified Halifax about my husband's death on 25.1.12 I was informed that payments could still be made into the joint account.

Why was I not told that this payment had been refused? I am now £1200 worse off until the widowed parents' arrears have been credited. Needless to say I will not be using a Halifax account.

My tax code is calculated on the basis of receipt of the extra bereavement allowance which I have not had for the last 3 months.

On a separate note I have been advised that all correspondence should be in writing. You have my email address. Please email me rather than use 2nd class post which has been done in the past in order for this matter to be dealt with speedily.

I am still incredulous about the catalogue of errors in what should be a straightforward procedure at a very difficult time.

Yours sincerely

V French

On the 19th March we wrote again to Claire and Mr Horta-Osorio to say that Vicky had tried to ring Damon but it had gone to a recorded message saying it is a switchboard number now closed. We also pointed out that the complaint was and still is, with the Bereavement Service Centre.

We added that we had emailed on the 13th March regarding more incompetence and not had any response. Rude and upsetting but not surprising.

Damon wrote again. The letter was dated the 12th March. In it he apologised for Vicky not being able to 'phone him and he had rectified the error. Interesting that this letter was written the day before the email informing Halifax of this difficulty. He apologised for the error in his letter. They were unable to arrange for a letter to be sent from the Bereavement Service Centre as the apology was offered by the whole bank. Feedback had been given.

Damon had been in contact with Vicky regarding the above and they had agreed a further £100 to compensate for the financial losses.

On the 23rd March Penny wrote after speaking with Vicky. They couldn't find any trace of the payment. If Vicky wanted the bank to pursue the matter she would have to contact the department of Work and Pensions and ask them to conduct a BACS trace on the payment. She apologised for the fact that Vicky had received a cheque book in her husband's name and a new one was being sent out. The account was credited with a further £50.

A story of terrible customer service and the efforts one has to undertake to rectify matters. The total of £650 perhaps reflects that but I do wonder what the Financial Ombudsman would have said. However, given the circumstances it was sensible to accept the offers.

Bank unauthorised transactions

If you notice a transaction that you did not authorise, notify the bank immediately who should refund the money straight away unless it can be proven that; you authorised the transaction (your bank cannot say that use of your password, card and PIN conclusively proves you authorised a payment); you are at fault because you acted fraudulently or, you deliberately, or with 'gross negligence', failed to protect the details of your card, PIN or password in a way that allowed the transaction; you told your bank about an unauthorised payment 13 months or more after the date it left your account.

If the bank refuses to refund the money it should explain why. You then have the option of taking the matter to the Financial Ombudsman or Small Claims Court.

You may have to pay the first £50 if your card was lost or stolen. However, you are not liable for any unauthorised transactions after you have informed the bank of loss or theft.

Direct Debit Guarantee

Your bank or building society monitors and protects the efficiency and security of your direct debit. Those using the system go through a careful vetting process before they're authorised, and are closely monitored by the banking industry. The efficiency and security of direct debit is monitored and protected by your own bank or building society.

If there are any changes to the amount, date or frequency of your Direct Debit the organisation will notify you (normally 10 working days) in advance of your account being debited or as otherwise agreed. If you request the organisation to collect a payment, confirmation of the amount and date will be given to you at the time of the request.

If a mistake is made with your direct debit you are covered by the Direct Debit Guarantee.

If an error is made in the payment of your Direct Debit, by the organisation or your bank or building society, you are entitled to a full and immediate refund of the amount paid from your bank or building society.

If you receive a refund to which you are not entitled, you must pay it back when the organisation asks.

According to the Financial Ombudsman, common fob offs made by banks and building societies when a direct debit is wrongly paid are; "The customer didn't give enough notice", "We don't operate the direct debit guarantee", "You'll have to contact the originating company for a refund" and "The guarantee doesn't apply – because you haven't suffered a loss". None of these are correct and should you not receive a refund take the matter to the Financial Ombudsman.

TEMPLATE: **Direct debit incorrectly paid**

Dear [*xxx*]

Re: [*Account number*]

On the [*date*] I wrote to you informing you to stop my direct debit to [*company name*]. On the [*date*] [*£xx*] left my account as a direct debit. Please refund this amount under the Direct Debit Guarantee Scheme.

Yours [*faithfully/sincerely*]

TEMPLATE: **Bank/building society refusing to refund direct debit error**

Dear [*xxx*]

Re: [*Account number*]

Thank you for your letter of [*date*] informing me that you will not be refunding the direct debit incorrectly paid to [*company name*]. I am covered by the Direct Debit Guarantee Scheme. The reason you provide [*insert reason*] does not exclude you from this.

Please refund the [*£xx*] incorrectly taken from my account within seven days and confirm this in writing. If you are unable to do this, please provide a letter of deadlock so that I can pursue the matter through the Financial Ombudsman.

Yours [*faithfully/sincerely*]

Real example of complaining to a bank about Misrepresentation

When we went on holiday to The Philippines I used the Money Saving Expert *travelmoney.moneysavingexpert.com/* (Martin Lewis MSE) website to compare rates for money. The best deal was NatWest. So I bought the Pesos. When I went to take the money we hadn't spent to be changed the assistant told me that they couldn't exchange without charging commission which was not what it said on the website. A breach of the Misrepresentation Act 1967 then. Nat West staff wouldn't have it though.

Nor when I went back again to see someone senior!

So, obviously I did not pay the commission. I wrote. I pointed out the error of their ways. Namely that they stated no commission fees on the website and that I would be informing Martin Lewis so that MSE could take NatWest off the site. I expected redress for having to make another journey, parking costs, time wasted on this matter and the inconvenience. They wrote acknowledging the mistakes and asking me to 'phone them to discuss the matter. I don't do 'phoning for the variety of reasons outlined in the tips. So I wrote again. I made it clear that I would not be wasting any more time discussing the matter, all the details were in the letter and I suggested they ensured that when I took the money back that staff were properly informed and that I received adequate redress. Two trips and three letters I'll have good redress thank you.

NatWest gave me £250. The amount I was exchanging was less than £100. However, the amount reflected their concerns about my informing Martin Lewis methinks!

Although the story above is a success story, it does show how a consumer should not just give up. 2 trips and 3 letters, most people wouldn't even bother with one letter never mind 3. However, this shows that it is worth complaining as well as it being the principle of the thing.

Never ever just give in to bad service. If they say no commission for exchanging money ensure that they keep to the promise. They are breaking the law if they don't. It's because people can't be bothered to complain and take the time to write a letter that bad practice continues.

PayPal

From 17 June 2014 you now have 180 days to report an issue. It used to be 45 days from when payment was made. PayPal also extended its UK buyer protection to cover digital goods, services, tickets and other goods "you don't usually hold in your hands" – e.g. music and film downloads, holidays or car rental.

If an eligible item that you've bought online doesn't arrive, or doesn't match the seller's description PayPal's Buyer Protection Scheme will reimburse you for the full amount of the item plus postage and packaging costs. Buyer Protection covers all your online purchases, on eBay or on any other website, when you use PayPal.

If you use your credit card to pay for something through PayPal and the funds go direct to the seller, then as long as the company you're buying from has a 'Commercial Entity Agreement' with PayPal you may still be able to claim under Section 75 for any misrepresentation or breach of contract.

If PayPal sees in favour of the seller and doesn't refund your money you may still be able to claim from your credit card company if you use a credit card to pay PayPal. But see the last paragraph in *Credit cards* below for the problem here.

If you need to take an issue further it may be possible to take a complaint about PayPal to the Financial Ombudsman. But not all of PayPal's services are covered and it is not clear which ones these are. Despite PayPal operating from Luxembourg, and contrary to popular belief, it is possible to take PayPal to the Small Claims Court. This seems a route people have taken to access their money when PayPal have frozen their accounts. The UK address is in the back of this book.

Credit cards

If you have a problem with an item you have bought or service you have received you can contact your credit card company. You may want to do this for example when the company has gone bust, is refusing to give you a refund or does not respond to communications from you. You have a right to be refunded if you make a claim within 6 years (5 in Scotland) using Section 75A of the Consumer Credit Act 1974.

Purchases over £100 and less than £30,000 are covered. You are covered if you pay as little as 1p but the item costs more than £100.

In 2007, the House of Lords ruled that Section 75 has no territorial limitations, therefore, cardholders who use their credit cards to make purchases abroad are protected in the same way as in the UK. So, purchases made on a credit card may also be covered under Section 75 when; goods or services are purchased from a foreign supplier whilst the cardholder is abroad, purchased from a foreign supplier for delivery to the UK, or purchased from a foreign supplier or agent who is temporarily in the UK.

Completing a credit card transaction through a third party payment service means that the credit card provider and the seller are no longer in a direct relationship so are not equally liable. This applies therefore to services such as PayPal, Amazon Marketplace, Worldpay and Google Checkout.

In the UK, where you are entitled to specific statutory protections (i.e. those listed in chapter 5 *Consumer Rights*) the credit card company is a second party to the purchase and is therefore equally liable in law if the other party defaults or goes into liquidation. However under Section 75 Consumer Credit Act 1979, the purchaser loses this legal protection if the card payment is processed via PayPal.

TEMPLATE: **Gaining a refund from a credit card company**

This is a very basic template, you will need to fill out details and provide evidence if necessary.

Dear [*xxx*]

Re: [*Account number*]

On the [*date*], I purchased describe [*item/service*] for [£*xx*] However the [*xxx*] has developed a fault (or describe the service failures). [*Xxx*] where I bought the [*item/ service*] has *rejected my request for a refund/not responded to communication (detail it) / has gone bust.*

Therefore, under Section 75 of the Consumer Credit Act 1974 please refund me the full amount of [£*xx*].

Should you need any more information to back up this claim please do not hesitate in contacting me.

I trust that I will receive confirmation of the refund within 14 days.

Yours [*faithfully/sincerely*]

Should the credit company ignore or reject your request, write again asking for a "letter of deadlock" so that you may go to the Financial Ombudsman. You can then take the matter to the Financial Ombudsman to make a decision. You are still able to go to court if you are not happy with that decision.

Credit card unauthorised transactions

Should you notice a transaction that you don't recognise on your statement contact the company immediately. One of the few times I would advise 'phoning as this is the sort of thing where time could be crucial. There are various reasons that an unauthorised transaction may appear; a company may have inadvertently taken two payments or your card could have been cloned. Then write a letter enclosing any evidence to show that the transaction could not have legitimately been made by you.

Should your card be stolen you should report it immediately by telephone. If transactions appear on your statement that occurred after the loss contact the credit card company immediately. You should be refunded, if not, write.

In both cases above if the credit card company refuses to agree and refund you, ask for a letter of deadlock and then you can take the matter to the Financial Ombudsman to investigate and/or go to the Small Claims Court.

TEMPLATE: **Unauthorised transactions on a stolen card**

Dear [*xxx*]

On the [*date*] my credit card was stolen and I notified you immediately. In this conversation you informed me that the following transactions had been made which were not authorised by me:

[*Detail*]

Please could you ensure that I am credited for the total amount above and write to confirm that this has been undertaken. I would appreciate your doing this by return.

Yours [*faithfully/sincerely*]

TEMPLATE: **Unauthorised transactions**

Dear [*xxx*]

On the [*date*] a debit was made for [*£xx*] to name of [*company*]. On the [*date*] I telephoned you to inform you that I did not authorise this transaction. Please find [*enclosed/attached*] evidence that this is the case. [*Detail the evidence e.g. out of the country*].

Please could you ensure that I am credited for the total amount above and write to confirm that this has been undertaken. I would appreciate your doing this by return.

Yours [*faithfully/sincerely*]

Real example of complaining about credit card charges

This is similar to the banks example above regarding going into the red. I have various different credit cards and at one time or another I have forgotten to pay off the amount or I hadn't received the bill to remind me. I always pay my bill in full, so when I receive charges for not paying by the due date I always complain.

I wrote explaining that I had not received the bill or it was an oversight and that this was evidenced because I always paid in full. Always ending with informing the company of my long standing loyalty and that if I did not receive a refund of the charges I would investigate moving my business to another company. Each time I received a full refund. I now pay by direct debit so the problem doesn't occur again!

So I would always urge you to complain when you think the charges unfair. However, I think it unlikely that you would get any refund if you didn't always pay in full or there weren't some clear exception to the usual way you pay off your card. My complaints worked with Sainsbury's Mastercard, Tesco Mastercard, Amazon, Marks and Spencer and Halifax.

Real example of using Section 75 of the Consumer Credit Act 1974

Many years ago we had some curtains made by a furniture and furnishings company. We paid the deposit on a credit card. The company wanted cash for the remainder which we wouldn't pay. Even though we would have been covered because we used the credit card for a deposit we knew something was wrong and if they were going to fleece customers by getting cash and not declaring it to receivers at a later point we would not let them get away with it! We won and the curtains were put up. They were not satisfactory. The swags and tails were different to the curtains and poorly hung.

As expected, as soon as I tried to get our money back, I could not get any response. Had we have given them cash they would have done a runner with it one assumes. Many people who were left out of pocket I'm sure would be pleased that at least the owners didn't pocket over £1,000 in cash.

So, I contacted the credit card company. I had to get an independent report and then returned the curtains to the warehouse. Quite ridiculous given that we knew that no-one was there but the credit card company insisted. So the curtains were sent back via a courier company (which messed up the delivery by not doing it within specified time and I got my money back for that too!) The curtains were brought back to us as undeliverable. The credit card company paid up.

Also useful to know is that this Act covers store cards. If the credit card company refuses to help, report it to the Financial Ombudsman.

See also chapter 11 *Insurance* and chapter 12 *Holidays and Flights* for more examples of how to use this Act.

Chargeback

Purchases bought on debit cards and below £100 are not covered by the Section 75 of the Consumer Credit Act 1974. Chargeback, although not part of any act of law, is a voluntary scheme based on scheme rules set by card issuers such as Mastercard and Visa. Because it isn't set in law you should use the Consumer Credit Act 1974 where possible, otherwise Chargeback can be applied for similar situations.

You will need to make the request within 120 days of the transaction date. Bear in mind that this scheme is much less well known than the Section 75 rule and so many staff might not know of it if you ring the bank. My advice therefore would always be to write.

If the bank/credit card company rejects your claim and/or you are unhappy with the process you can take the matter to the Financial Ombudsman but not to court.

Financial Ombudsman

Banks must deal with your complaint within 8 weeks (or explain what it is doing in this time and if it is to take longer, why). Follow their complaints procedure. If you are unhappy with their response and cannot gain a resolution within that time, request a "Letter of deadlock". It must be after 8 weeks from your initial letter of complaint, or you must have this letter, in order to take the matter to the Financial Ombudsman.

Write to the Financial Ombudsman outlining your complaint. You will need to fill out their simple 3 page complaint form, and send in any evidence. The time it takes can be anything from a few months to two years (although that long is rare and usually refers to complex PPI claims). 6 months appears to be the average.

If you wish to claim for a sum on top of any money that is due to you, check the Financial Ombudsman's website for examples of awards and levels you should look at. There is no set amount but there are guidelines for limits on what will be paid for certain types of mistakes/inconvenience. Anything up to £150,000 can be paid.

The Financial Ombudsman has a "voluntary jurisdiction" to allow businesses to sign up for certain types of complaint not otherwise covered by their compulsory jurisdiction. This includes:

- *Banks and general insurance companies based in Europe* and not regulated by the FCA – dealing predominantly with consumers in the UK.

- *Investment companies based in Europe* and not regulated by the FCA – dealing predominantly with consumers in the UK.

- *Mortgage and insurance intermediaries* that wanted to be covered by the ombudsman before they became regulated by law by the FSA (at which point they were covered automatically by compulsory jurisdiction).

- *Certain firms regulated by the FSA from 1 December 2001* (the date called "N2") that were not members of one of the predecessor ombudsman schemes but wanted to be covered by it for complaints about events that happened before "N2".

- *National Savings & Investments (NS&I)* – following the statutory abolition of the former Independent Adjudicator for National Savings & Investments.

- *PayPal* (from 2 July 2007) but the Financial Ombudsman does not provide details of what parts of PayPal services are covered.

- *Post Office Ltd* – for disputes relating to foreign exchange and postal orders

- *Freight-forwarders and storage companies* – for insurance-related complaints from retail customers.

I have used the Financial Ombudsman a few times and have always found it a very easy and straightforward process and staff are helpful.

TEMPLATE: **Deadlock letter request**

Dear [*xxx*]

Re [*complaint*]

On the [*date(s)*] I wrote to you regarding my complaint. I asked for [*detail*] to be undertaken to resolve the issue. I am not satisfied with your response so I am now taking this matter to the Financial Ombudsman.

Please supply me with a letter of deadlock.

Should I not receive this within 14 days I will assume that you are in agreement and proceed to the Financial Ombudsman with no further reference to you.

Yours [*faithfully/sincerely*]

Real example of using the Financial Ombudsman

Sadly, yet another Halifax story. Seven years ago when I was pregnant and made redundant ('tis okay that wasn't a complaint! The contract ended at the right time and I wanted the redundancy! Imagine the problems they would have caused for themselves if that hadn't been the case?!) It meant that I could pay a lump sum off my mortgage and I did so. I paid a few thousand and asked for the bank to reduce the term and not the amount.

What Halifax did then was quite incredible really. Someone from Halifax wrote to me and told me that I had missed a payment. Huh? Obviously I hadn't! So I wrote to them providing details. Unbelievably they did this a further two times AND charged me £45 per letter! I wrote to them each time and charged them for my letters.

So I went through the Financial Ombudsman and claimed for inconvenience. I won. I never did find out what or why their systems were so appalling. That year though I believe Halifax was the most complained about company to the Financial Ombudsman.

Pensions

If you have a complaint about a state pension contact the Pension Service Helpline. Explain your complaint and what you want to put it right. The Pension Service tries to resolve your complaint over the telephone. If it is unable to do so it will contact you within 15 days. If you remain unhappy with the response you can contact the Director General of Operations for the Department for Work and Pensions who will respond within 15 days. If you are not satisfied with this response you can take the matter to the Independent Case Examiner which is impartial and free. You can then take the matter to your MP and ask for the case to be referred to the Parliamentary and Health Ombudsman. You may get a special payment if you've experienced unfair treatment or suffered financially.

For other pensions contact your pension provider directly and make your complaint to them. The Pensions Advisory Service (TPAS) which is an independent non-profit organisation providing free information, advice and guidance on the whole range of company, personal and stakeholder schemes can also help try to resolve the issue and you should contact them before proceeding to the Pension Ombudsman.

The Pension Regulator website is also useful for (in the case of work based pensions) providing information on whistle blowing, such as mis-administration on your scheme. You can also complain about the Pension Regulator.

If your complaint is against the trustees or managers of an occupational pension scheme, ask them to deal with your complaint under the scheme's internal dispute resolution procedure (IDRP). By law, the Ombudsman cannot investigate your complaint until it has been through this procedure.

If you are not happy with the response from the pension provider then you can take the matter to the Pension Ombudsman. If not happy with the decision you can appeal to the High Court in England and Wales, the Court of Session in Scotland or the Court of Appeal in Northern Ireland. Any appeal will need to be on a point of law and made within short time scales.

Pension Ombudsman

The pension Ombudsman can investigate occupational pension schemes (which are linked to someone's employment) and individual pension arrangements, such as personal pensions. If your complaint was about how the pension was sold to you then you need to use the Financial Ombudsman.

Once you have gone through the company's complaint procedure and contacted TPAS you can contact the Pension Ombudsman.

Payment Protection Insurance

PPI for short. Designed to cover debt payments if you can't work. Thousands of people have been mis-sold. If you think you have been mis-sold do not pay a firm to claim the money for you. The process is very straightforward and there is no reason why you should part with any of the money that you are owed.

There is masses of information on PPI mis-selling on the internet. One of my favourite websites, *Money Saving Expert* (Martin Lewis), provides all the resources you need to make a claim. There is no need for me to reproduce it all here as it would be a book in itself.

HMRC

The number and types of complaints that one can make against the HMRC, such as tax codes, tax credits, tax paid, child benefit, self-employment are obviously vast. You will need to contact the relevant department (look online) and ask for the relevant complaint procedure. Generally speaking you will need to put your complaint in writing, include your National Insurance number, any reference number the HMRC has given you and your unique tax payer reference if you are self-employed. Describe what went wrong, dates, names of any people you have had contact with regarding the issue(s), the effect of the errors and what you want done to put it right.

Write to the relevant department and you should be assigned a complaint handler. The HMRC can refund any costs you have incurred such as postage, 'phone calls and professional fees. If it has made an error and it has caused you significant stress and worry it may make a payment to reflect this.

If you are not satisfied with the response take the matter to the department director. If not satisfied with this then ask for the independent adjudicator to look into the complaint within six months of your final correspondence with the director's office. The adjudicator is free and unbiased. Once you have exhausted these avenues you can ask your MP to refer your case to The Parliamentary and Health Service Ombudsman.

TaxAid advises people on low incomes with tax affairs and Tax Help for Older People also advises older people. (Details in chapter 27 *Useful Contacts*).

8 UTILITIES

ENERGY

There have been many reports over the last few years regarding poor practice in the energy market, such as mis-sellling, putting people on the wrong tariffs and over charging. Companies are bound by the same laws as suppliers of other services.

Following Ofgem investigations, if you have switched suppliers in the last couple of years with a company representative rather than online, you may have been mis-sold. It may be worth checking to see if the company has a compensation package.

Ofgem is the Office of the Gas and Electricity Markets, which supports the Gas and Electricity Markets Authority (GEMA), the regulator of the gas and electricity industries in Great Britain. The Authority's powers and duties are largely provided for in statute (such as the Gas Act 1986, the Electricity Act 1989, the Utilities Act 2000, the Competition Act 1998, the Enterprise Act 2002 and the Energy Acts of 2004, 2008, 2010 and 2011) as well as under rulings of European Community legislation in respect of energy regulation. GEMA oversees Ofgem's work and provides strategic direction.

Energy suppliers must have a procedure for dealing with complaints. This should be available on their website or by telephoning them. The procedure should include names and contact details of all available sources of independent help, advice and information.

If you have a complaint about your electricity, contact the supplier in the first instance. If you think you are entitled to compensation, contact your regional electricity distributor within three months of getting your power back on (if they haven't contacted you). Your regional electricity distributor may not be the same as the company that supplies you with electricity. There are fixed payments for various issues.

The big six companies must resolve a complaint within 8 weeks (12 weeks for smaller companies). The customer needs to be part of this process, providing any information requested. If it is not resolved within this time the supplier must produce a letter of deadlock. Once this is received the customer can take the complaint to the Energy Ombudsman. (In Northern Ireland, you should contact the Consumer Council for Northern Ireland).

The Priority Services Register is for vulnerable people (people who are of pensionable age, are registered disabled, have a hearing or visual impairment, or have long term ill-health) and includes lots of benefits including entitlement to a free annual gas check, priority reconnection and free advice. Register with your supplier.

Ofgem Standards of Conduct

In August 2013 Ofgem put new Standards of Conduct into place. They require suppliers and any organisations that represent them, such as brokers or third party intermediaries, to ensure that each domestic customer is treated fairly. They cover three broad areas:

Behaviour:
suppliers must behave and carry out any actions in a fair, honest, transparent, appropriate and professional manner.

Information:
suppliers must provide information (whether in writing or orally) which is:
- complete, accurate and not misleading (in terms of the information provided or omitted);
- communicated in plain and intelligible language;
- related to products or services that are appropriate to the customer to whom it is directed; and
- fair both in terms of its content and in terms of how it is presented (with more important information being given appropriate   prominence).

Process:
the supplier must:

- make it easy for the consumer to contact them;
- act promptly and courteously to put things right when they make a mistake;

- otherwise ensure that customer service arrangements and processes are complete, thorough, fit for purpose and transparent.

Four "core" tariffs per fuel (electricity and gas) will be the limit that any supplier can offer. This will apply to each payment type. Suppliers will be allowed to offer these tariffs to collective switching schemes. They will also be able to offer extra fixed term tariffs into schemes that meet their criteria.

Standing charge and a single unit rate for all tariffs and suppliers can set the standing charge at zero if they wish.

Dual fuel and online account management discounts remain. They will not be considered as "core tariffs" but as a discount. They will be simplified and will apply uniformly across all tariffs as £/pence per year. For example, a supplier would be able to offer a direct debit customer a choice of no more than four electricity and four gas tariffs. The customer could then choose a dual fuel discount and an online account management discount.

Existing, expensive "dead tariffs" (i.e. tariffs that are no longer marketed) – customers must be transferred onto the cheapest variable rate. A supplier will only be able to keep consumers on dead tariffs if they are cheaper, or as cheap, as the supplier's lowest standard or evergreen tariff.

Ban on increasing prices on fixed term deals or making other changes to fixed term tariffs (except trackers or structured price increases set out in advance which are fully in line with consumer protection law).

Ban on rolling forward household customers onto fixed term contracts without their consent.

42-49 day window before customers' end date of their fixed term tariff for them to decide if they want to stay with the supplier or switch.

Requirement to give all customers personalised information on the cheapest tariff offered for them. This information will appear on each bill and on a range of other customer communications.

All information suppliers send to consumers is to be simplified, more engaging and personalised to them.

Tariff Comparison Rate (TCR) – all suppliers' communications to provide "at a glance" information to help customers compare tariffs. The TCR will be similar to the APR comparison rate used with credit cards. Ofgem is also requiring suppliers to provide personalised estimates which take account of a customer's usage to enable them to compare tariffs more accurately when switching.

Tariff information label will set out key terms and conditions as well as relevant information to help consumers compare across suppliers.

Quality of Service Guaranteed Standards

The Quality of Service Guaranteed Standards are guaranteed standards of service levels that must be met by each distribution company. The Direction was made by GEMA and took effect in October 2010. These standards have been set to guarantee a level of service that it is reasonable to expect companies to deliver in all cases.

If the distribution company fails to meet the level of service required, it must make a payment to the customer subject to certain exemptions which are:

- severe weather makes it impossible to restore the supply
- strikes or industrial action
- you're out when the energy company visits and you knew they were coming
- you cancel an appointment.

Payments under the guaranteed standards compensate for the inconvenience caused by loss of supply. They are not designed to compensate customers for subsequent financial loss.

Ofgem monitors and enforces the guaranteed standards relating to quality of supply.

The guaranteed standards cover 12 key service areas, including supply restoration, connections and voltage quality, and for the consumer cover situations when:

- you report a faulty prepayment meter to your supplier and someone is not sent to repair or replace it within a specified time
- the supplier doesn't arrive within agreed time slot for a visit to your home
- the supplier doesn't respond to your written enquiries within a certain time limit
- gas supply is interrupted because of a fault - you may be entitled to a compensation payment, depending on for how long it is off. It must be restored within a specified time depending on the weather and the number of homes affected.

- the supplier does not give two days or more written notice when an electricity distributor plans to interrupt your supply
- a gas transporter digs up your garden or driveway and any damage caused by the work is not made good within ten days
- you are on the Priority Services Register and your gas supply is interrupted but you are not given alternative heating and cooking facilities within four hours.

Back billing

From 1 May 2018 all energy suppliers had to follow Ofgem's back billing rules. Before then it was only the "big six" who, according to Ofgem, did not always follow the principles. If the supplier is at fault for not sending you a bill for more than a year, (and this could be for a number of reasons including, not dealing with requests from you about a faulty meter or account and subsequently allowing a large debt to build, failing to process a direct debit or just failing to send you a bill) then you do not have to pay. There are some circumstances when this doesn't apply, such as if you make no attempt to make a payment. Should the company not honour this principle then follow their complaints procedure.

Cold weather payment

This is different to the Winter fuel payment. If you receive certain benefits and the temperature was forecast to be or is zero degree celsius or below for seven consecutive days you will receive £25 for each 7 day period between 1 November and 31 March. You can check if you are eligible and whether you will receive the payment (you do not need to claim, it will be automatic) on the Government Cold Weather Payments page. Details for how to claim if not received are also on the site.

Real example of a complaint about gas being cut off

There had been some gas works undertaken in our road for some weeks. Starting on the 14th December we were without gas for 3 days. It was extremely cold, around the time of the snow and we were given 2 small electric heaters, a further heater the next day and 2 electric hobs. It was only by chance that we were not without heat for longer. When we had been without gas for all of the 14th and it was about 5pm I went outside to ask the workmen when my gas supply would be back on. They told me that I should have gas and that when they had put the cameras down our house was showing as fine and being served from across the road (where pipes were not being replaced).

I wrote and stated that as per GS13 of the National Grid Standards I was not provided with notification of interruption of supply at least 5 days in advance. In fact I was not given any notification. Had I been, I would have been able to make alternative arrangements, including taking my two year old to a warm house and not wasting food.

The heaters gave little heat compared to a normally fully centrally heated house and I was unable to cook the meat I had defrosted (so couldn't refreeze). I had a two year old which made the situation worse as it was essential that he was kept warm. We had to have the heaters on full blast for the entire time we were without gas supply at obviously great cost to us. Electricity costing more than gas. I expected to be compensated for the 3 days we were without supply which I believed to be £30 plus £30 for each 24 hours without supply, plus the increased cost of running 3 electric heaters.

I received £140. (Under GS14 they had to respond within 10 days, sadly they did!)

Here's a tip for preventing complaints and if you don't do it already then shame on you! Always give your tradesmen/women tea, coffee and biscuits! I kept those poor very cold men in tea and biscuits whilst no-one else for many doors up and down did. Guess whose gas got put on first?

Real example of a complaint about gas works causing a power cut and property damage

Dear xxx

Re works in xxx Rd

I am writing regarding ongoing works carried out by the National Grid on xxx, Essex. The work undertaken by your teams has caused my family much distress, inconvenience, loss of services to our home and some unnecessary costs have been incurred. There are a number of incidents that contributed to the appalling situation.

National Grid commenced work adjacent to our home on Monday 22nd October 2012.

That afternoon, the workers damaged the water main resulting in us having no water services until late Tuesday morning. My family had to travel to our wider family in Upminster (10 miles away) to eat and wash as obviously we did not have water to do so.

Electricity was also cut through the night, and reconnected by morning.

On Wednesday 25th, our phone line was cut off. On investigation by BT, the fault was traced to a severed line 40 metres from our home, i.e. where your team had conducted ground works and had severed it. BT was unable to reconnect the line until 6th November (12 days), due to being unable to gain access to the specific area of the fault because of your works. National Grid engineers then filled in the hole where the severance had occurred causing BT to re-dig the hole and take extra time to reconnect the line.

I frequently work from home, so 'phone and internet access are essential for us to live our normal life. This disruption meant that I had to travel into London to head office to be able to work at a cost of £28 a day for the 9 days. We have a pre-paid home delivery service with Tesco for deliveries twice a week. Because we had no internet connection we were unable to do our twice weekly shop for that period. We therefore had to travel to shop being put to further inconvenience in addition to being out of pocket with delivery service.

When we discovered what the road works were for (i.e. to replace the gas mains) in xxx, we asked your engineers if there would be a disruption to our gas supply, we were told no.

On 6th November the gas supply was cut off without warning. We contacted British Gas (our supplier) as we did not know that the break in service was due to National Grid works. We did not know if there was a gas leak that caused the outage. The BG engineer discovered that the outage was due to your engineers 'not knowing that number 7 was connected to that main'. I was, and am, shocked that the engineers, working on gas mains are unaware of what houses are connected to what pipes! Unbelievable!

We returned from work the following day (7th November) to find our front garden had been dug up to replace gas pipes, we received no prior notice of this. We were not given any warning and as yet have not received any explanation for it. This further break in supply meant that we had to travel again to family to wash and keep warm for the evening. We slept in a cold house that night and next morning, used kettles to provide hot water for washing before work and school.

My wife suffers from an allergy to cold; Urticaria. She had a flare up of the condition which lasted over 24 hours. We have two young children who we worried about keeping warm.

The gas supply was reconnected at approximately 9pm on 7th November. Our garden had an exposed trench 2ft wide by 2ft deep for 6 days, it has since been filled in, but remains behind safety barriers and has yet to be turfed to repair the damaged lawn. Under GS2 of the Gas Standards I am entitled to £50 for this and £50 for each 5 days after that until it is put back to the original state.

I was not provided with notification in advance of interruption of supply at least 5 days in advance (as per GS13 of NG Standards). In fact I was not given any notification.

In summary, the Gas Standards have been broken by not providing notice of loss of gas and my garden has not been put back to its original state. I am entitled to redress for this as detailed above. In addition I expect to receive redress for my out of pocket expenses which include cover for 3 Tesco delivery service charges and transport costs for travel to work and to family. I also expect to receive redress for the immense inconvenience of being without gas, electricity and telephone/internet access for a wholly unacceptable length of time.

I look forward to hearing from you. Under GS14 of the Gas Standards I am entitled to a response within 10 days. Should I not be fully satisfied with your response I will not hesitate in taking the matter further which will include, but not be limited to, contacting Trading Standards and the Energy Ombudsman.

Yours Sincerely

John received £300.

Electricity and gas meters

Meters are checked for accuracy before being installed. However, errors do occur. If you believe that the meter is registering inaccurately turn off all your appliances and see if the meter is still recording usage. If so, write to your supplier to complain.

TEMPLATE: **Faulty meter**

Dear [*xxx*]

Re: [*account number*]

My meter for my [*electricity/gas*] is currently showing a reading of [*number*]. I do not believe that this is accurate.

The bill in question [*date*] for [*£xxx*] is significantly higher than it should be [*include any further relevant details here e.g. being away from the property for any length of time or a bill showing higher than your winter bill etc.*].

I inspected the meter with all my [*electrical/gas*] appliances turned off and noted that it continued to register [*number of units*] of consumption. This is evidence therefore that either the meter is faulty or that there is some other problem. Whatever the reason, the bill is not a true reflection of the [*electricity/gas*] used. I request that you carry out a test on the meter at my home.

I look forward to hearing from you with a suitable date for the test to be carried out.

Yours [*sincerely/faithfully*]

TEMPLATE: **Over-charging**

Dear [*xxx*]

Re: [*Account number*]

On the [*date*] I received a bill for energy usage between [*start date*] and [*end date*] and I have been charged the sum of [*state amount that has been charged*].

The [*energy consumption/meter reading*] stated on the bill is inaccurate because [*bullet point reasons for challenging the bill evidence which supports your complaint e.g. time away from the property*].

I trust that you will look into this matter and send me a revised, accurate bill along with confirmation that I have been credited with the difference and records are updated.

I look forward to hearing from you within the next 7 days. Should I not receive a satisfactory response I will not hesitate in taking the matter further. This will include, but not be limited to, reporting the matter to the Energy Ombudsman.

Yours [*sincerely/faithfully*]

Switching energy

For anyone who doesn't just let their car or house insurance renew each year, switching energy supplier is the same principle. If you do just let your house and car insurance renew it is likely to be costing you hundreds of pounds a year. Never has a renewal been the cheapest quote for me in over 25 years of driving and only once for the house!

If you haven't switched for many years, the chances are you are paying way over the odds for your energy. I look to switch every year and I think there was only one year when I didn't change and that was when I was with a company which informed me when I could find a cheaper tariff with them.

Don't switch with someone on the doorstep though! That's highly likely to be the poorest solution. However, since 2010 the big 6 have agreed with Trading Standards not to call on doors where there are "No Cold Caller" signs. So, should you have a sign and someone calls, take the employee's name and details and report him/her to the company. You may get compensation for the inconvenience. If an energy salesperson has forged a signature on your contract, you're entitled to £250 compensation.

Since 2010 energy companies have to send you an annual statement which will have all the information you need to switch, i.e. consumption over the year. Even if you don't have this you can still use the information from old bills. You can usually sign up to look at your account online, so you can use that if you don't keep paper statements. Go to any of the switch sites, type into your favourite search engine "switching energy suppliers" and take your pick. It is always worth checking more than one. The Money Saving Expert website is great. On the energy section you will be taken painlessly through comparing prices. Then sign up for the email on that page. You can set a minimum for how much you want to save a year before switching and you will automatically get an email telling you that you could save this amount and to look at switching. So you can switch and forget about it until you get an automatic email telling you that you could save by switching.

Switching should take a maximum of 6 weeks.

If you have been switched to a new energy supplier without your consent, (known as an erroneous transfer) you can complain to your old or new supplier. If complaining to one doesn't work, you can complain to the other.

TEMPLATE: **Problems switching**

Dear [*xxx*]

Re: [*Account number*]

On the [*date*] I requested that [*gas and/or electricity supplier name*] switch my supply to you.

The switch was completed by [*detail how the switch was undertaken e.g. phone/ switching site etc*].

I was advised that the switching process would take [*number*] weeks which has now passed and I have still not received confirmation that the switch has been completed.

Please confirm by return, when the above switch was completed, or alternatively the date on which the switch will be completed, along with an explanation for the delay. I expect some redress for the poor service and inconvenience.

I look forward to hearing from you. Should I not be fully satisfied with your response I will not hesitate in taking the matter further. This will include, but not be limited to, taking the matter to the Energy Ombudsman.

Yours [*sincerely/faithfully*]

TEMPLATE: **Erroneous transfer**

Dear [*Sir/Madam*],

Re: Erroneous transfer [*account number*]

I am writing to you as my energy supply has been transferred to a new supplier without my consent. I would like you to take back my supply and bill me as if I never left, as provided for in the Erroneous Transfer Charter.

It may be helpful to know that my meter serial numbers are [*xxxx*] and [*xxxx*].

The supplier who has taken over my supply is [*xxxx*].

Please apply to have my supply returned as an erroneous transfer and ensure that the account continues to be billed as if I never left. Please also ensure that any errors on the distributors database which could lead to this problem reoccurring are rectified.

I look forward to hearing from you within seven days.

Thank you.

Yours [*sincerely/faithfully*]

Energy Ombudsman

Ombudsman Services runs the ombudsman service for the energy sector and has been approved by Ofgem.

The services covered are: Gas complaint, Electricity complaint, Dual fuel, Connections, Feed-in tariffs FITS, Green Deal, Solar panels, Insulation, Heating, Gas bill, Energy bill, Electricity bill

Request a deadlock letter from the company if you remain unsatisfied. If the company does not provide this or 8 weeks has passed you can then take the matter to the ombudsman. It will work to resolve the matter and if simple can offer to try and resolve it over the 'phone or email with the company in under 5 days and the resolution can be agreed by both the company and you. If the ombudsman decides that it will take more than 5 days, the company will be asked for more information and the ombudsman will prepare an investigation plan and propose a resolution to you and the company. Both of you can offer more information at this stage before the ombudsman makes the final decision. Decisions are legally binding in court and the company has 28 days to comply with the ombudsman's decision(s). The customer can be awarded up to £10,000 to return you to the position you would be in had the mistake not occurred and can reflect the trouble to which the company has put you.

WATER

Water companies are regulated by Ofwat. Each water company must follow the Guaranteed Standards Scheme which is a statutory scheme that provides compensation in the event of service failure. Each water company must have a complaint procedure in place. In addition each company must have various codes of practice including its customer code of practice and other codes covering domestic leakage, debt recovery and pipe laying. They also have to have a published charges scheme – this outlines the charges the company has to apply for different groups of customer. All companies are required to have complaints procedures and all the above must be covered by Ofwat.

Ofwat regulates the water and sewerage sectors to drive improvements in service. It monitors each company's performance, comparing service across the industry and supporting best practice. It will also take action against any company that fails to provide the level of service customers expect.

The guaranteed standards scheme includes standards about how a water company must:
- make and keep appointments
- maintain the right water pressure
- deal with interruptions to the supply
- answer account queries and complaints.

The standards don't apply in certain situations – e.g., if the problem is caused by severe weather conditions, industrial action or someone else's actions. If a company doesn't agree to your request to pay bills in a different way, it must tell you within five working days or pay compensation of £20. The water company must pay compensation if essential household water supplies are interrupted because of an emergency drought order. This is part of their licence conditions.

Water companies should usually supply water at a minimum of seven metres static head, unless low pressure is due to drought or essential maintenance work. If the pressure falls below this for an hour or more on at least two occasions in a 28 day period, you're entitled to a payment or credit of £25. Only one payment of £25 can be made in any one financial year. If the fall in pressure is due to industrial action or someone other than the water company then no payment will be made.

Water companies should provide a minimum of 48 hours notice of any interruption to supply and provide details of when it will be restored. If it does not or does not restore supply by the specified time then you are usually entitled to £20 compensation and a further £20 compensation if you don't receive the first £20 within 20 days. In cases where an emergency such as a burst pipe has caused interruption the company must restore the water within 12 hours although this rises to 48 hours if it is a strategic main pipe. The company must tell consumers as soon as possible regarding where an alternative water supply can be obtained, when it plans to restore the supply and a telephone number for more information.

If the supply is not restored by the time the company says it will be, compensation is due. £20 for the first 24 hours and £10 for each further 24 hour period the supply remains unrestored. If the interruption lasts more than 12 hours, the company should provide an alternative supply, for example, bottled water or tankers in the street known as bowsers.

If effluent from a sewer vested in a sewerage company enters a customer's building the company must make an automatic payment of the sum equal to the customer's annual sewerage charge up to a maximum of £1,000. If the payment the company is required to make is less than £150, the company must pay the customer £150. (There are some exemptions such as exceptional weather conditions or industrial action by the company's employees).

If effluent from a sewer, which is vested in a sewerage company, enters a customer's land or property, the company must make a payment of the sum equal to 50% of the customer's annual sewerage charge up to a maximum £500. The customer must claim the payment from the company within three months of the incident. The company must make a minimum payment of £75.

The company will consider the effects of the leakage such as damage and length of time of flooding before agreeing the amount.

For both leakage types, payment must be made within 20 days or an additional amount is due. Any disputed claims for payment under this scheme can be referred to Ofwat.

For Scotland write to the Scottish Water and Sewerage Customers' Council, Northern Ireland, the Water Services Office of the Department of the Environment and for England and Wales, OFWAT – where guidelines are similar.

The standards clearly state that the scheme does not affect any legal rights to compensation that customers may have.

If you are not satisfied with your water company's response you can take the matter to the Consumer Council for Water and ultimately the Parliamentary and Health Service Ombudsman. In Scotland the Scottish Public Services Ombudsman and in Northern Ireland the Consumer Council.

TEMPLATE: **Break in water supply**

Dear [*xxx*]

Re: [*Account number*]

On the [*date*] my water supply was interrupted for [*xx*] days. The Guaranteed Standards Scheme states that I am entitled to compensation for this interruption. *(If applicable add the next 2 sentences)* I [*enclose/attach*] receipts for the remedial work necessary due to the damage that arose due to insufficient water. I also enclose/attach reports from the repairers outlining the need for the work due to the water interruption.

I look forward to receiving your proposal for compensation within the 20 days. Should I not be fully satisfied with your response I will not hesitate in taking the matter further. This will include, but not be limited to, reporting the matter to the Consumer Council for Water and Ofwat.

Yours [*sincerely/faithfully*]

TEMPLATE: **Sewage entering a building**

Dear [*xxx*]

Re: [*Account number*]

On the [*date*] effluent from one of your sewers entered my property and caused the following damage: [*bullet point details*].

I [*attach/enclose*] photo of the damage.

Under the Guaranteed Standards Scheme I am entitled to compensation equal to my sewerage payment which is [£*xxxx*].

I look forward to receiving your proposal for compensation within the 20 days. Should I not be fully satisfied with your response I will not hesitate in taking the matter further. This will include, but not be limited to, reporting the matter to the Consumer Council for Water and Ofwat.

Yours [*sincerely/faithfully*]

The Drinking Water Inspectorate (DWI) was formed in 1990 to provide independent reassurance that public water supplies in England and Wales are safe and drinking water quality is acceptable to consumers. It checks that the water companies in England and Wales supply safe drinking water that is acceptable to consumers and that it meets the standards set down in law. In Scotland the Drinking Water Quality Regulator for Scotland (DWQR) ensures that drinking water in Scotland is safe to drink. These regulators do not deal with billing and compensation issues.

Water companies test the water every day. Inspectors from the DWI and DWQR independently check these tests and audit water company laboratories. If any one of the millions of tests each year fails the standards then inspectors require the water company to make the necessary improvements to drinking water quality. They also go out on site to check that improvement work is completed on time. In addition to this they inspect those aspects of water operations which ensure drinking water is safe at all times.

Consumers can also get water tested through an approved laboratory but will have to pay for this.

9 VEHICLES

A sector which often appears a law unto itself and from which can be very difficult to gain redress.

Garages often try to fob you off with "contact the manufacturer". Don't. Many garages are members of Trade Associations which you can contact and if you still don't get any joy you can go to the Small Claims Court.

When you choose a garage you should look to see if it is a member of a trade association and if any doubt about the authenticity of the sign you can contact the trade association to check. You can also look online to find garages which are members of the association.

The Motor Ombudsman is an impartial self-regulatory body. Its members follow codes of practice and these have been approved by the Trading Standard Institute Consumer Codes Approval Scheme (CCAS). The scheme approves Codes of Practice that set out a minimum standard for their members.

- *The New Car Code of Practice* covers 99 per cent of all vehicles sold within the UK. It sets the standards for new cars which their members must follow. The code commits their members to providing honest and fair sales and warranties written in plain English.

- *The Service and Repair Code* has over 7,800 garages subscribed. This code commits members to providing open and transparent pricing policies and honest and fair services.

- *The Vehicle Warranty Products Code* aims to drive up standards across a wide range of automotive warranty and insurance products, by committing subscribers to higher standards than required by law. The code ensures members warranty products are clear and not misleading and that clear information is given at the point of sale.

If you have a complaint about a member of The Motor Ombudsman and they haven't resolved your complaint satisfactorily, you can contact The Motor Ombudsman for advice. They will help you resolve your dispute for free using their own conciliation and advisory service. If the matter still can't be resolved, The Motor Ombudsman can offer you legal arbitration for a fee, or of course you can go through the Small Claims Court.

If you know that the garage or dealer is a member of The Motor Ombudsman you could add a paragraph referring to this scheme to the following template letters of complaint. You could say that you will be informing The Motor Ombudsman of the breach naming the relevant code above or that you would be willing to go through their arbitration scheme to avoid legal action.

New Cars

If you want to reject a new car you should do so very quickly. Unlike buying a faulty kettle that you could take back after a few weeks and expect a full refund, a car depreciates in value and this will be reflected in any refund and no doubt be a matter of argument. In court too the judge may say that you have kept the car too long to expect a full refund. You are covered by the amended Sale of Goods Act 1979 (Sale and Supply of Goods Act 1994)/Consumer Rights Act 2015 and so if it is not fit for purpose, of satisfactory quality or doesn't fit the description then you are fully entitled to expect the retailer to come and pick up the vehicle and give you a full refund. You do not have to accept a repair. If you have had the car too long to return it you can reasonably expect a repair.

You should expect the dealer to pick the car up from you if you are getting the full refund but make sure the cheque has cleared first!

You might choose to accept a repair, or already have had to have a repair, for which you want redress. You can do this whilst retaining your rights under the Sale and Supply of Goods Act 1994/Consumer Rights Act 2015.

A new car, a real complaint example

A few years ago my mother bought a Smart car. A couple of months later my brother noticed that the front near side tyre was flat. (The car hadn't been driven for a while because my father had been seriously ill). My mother therefore called Smart Assistance who sent someone out for recovery. A garage repaired what had appeared to have been a slow puncture. The repair had cost £12.00.

A couple of months later my mother went to drive the car and the battery (original battery) was flat. Again, she telephoned Smart Assistance. The battery was put on charge and she was told that everything was fine and to leave the engine running for 20 minutes. She then went out in the car to a local garden centre. She went back to her parked car after three quarters of an hour to find the battery flat. She 'phoned Smart Assistance once again and they again sent out a recovery vehicle. The man replaced the battery and charged her £53.00. She then telephoned Mercedes and explained what had happened and asked if this was under the warranty. I don't much care for warranties. My mother was entitled to a full refund as the car was sold as satisfactory and in good running order. It was not. I believed that Mercedes was therefore again in breach of the Sale and Supply of Goods Act 1994 so a full refund is what she would get!

Later they 'phoned back to say that Head Office, as a goodwill gesture would give her back half of the amount and refunded £26.50.

Following that, the car had been running well until a month later. My mother drove the car for six days but then the battery was flat. She 'phoned Smart Assistance yet again. Their engineer found the battery to be faulty. He tested everything including the alternator etc. He said she would have to take the car back to another garage (which is about an hour from where she lives). He then drove her to her local Mercedes garage after charging the battery. She spoke to someone and they said they'd call the following day. They didn't and she had to 'phone them. She was told that there had been a problem and that the battery was not only faulty but their suppliers had sent a wrong battery to replace it, and could she should 'phone the following day.

My mother was told that they hoped the right battery would be in by Monday 21st and that it would cost her £147.00 and she could come and pick the car up.

This is where I stepped in. I didn't want her to; have to go and get the car; pay for the puncture repair; pay for the faulty battery; pay for the new battery and I wanted her to be refunded fully for the first one and something for the inconvenience of course!

We requested a full refund and return of the vehicle. The car had been owned for a few months so this was never going to be agreed but I went for it in the hope that we at least got some redress and something for the inconvenience.

19/11/11 Wrote to Mercedes detailing the above. The slow puncture, the flat battery and the poor customer care. Clear breaches of Supply of Goods and Services Act 1982.

23/11/11 Response from General Manager, stating that he couldn't comment on the slow puncture and that two months was too long to decide where the fault lay. Smart Assistance used an independent breakdown company who did not supply a Mercedes-Benz battery - they couldn't guarantee parts from a third party. He had instructed them to replace the battery "... and the only cost to [my] mother would be the money previously refunded to her as a goodwill gesture for the first battery." (Yes he did word it like that). The battery should be charged every 3-4 weeks. He believed there were no grounds for complaint or return of vehicle.

23/11/11 In response to this, I emailed the MD stating that my point regarding the Sale of Goods Act 1979 (amended) remained. My point that the WHOLE amount should have been paid was ignored. It is wholly irrelevant that an independent sub-contractor fitted the battery. I did NOT agree that once Mercedes was involved everything was done to look after my mother's interests. It was unclear as to whether the supply of the new battery was at the charge that she had already paid. The battery in the first instance was recharged and yet had to be replaced. It was pointed out that the battery was not charged by my mother which provided opportunity to make yet more complaints. When the car was sold to my mother she was told that the battery was in the boot. The front grill comes off to show the coolant system and windscreen water bottle. She was told that there was no spare tyre because there is no room but the battery was under the front seat. She was told that it was possible for one person to get at it. As a small 70 year old woman she would never have the strength to pull back the carpet let alone the protective cover. Therefore she was misled. She had actually had to hold this cover back 3 times for mechanics and the polystyrene is now broken by the first mechanic. So a) she was given misinformation b) the mechanics have shown that one person cannot do it and c) one mechanic actually broke the polystyrene. I reiterated the law and the redress I expected.

25/11/11 MD responded with £12 refund for the puncture repair. The 50% refund on the battery increased to 100%, but he said that she was getting 150% back! The polystyrene break was to be seen to.

25/11/11 thanked MD for the £12, my mother paid 50% of the amount £26.50. He stated that she was to be given 150% of the amount so told him that I assumed therefore that this included a further £53 for the battery to cover the extreme inconvenience caused by misinformation and faulty parts. She obviously had not had 150% given that the first battery should not have been needed and the second was due wholly to faulty fitting of it! Anything other than this was a) not reflective of the law and b) not "correct and fair given the inconvenience caused". I believed a figure nearer £100 would be more reflective of the inconvenience and stress caused plus the remaining £26.50 which was owed to my mother.

25/11/11 MD responded with offer of £165 (£53 battery refund + £100 goodwill + £12 puncture repair) and repair of polystyrene tray and return of the car.

Now clearly, this took some perseverance. It took one letter and two emails before I gained the redress I believed was due and obviously the correspondence had much more detail and was longer than A4 in each instance. So yes, it is time consuming, yes companies do make it difficult and will try and fob you off but, yes it was worth it. Remember my mantra "It's the Principle of the Thing". The above example shows you that with perseverance and knowledge of the law you can gain redress, even with cars!

TEMPLATE: **Rejecting a new car**

Dear [*xxx*]

Re: [*Registration of the vehicle*]

On [*date*] I purchased a vehicle with the above registration. I am rejecting this vehicle for the following reason(s):

[*Bullet point the defects*]

Under the Consumer Rights Act 2015 I am entitled to goods of a satisfactory quality. The fault(s) developed show that [*it/they*] [*was/were*] there at the point of purchase and therefore you are in breach of contract and I request a full refund.

Please provide details of when I can receive this refund and propose dates and times when you will be able to collect the vehicle.

Should I not be fully satisfied with your response I will not hesitate in taking the matter further. This will include, but not be limited to, [*insert relevant trade association if a member, social media if appropriate, Trading Standards and the Small Claims Court for claims up to 100k*].

I look forward to hearing from you within seven days.

Yours [*sincerely/faithfully*]

TEMPLATE: **Requesting a repair to a new car**

Dear [*xxx*]

Re: [*Registration of the vehicle*]

On the [*date*] I purchased a vehicle with the above registration. The car has developed [*a/some*] fault(s): [*insert fault(s)*]. Under the Consumer Rights Act 2015 I am entitled to goods of a satisfactory quality that are fit for purpose. As [*this/these*] fault(s) have developed it demonstrates that [*it/they*] [*was/were*] there at the time of purchase. As such you are in breach of contract and I am legally entitled to a refund. However, on this occasion I am willing to accept a repair whilst retaining my rights under the aforementioned Act.

Please provide details of how and when you would like to arrange for [*this/these*] repair(s) to be undertaken.

I look forward to hearing from you within seven days.

Yours [*sincerely/faithfully*]

Second hand cars

Undoubtedly you would not expect a second hand car to be in as good a condition as a new car! However, when buying from a dealer you still have the same rights under Consumer Rights Act 2015 (Sale and Supply of Goods Act 1994 for items prior to 1st October 2015) and the car should be roadworthy.

If you find a defect that wasn't pointed out to you at the time of purchase you should inform the dealer immediately (usually within less than a couple of weeks). After this time a refund will significantly reflect the difference between market value and the price you paid for the vehicle. You should expect the dealer to pick the car up from you if you are getting the full refund but make sure the cheque has cleared first!

When buying a second hand car you might look more favourably at a warranty scheme to work like an insurance policy but check everything in it with a fine-tooth comb.

When buying a second hand car from a private seller your rights under the Sale of Goods Act 1979/Consumer Rights Act 2015 still cover you. However, a private seller is only bound to give you truthful answers to questions you ask about the car, unlike car dealers they are not obliged to give details of the car if those details aren't requested. You can ask for a full refund or you ask the seller to pay for what is needed for the car to match the description. If the seller refuses to do either of these things then the only option open to you is the Small Claims Court.

A second hand car, a real complaint example

A friend of mine had issues with a second hand car she bought and the owner of the garage wouldn't reimburse her. This included what appeared to be a problem with the MOT certificate. The owner had also tried to pass off the problem as the MOT garage's fault and so I wrote this letter for her and she got everything requested:

Dear Joe,

I have now sought legal advice regarding the situation with the car I purchased from you.

Under the Supply of Goods and Services Act (1982) and the amended Sale and Supply of Goods Act (1994) my contract is with you and not the garage you used to undertake the MOT test, as this formed part of my agreement to purchase the car. My garage identified 12 faults on the following day. It is highly unlikely that these faults could have developed within less than 24hrs from when the MOT was undertaken and the car stayed in your garage. One can only assume that there must be a problem with the MOT and I shall be reporting this to the relevant authorities. Clearly the car was neither of satisfactory quality, nor fit for purpose when I collected it. I also believe that the Misrepresentation Act (1967) has been breached due to the apparent speedy appearance of 12 faults which would cause a car to fail its MOT test within less than 24hrs.

I am fully entitled to my money back for the above reasons or a full repair to make good the necessary work. However, due to the nature of the work and the issues with the MOT I will exercise my right, under the Sale and Supply of Goods Act 1994) to put right the work and bill you for this.

My garage has quoted £200.00 to cover all the work. However, this does not include fixing the CD player which I have informed you is also not working and I will be seeking a price and redress from you for this.

You were recommended to me by a friend as a car centre that was legitimate and able to provide a good product and service. Aside from all the faults with the car and MOT, I have been very disappointed with the lack of communication (not returning 'phone calls) and the length of time I have been kept waiting on more than one occasion when previously told things would be ready.

I am legally entitled to a full refund but on this occasion am willing to accept the repairs being undertaken.

I look forward to hearing from you within seven days. Should I not be fully satisfied with your response I will not hesitate in taking the matter further. This will include, but not be limited to, informing Trading Standards and VOSA of the issues, sharing our experiences on social media and various internet review sites and seeking redress through the Small Claims Court for the £200.00 plus £35.00 Court Fee and expenses.

Yours sincerely,

TEMPLATE: **Rejecting a second hand car from a dealer**

Dear [*xxx*]

Re: [*Registration of the vehicle*]

On [*date*] I purchased a vehicle with the above registration. On [*date*] I discovered that the car has [*a/some*] defect(s). I enclose an independent report showing that the car is unfit to drive.

Under the Consumer Rights Act 2015 I am legally entitled to goods of satisfactory quality that are fit for purpose and are as described. This is a clear breach. The wording of the advertisement for this car led me to believe that the car was in good running order. As it clearly was not I believe that that you are also in breach of the aforementioned Act and the Misrepresentation Act 1967 for misdescribing the vehicle and Consumer Protection from Unfair Contract Terms 2008 for misleading advertising.

I am therefore rejecting the vehicle and expect to be fully reimbursed for the full purchase amount [*£xxx*] and for you to collect the vehicle.

Please provide details of how I will be reimbursed. Once funds have cleared we will make arrangements for you to collect the vehicle.

I look forward to hearing from you within seven days. Should I not be fully satisfied with your response I will not hesitate in taking the matter further which will include, but not be limited to, seeking redress through the Small Claims Court and reporting you to Trading Standards.

Yours [*sincerely/faithfully*]

Clocking

Clocking is the illegal practice of reducing a vehicle's recorded mileage by tampering with the odometer. Should you find that the odometer has been clocked without any indication that this may have been the case, contact the dealer. As well as being able to claim for the car not being as described under the aforementioned Act you can also use the Misrepresentation Act 1967. You can also threaten to inform Trading Standards.

TEMPLATE: **Rejecting a clocked car**

Dear [*xxx*]

Re: [*Registration of the vehicle*]

On [*date*] I purchased the above vehicle from you. The car showed [*xx*] miles on the odometer. I have since discovered from documentation relating to the car that the mileage is significantly higher than this, which would suggest that the odometer has been altered.

The Consumer Rights Act 2015 states that goods must fit their description. The mileage was stated as [*xxx*] when the accurate figure is more than [*xxx*], so this is a clear breach. You are also in breach of the Misrepresentation Act 1967 for misdescribing the vehicle and The Consumer Protection from Unfair Trading Regulations 2008 for misleading advertising.

I look forward to hearing from you within seven days. Should I not be fully satisfied with your response I will not hesitate in taking the matter further which will include, but not be limited to, seeking redress through the Small Claims Court and reporting you to Trading Standards.

Yours [*sincerely/faithfully*]

Garage Servicing

The Consumer Rights Act 2015 (Supply of Goods and Services Act 1982 prior to 1st October 2015) covers vehicle repairs. So should you believe that the repair that you have received is not of satisfactory quality or hasn't been undertaken in a reasonable length of time you can assert your legal rights and request a refund or that the job is undertaken properly. This includes when a vehicle does not function satisfactorily a few days later due to the repair. Should the garage refuse to refund or redo the job you can go to arbitration through the trade association if it is a member. For peace of mind you might always want to check that a garage is a member before taking your vehicle to it. You should always give the garage a chance to put things right as you have a legal obligation to keep costs to a minimum. You should also be compensated for out of pocket expenses such as using different transport when the garage undertakes the job again but you must keep this to a minimum.

Always agree a price, preferably in writing, before work is undertaken. You may also wish to agree on a maximum total cost for incidental small items which can be incurred without having to call you. If you haven't done this and you feel that you are overcharged then you should get estimates for the work from other garages to use as evidence. If you are forced to pay, ensure that you state, (in writing as usual is best), that you are paying under protest.

If a garage damages your vehicle then this is a breach of the Consumer Rights Act 2015 (Supply of Goods and Services Act 1982 prior to 1st October 2015) and the garage must pay to put the damage right unless it can prove it was not responsible.

If the garage claims that it is not responsible for vehicles left in its possession it is in breach of the Consumer Rights Act 2015 (Unfair Terms in Consumer Contracts Regulations 1999 for servicing before 1st October 2015).

TEMPLATE: **Service complaint**

> Dear [*xxx*]
>
> Re: Servicing of car registration [*xxx*]
>
> On [*date*] you undertook a service on my vehicle. When I collected it, I was informed that a full service had been undertaken and that you had discovered a [*fault describe*] and had repaired it accordingly. You charged [£*xxx*].
>
> On date the car developed [*a/some*] fault(s) [*insert fault(s)*] resulting in the car being unfit to drive and I had to get it immediately repaired at a cost of [£*xxx*]. I [*enclose/ attach*] a copy of the invoice detailing the work which was undertaken.
>
> Under the Consumer Rights Act 2015 I am entitled to services being undertaken with reasonable skill and care using parts fit for purpose and of satisfactory quality. The faults detailed show that you are in breach of this contract and therefore I expect to be reimbursed for the above cost of repair.
>
> I look forward to hearing from you within seven days. Should I not be fully satisfied with your response I will not hesitate in taking the matter further. This will include, but not be limited to, seeking redress through the Small Claims Court.
>
> Yours [*sincerely/faithfully*]

TEMPLATE: **Service over charge**

Dear [*xxx*]

Re: Servicing of car registration [*xxx*]

On [*date*] you undertook a service on my vehicle. I was told that this would cost [£*xxx*]. This formed part of a verbal contract. On collecting the vehicle I was charged [£*xxx*].

Whilst I believe that your quote formed part of a verbal contract I am also covered by the Consumer Rights Act 2015 in that I need only pay what is considered a reasonable amount. I have therefore gained two quotes for the work from two different garages. One quotes [£*xxx*] and the other [£*xxx*].

Either:

Therefore I am prepared to pay you [£*xxx*] based on the other garages' quotes and your original quote.

Or:

Therefore I expect a refund of [£*xxx*].

I look forward to hearing from you within seven days. Should I not be fully satisfied with your response I will not hesitate in taking the matter further. This will include, but not be limited to, seeking redress through the Small Claims Court.

Yours [*sincerely/faithfully*]

TEMPLATE: **Garage damaging a vehicle whilst in possession of it**

Dear [**xxx**]

Re: Car registration [**xxx**]

On [**date**] you undertook a service on my vehicle. I collected it on [**date**]. On collection I found damage to my car caused whilst it had been in your possession.

Under the Consumer Rights Act 2015 I am entitled to services being undertaken with reasonable skill and care. The damage caused clearly shows that this Law was breached.

[*If appropriate include the following paragraph:*

You claim that you are not responsible for vehicles left in your possession but this is a breach of the Unfair Terms in Consumer Contracts Regulations 1999.]

I look forward to hearing from you within seven days regarding how you will be putting the matter right. Should I not be fully satisfied with your response I will exercise my legal right to get the necessary work undertaken by another garage and charge you for this work. Should you not reimburse me for this I will seek redress through the Small Claims Court.

Yours [*sincerely/faithfully*]

10 RESTAURANTS, HOTELS, PUBS AND CAFÉS

See the section on *Holidays and Travel* with regard to accommodation. When you make a booking for accommodation or eat out you have entered into a contract and are covered by consumer law for any breach.

Bookings

A booking for a meal should be honoured. If it is not, speak to the manager and try to come to some agreement – perhaps a free drink while you wait for the table. If this cannot be done then ensure you inform the manager that you will be taking the matter further to claim compensation. If the booking was for a special occasion then this could be reflected in any compensation claim. Make sure that the establishment knows that the booking is for a special occasion and what that is. You can claim for loss of enjoyment and disappointment. You can also claim for out of pocket expenses such as travel. In theory you could take the matter to court but I would advise only doing this where you have clear evidence that the establishment was aware of the occasion and there was significant inconvenience, otherwise it is very subjective and risky. There are alternatives to court though, see chapter 25 *Small Claims Court* for more.

Do try to find an alternative and evidence your attempts when complaining. Remember a booking works both ways and whilst an establishment is in breach of contract if it fails to keep a booking it could, in theory, charge you for not keeping a booking!

TEMPLATE: **Booking not honoured**

For purchases prior to 1st October 2015 quote "Supply of Goods and Services Act 1982"

Dear [*xxx*]

Re: Booking [*reference*]

On [*date*] I booked a table for [*xx*] for [*date and time*]. I informed you that the booking was for a special occasion. [*Detail*]. However, on arrival we were told that there was no record of the booking. No alternative or compensation was offered.

The Consumer Rights Act 2015 demands that services should be carried out with reasonable skill and care. You are therefore clearly in breach of this. [*I/we*] incurred the following costs for which [*I/we*] [*enclose/attach*] evidence: [*Detail, such as travel*]. As the booking was for a special occasion I am also claiming for loss of enjoyment, considerable disappointment and the inconvenience caused and believe [*£xxxx* reflects this. [*Describe how you came to this amount (or if unsure leave out put a full stop after "caused" and cut the rest of the sentence).*]

I look forward to hearing from you within 7 days regarding an offer of compensation. I will be sharing the experiences on review sites and should I not be fully satisfied with your response I will take the matter through the Small Claims Court to reclaim my losses.

Yours [*sincerely/faithfully*]

When it comes to unsatisfactory food or drink many of us, me included, feel awkward about complaining. Well, I never feel awkward about complaining but more specifically I mean never knowing what someone may do to your food if you send it back. Before the many good restaurant, café and pub staff throw their arms up and say "not me" we have all heard of stories of staff spitting on food and worse. Many have been on the media telling us what they do so it is a difficult decision. However, you must complain at the time to be taken seriously and to be able to follow up. Quote the Consumer Rights Act 2015 (or for bookings prior to the 1st October 2015 the Supply of Goods and Services Act 1982) which entitles you to food and service that reflects the establishment. Compare the place to a similar one serving similar food.

You do have the choice of refusing a replacement course and deducting the price of the unsatisfactory item from your bill. If you are made to pay under protest complain in writing later and if possible write "Paid under protest" on the bill and take a photo of it.

Do not eat the food that you are complaining about.

Now that most of us have our mobile 'phones with us it is possible to take photographs of food which can be used as evidence. Ensure that the photo clearly shows that it is from the establishment. You can of course, if technically savvy enough, get the location and date and time on it. Bear in mind that one person's view of what is satisfactory may be very different to another, so be sure of your claim to redress.

Real example of complaining about café service

My mother and I were in Dunelm and ordered and paid for 2 cream teas. It was a little after 1.30pm. Our money was taken and the assistant made the tea and then told us that there were no scones. We were told that there had been a rush on. A rush at lunchtimes for cream tea, in a department store?! We might have been in the lovely West Country but Dunelm is hardly the cream tea centre of the world!

The assistant then had to go and ask someone to do the refund. Eventually someone came and then took a ridiculous length of time to work out how to do the refund! In this time my mother had actually drunk her tea and my son eaten his biscuit! My tea had gone cold. Depriving me of my tea is not good…

I wrote to the manager and told him that although the assistant was polite, I did not see how there could have been a rush of cream teas over the start of the lunchtime period or how she could not have known that the last one had been served! It is also poor staff management for staff not to know how to issue refunds. (Note that this is a management fault NOT the fault of a member of staff – unless they have been shown of course.) While I was there complaining I also pointed out that in the ladies toilets neither cubicle had any toilet paper. Added the usual "I won't use your services again and would be interested in feedback" and waited.

A few days later I got a very nice letter back. The Manager was very apologetic. Someone hadn't done the ordering properly, training was being undertaken and the letter stated that we could have £10 to spend on the next visit. So I sent the letter to my mother and she took her friend there one day.

TEMPLATE: **Served food complaint**

For purchases prior to 1st October 2015 quote "Supply of Goods and Services Act 1982"

Dear [*xxx*]

Re: [*Date of meal*]

On [*date*] our party of [*xx*] ate at your restaurant. We were appalled by the food we were served. [*Describe the factors in bullet points.*]

Under the Consumer Rights Act 2015 I am entitled to services carried out with reasonable skill and care. Food should be as described and of a reasonable standard. This was clearly not the case

I complained at the time and requested a deduction in the bill as is my legal right However, this was refused and I paid under the strict understanding that I was paying under protest. I enclose a copy of the bill.

I therefore expect to be fully compensated for this meal. [*If applicable add the following*] The meal was for a special occasion [*detail*] so I am also claiming for loss of enjoyment and disappointment caused.

I look forward to hearing from you within 7 days. Should I not be fully satisfied with your response I will not hesitate in taking the matter further which will include, but not be limited to, informing Trading Standards and issuing a summons against you in the Small Claims Court.

Yours [*sincerely/faithfully*]

Poor service would follow similar lines. If the service was so poor that it damaged any of your belongings, e.g. pouring food over your hand bag, then detail this in your letter and provide details of the cost of replacement/repair/cleaning.

You are legally entitled to not pay the service charge if service was poor. If the charge has been absorbed into the meal then you can deduct a reasonable amount e.g. 10%.

Real example of complaining about unsatisfactory drinks

Many years ago my partner and I went to a pub in North Weald. The pub had a cat. We had a drink. In one of them was a flea. How does one know it was a flea and not some other sort of insect? Well, if you put one between your fingers and press together any other thing of that size would die. A flea does not. We mentioned it to the landlord whose first reaction was to say "Are you a flea expert?" How rude. We left, reported him to Environmental Health which paid an unannounced visit and we sent the landlord a Christmas card and signed it from "The Fleas". The card was perhaps a tad unnecessary but it amused us.

The landlord should simply have refunded us the money or given us another drink. The pub had a cat and so the natural assumption was that fleas were in the carpet. It is of course possible that this was not the case but the landlord's rude and defensive attitude made us think otherwise and take the matter further. If a complaint is unusual or a landlord/manager/owner cares about his/her customers then s/he would not respond in such a manner. If you are being polite you should be met with politeness and if your complaint is valid (and ours was!) apology and redress.

Food poisoning

If you believe that you have a bout of food poisoning from an establishment where you have eaten then contact your doctor immediately. Proving that the poisoning was caused by the trader may be difficult but obviously it is made easier if more than one of you was affected. Under the Food Act 1990 it is a criminal offence for a business to serve food unfit for human consumption. You should therefore also inform the local Environmental Health Department.

Depending on the severity of the illness and your out of pocket expenses (such as loss of earnings) you may want to take legal advice regarding the amount of compensation to which you are entitled. In the first instance you can write directly.

TEMPLATE: **Food poisoning complaint**

For purchases prior to 1st October 2015 quote "Supply of Goods and Services Act 1982"

Dear [*xxx*]

Re: Meal on [*date*]

At [*time*] on the [*date*] my party of [*xx*] ate at your restaurant. [*Xx*] of us had [*detail*] and all of us were ill. I have been advised by my GP that the food poisoning was caused by the food in your restaurant. This is because [*detail the reasons such as only the people who had the chicken were ill*].

It is a criminal offence for a business to serve food not fit for human consumption under the Food Safety Act 1990 and as such I have informed the local Environmental Health Department.

Under the Supply of Goods and Services Act 1982 the food we received should have been made with reasonable skill and care. You were clearly in breach of contract and as such I am seeking redress for the pain, inconvenience and out of pocket expenses including [*bullet point detail*].

I am taking legal advice regarding the extent of the claim and will contact you with the figure as soon as I have it.

Yours [*sincerely/faithfully*]

Water

Personally, I object to paying for water. I am lucky to live in a developed country and therefore do not need to have bottled water. In addition I pay water rates therefore the water IS paid for! It is perfectly safe. People who drink bottled water for "health reasons" confuse me as there are no proven health benefits whatsoever.

The reason for including this here is because new licensing conditions came into force April 2010 ensuring that pubs, clubs and bars are obliged to provide free water where reasonably available. Annoyingly this does not include restaurants. However, it is illegal for a restaurant to try and pass tap water off as bottled water.

11 INSURANCE

Ensure that when you take out insurance that all the information you have given is correct. Should a company find out that you have lied on the form or any part of it is not correct, it is very likely that the company will not pay out.

Since April 2013 the onus has been on the insurer to ask you what it needs to know regarding an insurance product so it can figure out whether the policy's suitable for you. (Before then, it had to be volunteered.) So now, if the insurer didn't ask you the questions it needed to know to cover you and then says you are unable to claim you can take the matter to the Financial Ombudsman as mis-selling.

When you want to claim on your insurance you should claim as soon as possible. Contact your insurance company or broker to say that you wish to make a claim. You will usually be sent a form to fill out and return within a set time, usually 30 days.

Usually the company will send out an independent loss adjuster. S/he will ask you questions and establish the validity of the claim and provide a report to advise the insurance company on whether to reject the claim, pay in full or pay in part. You can also appoint a loss adjuster but you will have to pay for this.

If you disagree with the decision then follow the company complaint procedure. If you remain unhappy you can contact the Financial Ombudsman scheme. You usually have about six months to make a complaint from the time you have reached a deadlock with the insurance company. Awards made are not legally binding so if you remain unhappy after using this service you can still go to court. You might want to check that your insurance company is a member of the Ombudsman scheme before taking out a policy.

Watch out for the "automatic renewals" of insurance. I try to remember to ensure I inform them to not do this and keep a copy of that email. I have been known to forget or have only mentioned it on the telephone so there is no record and it is open to debate as to whether the call handler has noted the request. If this happens to you, write to them explain that you requested that they did not undertake an automatic renewal and that under the Consumer Contracts (Information, Cancellation and Additional Charges) Regulations 2013 you are cancelling the contract and you can also provide details of the company you have insured with if you wish. It's ridiculous that you do not get rewarded for being loyal - you get punished for not challenging. Until more people challenge then this practice will continue.

Never has a renewal been the cheapest quote for me in over 25 years of driving and only once for the house!

Real example of insurance company automatically renewing

We had our buildings and contents insured with Santander. I did not renew with it, choosing More Than (another story – see the complaint regarding quotes section below). However I noticed on the credit card bill that Santander had taken a renewal fee. I complained and Santander said that it was the broker and that another company would be in touch. The credit card bill clearly showed that Santander had been paid, so any contract was with it, or it had inaccurately taken money from my account.

I complained several more times via the online form. I received one (standard) email asking me to ring a 'phone number. I refused and sent many more emails all of which remained unanswered. Eventually I received a letter telling me that my complaint was being investigated. In the meantime I contacted my credit card company. Under Section 75 of the Consumer Credit Act 1974 I requested that I was refunded the money for two reasons. 1) I provided evidence to show that I had cancelled within the 14 day cooling off period afforded to me by various different laws and 2) had informed Santander several times that I did not want the insurance. I sent the credit card company copies of the emails and screen shots and within two days was refunded. A few days later Santander rang me asking for a call back. I don't do telephoning so didn't.

A few days after that Santander wrote to me to say that they had not received my emails. Although I had received 'thank you for your message' email auto responders, my messages apparently hadn't been passed to the right department. Yet another example of poor communication systems. A month on and the complaint hadn't reached them? I wonder if that is true, given that the first email from them told me that they weren't to blame and to contact the insurer. I received a refund plus £20 goodwill. Personally I believe that had I not contacted my credit card company, who acted within 2 days (well done Sainsbury's MasterCard), Santander would not have contacted me.

Comparison websites

See chapter 4, *Ensuring Your Complaints are Effective.*

Real example of complaint regarding quotes

This year More Than came out cheaper on the Money Supermarket comparison site. But this is when it got odd. I went through Moneysupermarket.com and got a reference number and password which did not work when I clicked to go through to the website. The quote included some cover which I did not wish to have. Secondly I tried to use Topcashback (excellent cashback site) and get a quote from More Than directly. This seemed to come to much More Than the Moneysupermarket.com quote! But it did not include the cover that I didn't want! It also requested details on specific items which were not included on the Monesysupermarket.com site. The Moneysupermarket.com quote listed certain other items and not others. Basically, the comparisons between the two sites were ridiculous and one could not change them either. So off went the email to the CEO as I felt that something was seriously flawed with their systems. Why can't you just get the same cover going through the comparison site as going direct? Why does it cost more going direct for a different cover and you can't use the cashback site when going through the comparison site for the cheaper quote? I stated that I wanted the price stated with moneysupermarket.com minus the cover I didn't want and to include the cover I did. I also expected to receive the £21.00 Topcashback to which I felt entitled. I got a new quote which was about £100 more than the other quotes in order to get everything I wanted, a cheque for the difference between the new quote and the cheaper Moneysupermarket.com one and the £21 cashback.

I'm not sure that any laws were broken here but I do think it is poor practice and would advise anyone looking at their insurance to explore all possibilities and to look at the comparison sites and then go direct. There was nothing misleading as they offered different things on each site, but it does show that you need to check just what you are getting cover for. Make sure you have the cover you want and contact the company if you see anomalies. My guess is that this practice is quite widespread and that we need to make sure that we are not being ripped off as well as ensuring that we have the cover that we want and need.

Contents Insurance

This insurance obviously covers the contents of your house and you may or may not have accidental damage cover. In the case of a theft ensure you inform the police immediately. Apart from the obvious reasons, your insurance company may refuse your claim if you do not do so.

You will need to check your policy for what is covered and excess etc. In theory if you have your contents and buildings insurance with the same company and damage has been caused to both the structure and contents, e.g. flood, there should be just the one claim. If you are using separate companies you will need to claim on each.

For accidental damage you will normally have to provide 3 estimates although in the bizarre contents insurance claim complaint example below we only had to give one.

TEMPLATE: **Rejecting offer**

Dear [*xxx*]

Re: [*Policy number*]

Thank you for your letter dated [*date*] making an offer of [£*xxxx*] for my [*damaged/ stolen/lost*] item. However I have found a valuation dated [*date*] that shows that the items was worth [£*xxxx*]. I have [*attached/enclosed*] this valuation.

In light of this new information I trust that you will re assess the claim and revise the offer within seven days.

I look forward to hearing from you.

Yours [*sincerely/faithfully*]

If the insurer doesn't offer more then send a similar letter threatening to go to the Financial Ombudsman.

Real example of accidental damage complaint

Don't be afraid to challenge insurance company procedures! If you feel someone has made a mistake they probably have. Last Christmas we sort of forgot a candle was burning! Luckily before it burnt the house down. It only burnt a couple of holes in the table and scorched it in other places. I telephoned the insurance company to request a claim form and was told that I would have to pay the £150 excess to the loss adjustor when he arrived. I don't think so! As the phone call was to a customer service representative I decided to write to the CEO of the insurance company. The correspondence went as follows:

23/01/14 emailed CEO, informed him that we had been told that an Assessor would come and we would have to give him a cheque for £150 which would be deducted from the amount paid out. Said what an appalling, outrageous and unfair system it appeared to be. We offered to send photos but this was declined. How on earth is anyone meant to make a decision about whether it is worth paying the excess and an increase in future premiums? You could look at the photos and give some indication, but this had been refused. Mentioned the Consumer Protection from Unfair Trading Regulations 2008 as I believed this to be an unfair commercial practice, misleading the consumer as to what they can expect. I attached the photos that were deemed unnecessary. I informed him that an Assessor could be sent and the excess deducted from the settlement should we choose to take it. Threatened the ombudsman and Small Claims Court.

24/01/14 response from someone in the CEO's team stating that he would like to arrange an inspection of the table by their contractor's Independent Inspections to see if the table could be restored. Offered us opportunity to arrange a report ourselves for which they would pay. Apologised that I was told I would need to pay the excess in the first instance, this should only be applied to a settlement.

28/01/14 emailed to say I had contacted restorers who have said that just by looking at the photos they can see that the table is beyond repair and the quote for providing a report with details of how much it would cost to replace will be £35 plus VAT. I reiterated that I was categorically told that the excess cheque had to be paid before we agreed to settle. This was queried several times because it sounded so ludicrous. The customer services representative was adamant that the cheque had to be paid to the assessor and I asked why this was. He clearly thought that this was the correct procedure so I was quite sure that this was not the first time it had been done and saw no reason why I should not take the matter further and expect redress for the inconvenience caused.

28/01/14 response to say go ahead with quote and that he would listen to the call and get back to me.

29/01/14 further email to say that I was correct and I had been advised as I said I had been! He had discussed the matter with the handler and apparently there was some confusion. With building repairs, they would expect their contractors to arrange to collect an excess before carrying out repairs but this would usually be after they had inspected damage and assessed the approximate costs. The handler was informed of the error and a significant misunderstanding about the claims process was put right. How you confuse a building with a table I am unsure. The report was accepted I settled and took the £25 goodwill gesture for the inconvenience.

Buildings Insurance

This will only cover specific damage and never maintenance! You will need to prove that damage was caused by the result of something specific. For example, weather reports, photos etc. Your claim will be rejected if the insurance company believes that damage was caused due to you not keeping your dwelling in a good state of repair.

TEMPLATE: **Rejecting insurance company's denial of responsibility**

Dear [*xxx*]

Re: [*Policy number*]

Thank you for your [*letter/email below*] dated [*date*] rejecting my claim against the above policy for [*describe damage*] on the grounds that [*quote their reasons*].

I reject your assertion that [*quote wording of the reasons claim is being denied*]. I also [*enclose/attach*] an independent report that shows that the damage was caused by [*insert wording from the report*]. This clearly shows that the damage was caused by [*insert cause*] and not, as you state [*quote insurer's claim of cause*].

I am therefore covered by the policy and expect to receive a full settlement. I trust that you will look into this matter as a matter of urgency. Should I not be fully satisfied with your response I will not hesitate in taking the matter further. This will include, but not be limited to, taking the matter to the Financial Ombudsman.

I look forward to hearing from you within seven days.

Yours [*sincerely/faithfully*]

Holiday Insurance

You should always take out travel insurance when going abroad. Use a comparison website and check the cover very carefully. In the EU you should also get an EHIC (replaced the old E111). (Beware of fake websites as with any site where you are handing over money). You'll either pay nothing for medical assistance, or at least reduce the level of upfront costs that you have to claim back later. Showing the card can reduce red tape and can help save time and hassle when trying to claim money back. Some insurance policies expect you to have the EHIC and won't pay for any expenses that the card would have covered. Sometimes the insurer will waive the excess if you have used your card. The EHIC covers required treatment for a pre-existing or chronic medical condition such as asthma or diabetes. Many insurers will not cover this and there are only a few companies/policies that will cover existing conditions.

You do still need travel insurance cover in addition to the EHIC because the EHIC is usually only accepted at state-funded hospitals and if you need assistance urgently and can only get to a private clinic, you will not be able to use the EHIC. It also doesn't cover mountain rescue should you need it!

Where the state-funded treatment is not entirely free, insurers will usually pay the outstanding costs.

The EHIC only covers medical costs so you need your insurance for any extra accommodation costs and repatriation.

If any state funded medical establishment refuses the card it is in breach of European rules. Should your EHIC be refused, try to get proof that you presented it at the time, as this could be key to getting the excess waived by your insurer. If you believe you've been incorrectly charged, contact the Department for Work and Pensions which may provide some reimbursement.

The bare minimum cover you need is for cancellation, curtailing of the holiday for a variety of reasons, illness/death at home or abroad, damage to home, called as a witness for court etc. You should also get property cover. You will want to be covered for delayed departure and/or luggage. In some circumstances you will want to claim from the airline directly. Always read the small print as to what is covered and what isn't before purchasing!

Your credit card accident cover, home insurance, (EHIC) or private health cover is not necessarily adequate. An emergency abroad can be enormously costly! For example if you need to be returned to the UK it could cost you thousands of pounds without sufficient insurance, e.g. (these costs taken from the DWP website):
- £35-45,000 – air ambulance from USA's East coast
- £12-16,000 – air ambulance from the Canary Islands
- £15-20,000 – scheduled flight, stretcher and doctor escort from Australia (figures supplied by FirstAssist Services Ltd)

The British Embassy or High Commission will not pay for this.

Take out your travel insurance at the same time as booking your holiday! It is usually cheaper to buy travel insurance yourself rather than using the site where you are booking your holiday. (Use one of the many comparison websites). Remember that it is now illegal for any site to automatically add any additional payments which appear as a default option.

I have not provided a template for this section as there are so many things that you could claim and be rejected for! Check terms and conditions and fill in the claim form carefully. Should you be dissatisfied with the offer or rejection, write to the company in a similar way to the templates above detailing your reasoning. Should you remain unhappy take the matter to the Financial Ombudsman.

Vehicle insurance

You must have vehicle insurance by Law.

When an insurance company settles with a motorist for full loss of their vehicle it is for what it deems to be the market value. Frequently motorists complain that the insurance company does not pay out the full value. Should you want to complain to the company about this, you will need evidence to show the car's worth. Such evidence might include copies of invoices for work that you feel increased the value, or sale prices of similar cars or an independent report.

If your vehicle has been in an accident and the insurance company offers what it thinks to be full market value but you want it repaired you can challenge the company. You will need an independent report; the RAC and AA, if you are a member, may be able to help.

Real example of complaint about car insurance administration

One year, Kwik-Fit came up the cheapest for us. So, I sent the proof of no claims and informed them NOT to renew automatically in 2014. That was on the 18/12/12. On the 11/01/13 I was emailed to ask for proof of no claims. So I sent it again on the 12/01/13. 3 days later they emailed me to ask for proof again. So, I tried to 'phone. I hate 'phoning because people get me so cross and there is no record of what is being said. Got one of those really annoying "press 5 and we will call you back" messages. I did and they didn't. So on the 21/01/13 I emailed again and this time I clicked on the "Request Read Receipt". Despite getting one AND on the 22/01/13 receiving an email saying it had been received and to ignore other correspondence, it got worse. On the 23/01/13 I received another letter requesting proof. (Dated 22/01/13). Later that day I received another email requesting proof! On the 25/01/13 I emailed informing them of my intent to take the matter further and received another email confirming receipt of the proof. The next day I received an email requesting proof. On the 31/01/13 I received a letter informing me that £15 had been added to my policy because I hadn't sent the proof.

So, in summary:
- I sent the proof of no claims twice.
- I informed Kwik Fit three times that I had done this
- Kwik-Fit asked 6 times for the proof.

I wrote to the Managing Director. I expected the refund and some redress and explanation for the ridiculous service. I got the refund (£15) and redress (£100) but no explanation. Someone 'phoned me after being told not to do so too. She then wrote and told me that they didn't receive the proof the two times it was sent. That didn't tally with receiving an email saying that it had been received. Additionally at the end of the year KwikFit decided automatically to renew my policy. I loathe this practice, they think it is okay because they wrote. Well it wasn't okay. I got £50 back plus the refund for the inconvenience. Never put up with this and then the practice might stop.

TEMPLATE: **Rejecting offer**

Dear [*xxx*]

Re: [*Policy number*]

Thank you for your [*letter/email below*] dated [*xx*] in which you make an offer of [*£xxxx*] for my claim in respect of the damage caused to my vehicle. However, I have obtained an independent report which values the car at [*£xxxx*] at the time of the accident. A copy of the report is [*enclosed/attached*].

I therefore reject your offer of [*£xxxx*] and trust that you will use this evidence in reassessing the claim.

I look forward to hearing from you within seven days. Should I not be fully satisfied with your response I will take the matter to the Financial Ombudsman.

Yours [*sincerely/faithfully*]

Private health insurance

Check the terms and conditions of your insurance policy. Health insurance is very complicated and what is and isn't included can vary greatly from one provider to another. There may be several exclusions listed when the insurance company won't pay out – such as specific conditions, diseases or treatments or if the condition or disease was pre-existing before you took out the policy. The company may also refuse to pay out the total amount if they think your practitioner is overcharging. In this case, you may have to meet the difference in costs yourself.

If you have a complaint about a health insurer take up the complaint with it first. If not satisfied with the response then take the matter to the Financial Ombudsman.

12 HOLIDAYS AND FLIGHTS

I could probably write another book just on all the different things one could complain about concerning holidays and no end of template letters! However, the main issues are covered below.

ATOL (Air Travel Organisers' Licensing) is a government-run financial protection scheme operated by the Civil Aviation Authority (CAA). All monies you pay for package holidays involving flights and holidays including a flight plus accommodation and/or car hire, must be protected under an ATOL licence. You will receive an ATOL Certificate at the time you make your payment, and you will need to keep the certificate safe.

ATOL cover means that if your travel company fails and your holiday can no longer go ahead you will be entitled to a refund if you are yet to travel and hotel costs and flights home if you are abroad with ATOL cover.

If you are not ATOL protected but book through a travel agent get your tickets as soon as you pay so that the airline should still honour your booking should the agent fail.

The ATOL scheme of financial protection covers flight-based holidays.

ABTA is the Association of British Travel Agents. If you buy a land or sea-based holiday such as coach, rail or cruise holiday from an ABTA member your monies will be protected by the ABTA scheme of financial protection. So, if your travel company fails and your holiday can no longer go ahead you will be entitled to a refund if you are yet to travel and hotel costs and transport home if you are abroad.

ABTA Members are bound to comply with the ABTA Code of Conduct, which ensures high service standards and fair terms of trading. Booking with an ABTA Member also gives you recourse should you have a problem or complaint with your travel company.

ABTA runs an arbitration scheme. It will help try and resolve any issues with you and the company. If it goes to arbitration there is a fee which varies dependent on the value of the claim. It also has a mediation scheme for member organisations. If your claim includes an element of minor illness or personal injury then this can also be considered by the arbitrator, but is limited to £1,500 per person.

The Package Travel and Linked Travel Arrangements 2018 covers the package holiday. The contract is with the tour operator and not the agent. However, should you specifically ask the agent to act on your behalf and s/he says that s/he has carried out a specific booking request and hasn't done so then your claim for this is against the agent.

The Package Travel and Linked Travel Arrangements 2018 provides that a package means the pre-arranged combination of at least two of the following components:
- *transport*
- *accommodation*
- *other tourist services* not ancillary to transport or accommodation and accounting for a significant proportion of the package. The definition includes a wide range of travel arrangements. Traditional package holidays described in brochures are covered, but it also includes tailor-made holidays where you have selected separate components.

Descriptions in brochures and online must be factually accurate and form part of your legal contract. So if the brochure says the hotel is quiet and no children are allowed there should be no children staying there. Accommodation quality and cleanliness should reflect the type of holiday and price paid. If you are unhappy with your accommodation you should complain about it to your representative as soon as possible (and complete one of their complaint forms) as the company should be given a chance to put matters right. You may still be entitled to redress of course. If however you do not complain at the time you will be asked why, if it was really that bad, you didn't ask to be moved.

The Package Travel and Linked Travel Arrangements 2018 and the ABTA code dictate that operators must take due care to ensure problems such as overbooking don't happen.

Under the Package Travel and Linked Travel Arrangements 2018, you can claim for loss of value (the difference in value between what you booked and what you got), out-of-pocket expenses, loss of enjoyment, inconvenience, or disappointment. There is no set formula for working this out as it is subjective but you should be reasonable and work it out logically.

TEMPLATE: **Misleading brochure descriptions**
For purchases prior to 1st October 2015 quote "Sale and Supply of Goods Act 1994"

Dear [*xxx*]

Re: [*booking number*]

I have just returned from the above holiday [*detail dates location etc*]. This holiday is described on page [*no.*] of your [*name and year of*] brochure.

The hotel was misleadingly described. It stated: [*bullet point and quote " " the parts with which you disagree*] but I experienced: [*bullet point the issues*].

I complained to hotel management and to the representative at the time but nothing satisfactory was done.

I believe that the details listed above in the brochure are misleading and breach The Consumer Protection from Unfair Trading Regulations 2008. The brochure's description formed part of our contract and as the description was inaccurate, you are in breach of contract. They also do not meet the Consumer Rights Act 2015 requirements.

Under the Package Travel and Linked Travel Arrangements 2018, in particular that which provides that "No organiser or retailer shall supply to a consumer any descriptive matter concerning a package, the price of a package or any other conditions applying to the contract which contains any misleading information." In addition it sets out the requirements as to brochures. In particular, the brochure must be legible, comprehensible and accurate.

As I am sure you are aware the regulation applies to both tour operators and travel agents and failure to comply is a criminal offence.

I am legally entitled to receive compensation from you for the disappointment and loss of enjoyment suffered, and for the additional costs incurred.

If you incurred any extra expense due to the issue include the following sentence: Due to the issues described above, I incurred the following expenses [*bullet point list*].

In accordance with the ABTA code (delete sentence if not ABTA members) I expect to receive an acknowledgement within 14 days. I then look forward to receiving your response within 28 days of the receipt of my letter as to how you intend to resolve my complaint.

> If within 14 days I am not fully satisfied with your response and offer of compensation, I will not hesitate in taking the matter further. This will include, but not be limited to, informing the ABTA Code of Conduct Committee, Trading Standards and issuing proceedings against you in the Small Claims Court without further notice including court costs and out of pocket expenses.
>
> Yours [*sincerely/faithfully*]

Booking a package holiday a real complaint example

Now, Adam booked the holiday via their website. Paid for it then was notified it cost a bit more, which he duly paid. (No, I would not advise doing that see below). Although he booked the holiday in July last year for a holiday in April, Sunmaster contacted him to say that they could no longer have the accommodation that they had booked and offered an alternative. But Sunmaster refused to refund and said that the alternative was like for like:

The original booking
Small hotel (Riad), only 6 rooms
No children allowed policy
Included Spa facilities
Suite over 2 rooms

The alternative
Large hotel, over 100 rooms
Advertised as a family resort, targeted towards families
No spa facilities
Apartment

I believe "No children allowed" and "Family friendly" are opposite ends of the spectrum. I don't think you need a maths degree to work out that there's quite a difference between 6 and over 100 rooms.

Adam challenged it and got told again no refund no other alternative. Adam then contacted the hotel directly and not only was it open, it also had his booking. Sunmaster apologised for the mistake with no explanation for what happened and the holiday went ahead. He complained again but got no response.

Although Adam and Melanie didn't actually complain about the rise in the cost of the holiday, I did. I pointed out that it was my belief that it was a breach of the Misrepresentation Act 1967. I also pointed out that there are many reviews on many forums and review sites saying a similar thing – you go through the process online then 'phone to book whereupon you are told that the price has gone up. Whilst I am aware that prices can fluctuate, they do not, and should not, change within minutes of following an online process/database. The process should be the same as with any other travel agent where you can complete the whole process online. In this case it was even worse as they had paid for the holiday. They were charged an additional £48.60. I also found that the Advertising Standards Authority had previously instructed Sunmaster "…to hold evidence to substantiate the availability of their holidays at the advertised prices". It would appear Sunmaster was not doing this. A contract is concluded when you pay (or agree to pay) and the seller gives you your goods or services. This is called consideration. This put Sunmaster in breach of their contract to supply a holiday to Adam and Mel. For this we claimed legally owed compensation.

Secondly. It was not a like for like property. Clear breach of the Supply of Goods and Services Act 1982. (SOGSA). Interestingly the alternative accommodation was just short of half the price for ten days on various holiday websites and staff should certainly not have insisted on no refund given the breach of laws. Sunmaster was also in breach of the Package Travel, Package Holidays and Package Tour Regulations 1992. Regulations 12 and 13 refer to alterations in the package holiday or to departure times or location.

Thirdly. I wanted some answers regarding why the accommodation was changed in the first place.

Fourthly. In the last correspondence from Sunmaster a member of staff said "I have demanded a thorough and full investigation and explanation from our suppliers for this mis-information and I shall contact you further in this regard and in due course." This was not the case as no further communication had been received. (Another breach of the SOGSA).

Fifthly. On arrival Adam and Mel found cause to complain again at the appalling administration and service from Sunmaster. To cut another long story short the taxi transfer was dreadful, getting lost, asking for payment and delaying their stay by several hours.

Finally! So, outlining all this and threatening to take Sunmaster to the Small Claims Court I added the details of time spent on the matter, the ignorance shown, and the relevant bodies to be notified if satisfactory redress was not received.

Requested amount
£48.60 difference in quoted and paid price
£35 court fees
£20 court expenses (travel)
£250 for loss of earnings due to contacting Sunmaster
£35 transfer costs
£25 for loss of holiday due to taxi failures
£50 for loss of enjoyment of holiday due to start/taxi failures
£200 for inconvenience and stress
£200 costs for witnesses (those who have gone through similar experiences with Sunmaster)
£100 for costs incurred whilst researching possibility of cancelling/postponing the wedding.
Total £963.60

Despite emailing the CEO there was no response. I emailed him a second time and gave him seven days. That email was effective and got a response. Offered £410, and a defence about terms and conditions (remember these can be challenged) and they didn't think they had breached any laws. I disagree but Adam and Melanie were pleased with their £410, the holiday cost just over £1000. One had to laugh, the response referred to Melanie with a different unknown surname, neither maiden or married names. So, I know I advise not to be sarcastic when complaining but sometimes, just sometimes, sarcasm just has to be used.

I included "I do not know what relevance your conversations with a "Miss Hunter" have to my case. Whilst I thank you and accept the offer of £410 I am concerned that the offer you are making includes a sum to a "Miss Hunter" we are not prepared to share any goodwill gesture with anyone else." "I expect to receive details about your investigation into the transfer in due course" plus a few other lines about not addressing some points and not believing they had truly looked at a satisfactory amount for redress.

They got a better response, still denying liability but offering a goodwill gesture of £710 (everything asked for minus associated court costs). It would suggest that they didn't want to go to court?

TEMPLATE: **Travel agent regarding requests not undertaken**

Dear [**xxx**]

Re: [**booking number**]

On the [**date**] I booked the above holiday with you. On the [**date**] I wrote to you regarding specific requirements [**bullet point these**]. On the [**date**] I received confirmation from you of this. However, [**detail the issues**].

You were under a legal contractual obligation to ensure that these specific requirements were made or inform me otherwise as per the Package Travel, Package Holidays and Package Tour Regulations 1992. You are therefore responsible for the disappointment and inconvenience caused.

I look forward to hearing from you within seven days regarding redress. Should I not be fully satisfied with your response I will not hesitate in taking the matter further. This will include, but not be limited to, informing ABTA, Trading Standards and if necessary starting proceedings through the Small Claims Court.

Yours [**sincerely/faithfully**]

Real Example of complaint about transfers

We booked a long week end in Majorca with Alpharooms. We paid for everything including the transfer. There was a shuttle bus or a super saver bus. One cost just £1 more per person so we thought we'd do that, maybe it was a private bus or at least smaller. Wrong. We weren't alone in thinking this. It appeared that everyone on that bus had booked the same bus, paying the extra £1 per person. But most people thought that it was only a couple of quid and forgot it methinks. However, I am not most people and remember, it's the principle of the thing. How many people paid this extra £1 and how much profit was made? Typically we were the last drop off. Hour and a half later we were dropped off. Someone has to be last but we thought they might pick us up last going back the other way round as we were less than half an hour away from the airport. When we got the time we would be picked up we found that this was not the case and we were to be picked up in the early hours of the morning with no breakfast! (We were all inclusive).

I fired off a quick email to Alpharooms asking what the difference was, why the bus couldn't go the other way and, given the time of our flight, why were we being picked up so early. Actually, even with allowing the hour and half for the journey it still got us there 3 hours before the flight! So I got the standard response about having to investigate. We were only there for a few days so I got seriously annoyed when I still didn't hear from them. We booked a taxi for the transfer.

Back at home I emailed the CEO and pointed out the unfairness and idiocy of the transfer times, the misleading of customers re transfer buses and the inconvenience. I got the full transfer costs back (both ways which was a couple of quid less than the taxi!) plus £10. I complained a bit more and got another £15 for the "potential loss" of breakfast. A total of £65.

After chasing for an explanation regarding the difference in prices of the transfer I was told "Alpharooms use various providers for the services that we offer. As a result some of the services are described in slightly different ways depending on the information we receive from our providers. The Super Saver Shuttle is the same as a Shuttle bus service; the difference is simply in the branding of the product" All well and good EXCEPT, the two shuttles were the same and were listed at exactly the same time with a difference in price of £1.

Real example of complaining about accommodation abroad

A couple of years ago we went to Thailand having booked accommodation in the UK. (Long gone are the days when we could just turn up and stay somewhere with a child now in tow!) We stayed in once place that was fine, but I was fairly sure that I had booked a superior room. My booking only showed the reservation not the actual room so I didn't have evidence with me of what I had booked. (Lesson learnt!) We had paid £110.40 which is 5,345.00 BAHT. The difference between the rooms was 900 BAHT (about £18). When we got home I checked and found that I had indeed booked a superior room.

I wrote to the Halifax stating that under the Consumer Credit Act 1974 I requested the difference paid because I had not received what I had paid for. Two weeks later I had not had a response and so I wrote to the CEO. I received a reply apologising for the lack of response and the full £110.40.

Travel money

See chapter 7, *Finance*, for a complaint about commission charged when there should have been none.

Remember that purchasing money on your credit card counts as a cash advance and you will be charged accordingly.

Real Example of complaint about an airline

A friend of mine used EasyJet for a holiday with her family a few years ago. Whilst there, her mother in law became seriously ill and they had to fly home. EasyJet wanted to charge £1000 for the flight home. In fact they got it for £700 by using an Internet cafe. That was for 4 of them one way on top of what they had paid! They, like I, thought that was exploiting the fact that they needed to get home before her mother in law died. Bear in mind of course that EasyJet would have sold their existing tickets on for more profit. Had her mother in law died whilst they were on holiday they would have had their money refunded.

When they got back Jo complained and got some standard response about prices and their Price Policy. They did say they would pay back the tax. Generous? No. Because they then backtracked on that saying it was a transfer. I disagreed. I also disagreed with them that my friend and her family should have to trawl the Internet with no help from the EasyJet Customer Representative. I disagreed that EasyJet should make a profit on the situation. I disagreed that Jo's family should not be compensated for the inconvenience and misinformation they were given. So, being quite disagreeable I put it in writing.

Now, Jo won't mind me telling you that her written English was rubbish, her emails informal including kisses. My email therefore she said "Scared the poo" out of her! She may have put it less eloquently.

I wrote an email for her to the CEO and pointed out the following:

1) I am fully aware that one takes a risk in flying with a budget airline and can expect to pay more if changes need to be made. However, charging such an extortionate amount more for a different flight I believe is profiteering.

2) The customer services representative stated that "Sometimes if a flight is not selling

as well as expected we would reduce the fare to encourage people to book." They booked at about 6.00pm for a 10.15am flight the next day. This contradicts what the representative says. There was little time left for people to book and to have 4 tickets available (and there were more) clearly indicates there was scope for these flights to be cheaper.

3) The original tickets were approximately £550 including the extras. The actual flights were about £90. They then had to pay an additional £675 (£1000 if booked directly at the desk). EasyJet would presumably have sold the original flight on for at least £675. That makes an additional approximate £1300 profit for EasyJet on top of the original acceptable profit. Nearly 250%! Stunning profiteering I believe!

4) EasyJet needs to treat all customers equally, so, does that mean it takes advantage of every customer who finds themselves in a difficult situation?

5) Why should it be cheaper at an Internet cafe trawling through flights than just transferring the flight dates directly with EasyJet?

6) The representative had offered to refund the tax and this offer was withdrawn as he said that they had transferred the tickets! More contradiction! This is incorrect, they bought new tickets and so they are entitled to at least the tax back. EasyJet even charged again for speedy boarding and baggage – how is THAT a transfer?!

7) The correspondence to date was forwarded and the point made that the last email hadn't even gained a response. (The one pointing out their contradiction).

8) EasyJet's guidelines on "Refunds and Cancellation fees" state that "In exceptional circumstances, however, EasyJet will consider issuing a credit in the event of the bereavement of an immediate family member provided that the claim and a copy of the death certificate are submitted by post to the EasyJet Customer Services Department." Not only were Jo and family not advised of this by the EasyJet representative, they were not advised of it by any Customer Representative on holiday or in correspondence. With a charge of £30 per customer, totalling £120 they should be refunded the £675 minus £120. A total of £555.

She got her £550 in EasyJet vouchers.

Denied Boarding Regulations

The Denied Boarding Regulation applies to passengers departing from an airport within the EU, whatever the airline is, and also applies to passengers departing from an airport outside the EU for an airport within the EU, if the operating air carrier is a Community carrier. (I.e. a carrier with a valid operating license granted by an EU state).

Under European regulations (EC261), passengers have significant rights if their flight is delayed, cancelled or they are denied boarding. These rights have been in place across Europe since February 2005 and the CAA is the national enforcement body for them here in the UK. The rights cover the following:

- Flight cancelled or delayed for several hours – the airline must look after passengers. It must provide food, drinks, and some communications. If passengers are delayed overnight, this also means providing them with a hotel and travel to and from it. (All these must still be provided even if the delay was out of the airline's control).

- Flight is cancelled – the airline must offer an alternative flight or a full refund. The passengers may also be entitled to compensation if the flight was cancelled less than 14 days before the scheduled departure.

- Denied boarding or "bumped" from a flight – the airline must offer an alternative flight or a refund. Passengers are entitled to compensation.

- If a passenger's flight is delayed by more than 5 hours and they no longer want to travel they are entitled to a full refund.

Regulation (EC) 261/2004 applies to all flights wholly within the EU/EEA or Swiss region, or departing an EU/EEA or Swiss airport, or arriving in the region and with an EU/EEA or Swiss airline. Under EU rules, airlines must pay compensation for cancelled or heavily delayed flights, however, they can escape this under some 'extraordinary circumstances'. This can include sudden severe weather events for example. Pilots turning up late, cancelled booking due to under booking etc. are examples of the airline at fault and so passengers can complain and get compensation.

The decisions made in the Huzar v Jet2 and Dawson v Thomson cases confirmed that routine technical difficulties are not extraordinary circumstances. Ron Huzar was delayed for 27 hours on a Malaga to Manchester flight. The delay had been caused by faulty wiring and Jet2 had claimed that this was unforeseen and categorised as an 'extraordinary circumstance'. In the Dawson v Thomson case, James Dawson was claiming for an eight-hour delay on a flight to the Dominican Republic in 2006; his claim was made in 2012. The airline refused to pay, citing the Montreal Convention, which limits claims to two years after an incident.

On the 31st October 2014 the Supreme court upheld the rulings at appeal. Delays caused by technical problems cannot be categorised as 'extraordinary' circumstances and airlines are liable for compensation. Consumers have up to six years after the flight to make qualifying compensation claims. A judge in Liverpool county court threw out applications on the 25th February 2015 by Jet2, Ryanair, Flybe and Wizz Air to keep claims on hold until a case in Holland about technical delays (Van der Lans v KLM) was decided. He stated that cases should be settled in line with existing passenger-rights rules.

Consumers who have had compensation claims rejected for either of these reasons can now re-submit the claims to the airlines as long as the delay was less than six years ago.

The airlines do not have to respond to complaints within an official time limit, so set them a date by which you expect to receive a response. At the very least a "holding letter" of investigation should be sent.

You are not covered for strikes but if you are delayed a day or so after a strike you may be entitled.

Compensation for delays is only due on flights arriving three or more hours late, except for flights of less than 1,500km. How much you are entitled to depends on how long the delay and how long the flight. It changes again if the flight is cancelled before/after seven days before you are due to depart. It does not reflect the price of the flight and is straight out compensation. Personally I don't like this, it buys into the "compensation culture". Genuine redress and goodwill gestures reflect time and amount spent on matters but these regulations do not take this into account and therefore there is a risk that the low cost airlines will be hardest hit and consequently have to put up their fares. I feel compensation should be reflective but whilst it isn't, the tables for amounts to which you would be entitled per flight are below:

Flight length	Arrival delay	Compensation due
Up to 1,500km, (all flights) e.g. Bristol to Milan	3 hours+	€250 (£219)
From 1,500km to 3,500km, (all flights) e.g. London to Tenerife	3 hours+	€400 (£350)
1,500+ km (flights within the EU only)	3 hours+	€400 (£350)
3,500km+ (flights between an EU and non-EU airport), e.g. Luton to Florida	3-4 hours	€300 (£263)
	4+ hours	€600 (£526)

You will also have cover from Section 75 of the Consumer Credit Act if you paid by credit card for anything costing more than £100. (See chapter 7, *Finance*).

Denied boarding or "bumped" from a flight compensation

Airlines will often ask for "volunteers" to not take the flight in return for compensation and this amount would be agreed with the airline at the time. If you are forced off due to overbooking it is the same compensation as if the flight were cancelled.

Flight length	Arrival delay	Compensation due
Up to 1,500km, (all flights) e.g. Bristol to Milan	Up to 2 hours	€125 (£109)
Up to 1,500km, (all flights) e.g. Bristol to Milan	2 hours+	€250 (£219)
1,500km – 3,500km (all flights), e.g. Glasgow to Ibiza	Up to 3 hours	€200 (£175)
1,500+ km (flights within the EU only)	3 hours+	€400 (£350)
3,500km+ (flights between an EU and non-EU airport), e.g. Luton to Florida	Up to 4 hours	€300 (£263)
	4+ hours	€600 (£526)

Flight cancelled 7-14 days before departure compensation

Rates are different for notice given and for when you arrive (even if the flight to which you have been changed is longer but gets you there earlier).

Flight length	0 - 1,500km, e.g. Bristol to Milan		1,500 - 3,500km, e.g. Glasgow to Ibiza		3,500km+, e.g. Luton to Florida	
Delay	Leaves 2hrs+ before, lands up to 2hrs after	4hrs+ late. OR leaves 2hrs+ before, lands 2hrs+ after	Leaves 2hrs+ before, lands up to 3hrs after	4hrs+ late. OR leaves 2hrs+ before, lands 3-4hrs after	Leaves 2hrs+ before, lands up to 4hrs after	4hrs+ late
Compensation	€125	€250	€200	€400	€300	€600
	£109	£219	£175	£350	£263	£526

Flight cancelled less than 7 days before departure compensation

Flight length	0 - 1,500km, e.g. Bristol to Milan		1,500 - 3,500km, e.g. Glasgow to Ibiza		3,500km+, e.g. Luton to Florida	
Delay	Leaves 1hr+ before, lands up to 2hrs after	2hrs+ late	Leaves 1hr+ before, lands up to 3hrs after	3hrs+ late	Leaves 1hr+ before, lands up to 4hrs after	4hrs+ late
Compensation	€ 125	€ 250	€ 200	€ 400	€ 300	€ 600
	£109	£219	£175	£350	£263	£526

Exchange rates correct at June 2019.

If you have problems with the response or don't get one, you can contact the European Consumer Centre Network, whose purpose is to offer assistance on cross-border EU contracts. The UK ECC is part of the European Consumer Centre Network, which is made up of 29 centres throughout Europe. Their aim is to provide advice and support to consumers who are shopping cross-border within the internal market.

If the company refuses to pay out you can take your case to the Civil Aviation Authority (responsible for the enforcement of consumer protection rules around issues like cancelled flights) after eight weeks. However, even if it rules in your favour, as a regulator it cannot oblige airlines to pay out. If your airline refuses to budge, the next step is to go to the Small Claims Court.

Some airlines are signed up to an Alternative Dispute Resolution body. You can look up which ones are signed up to what body on the CAA on their website. Some are approved by the CAA, others by EU Member States. Currently the CAA will deal with any airlines not members of an ADR scheme.

Connecting flights

If, due to a delay of less than 3 hours, you miss your connecting flight and so arrived at the final destination more than 3 hours late, you are entitled to compensation of between €125 and €600. However, this is only the case if you book both flights together at the same time.

Airlines will really fight this one! But in the Air France SA v Heinz-Gerke Folkerts & Luz-Tereza Folkerts 26/02/13 case the Judge ruled that

> "Article 7 of Regulation (EC) No 261/2004 of the European Parliament and of the Council of 11 February 2004 establishing common rules on compensation and assistance to passengers in the event of denied boarding and of cancellation or long delay of flights, and repealing Regulation (EEC) No 295/91 must be interpreted as meaning that compensation is payable, on the basis of that article, to a passenger on directly connecting flights who has been delayed at departure for a period below the limits specified in Article 6 of that regulation, but has arrived at the final destination at least three hours later than the scheduled arrival time, given that the compensation in question is not conditional upon there having been a delay at departure and, thus, upon the conditions set out in Article 6 having been met."

So quote that!

In March 2018 the UK Supreme Court ruled that airlines must pay compensation when passengers miss a connecting flight and arrive more than 3 hours late at a destination outside of the EU. Claudia Wegener v Royal Air Maroc SA 31 May 2018.

Brexit
If there is a no-deal Brexit there could well be disruption to flights around the time the UK actually leaves the EU. This is because the UK would not be part of the European Common Aviation Area and bilateral agreements need to be made.

At the point of writing it is not clear if a flight disruption would be considered as an "extraordinary" circumstance for the purposes of EU 261. I suspect it will be a matter to be fought in court. You should still get a refund but you may not get the compensation, consequential losses or admin fees. Check with your travel insurer as to whether your flight would be covered by Brexit issues.

The Government has said that in the event of a no-deal Brexit you will have the same rights under UK law in the event of denied boarding, cancellation or long delay of passenger air, rail, road or sea services.

TEMPLATE: **Delayed flight**

Put in the amount to which you are entitled using the tables above

---

Dear [*xxx*]

Re : Compensation claim for delayed flight [*booking reference number*]

I am writing regarding flight [*flight number*] on [*date*] from [*departure airport*] to [*arrival airport*]. The scheduled departure time was [*departure time*]. However, the flight arrived [*number hours late at arrival airport*].

Under EC Regulation 261/2004 I am claiming compensation for this delayed flight. The passengers in the party were:

[*Full names of everyone on your booking.*]

My scheduled flight length was [*number of*] kilometres, therefore I am seeking [*select from €250 / €300 / €400 / €600*] per delayed passenger in my party. The total is [*total compensation sum for all passengers*] for all passengers.

[*If appropriate include the following text*] During the delay the passengers in my party were not provided with any [*refreshments and/or hotel accommodation*]. Please find attached copies of receipts for the cost of purchasing our own. Please refund in full: [*bullet point everything you paid for and the costs*].

[*If claiming for both delay and other then add the following:*] The total compensation sought is [€ *total amount of all costs added together*] and I look forward to receiving the sterling equivalent.

I look forward to a full response to this letter within seven days. If I do not receive a satisfactory response I will not hesitate in taking the matter further which will include, but not be limited to, informing the regulator and if necessary starting proceedings through the Small Claims Court.

Yours [*sincerely/faithfully*]

Real Example of using the Delayed Flight Regulations

My mates, let's call them Janet and John, flew from Ibiza in 2012. Their flight was delayed more than 3 hours due to a technical fault. I found out about this a year later and duly wrote a letter for Janet and John in October 2013 to send to Thomas Cook. The response regarding the service was poor and took a long time. It also rejected the claim for compensation under the Delayed Boarding Regulations. Janet and John didn't want to take the matter further through the courts as it was debatable whether the technical fault was within Thomas Cook's control or not. I seethed about this for nearly a year, but then my time came to strike again!

In July 2014 the Jet2 vs Huzar case confirmed that technical difficulties are not extraordinary circumstances. So I wrote another quite short email including the following; "I have since taken legal advice. The decisions made in the Wallentin-Hermann vs Alitalia case 2009 and Jet2 vs Huzar case 2014 confirmed that technical difficulties are not extraordinary circumstances. Therefore my husband I are entitled to €250 each".

Within 24 hours Thomas Cook replied stating that "New information has become available and as a result of this the decision that was made originally has been changed. We work really hard to ensure that when a flight is delayed the disruption caused is kept to a minimum. Following this review, under EU Regulation 261/2014 compensation is payable on this occasion". A voucher for £409.37 was attached to the email. Janet and John were pleased. I wasn't. Compensation is compensation. You might accept a goodwill gesture as a voucher but not compensation. Within another 24 hours of my writing another email Janet and John had the money in their bank account!

So, it works. Use it and make sure you request compensation and not a voucher!

Accommodation booked separately

If your accommodation was booked with a UK travel company, then your contract will probably be with the hotel. But if the accommodation is part of a whole package, then the contract could be with the package travel company. Your contract is with the company to which you paid the money. The Consumer Rights Act 2015 (bookings made prior to 1st October 2015 the Supply of Goods and Services Act 1982) would be used. If the accommodation overbooks or does not provide services with reasonable skill etc. If you have to go to different accommodation due to overbooking you can claim from the hotel for breach of contract.

If you book accommodation directly with the hotel abroad then you will need to deal with the laws in that country including going to court in that country.

TEMPLATE: **Accommodation standard**

For purchases prior to 1st October 2015 quote "Supply of Goods and Services Act 1982"

Dear [*xxx*]

Re [*date of stay*]

On the [*xxx*] I booked accommodation for [*xx* people for the [*date*]. When [*I/we*] arrived I had cause to complain regarding [*detail/bullet point(s)*]. I have [*enclosed/attached*] photographs.

I complained to the manager at the time but the matter*(s)* [*was/were*] not resolved satisfactorily. I asked to be moved to another room and this was refused.

Under the Consumer Rights Act 2015 I am entitled to services to be undertaken with reasonable skill and care. The standard of cleanliness and quality to be expected from this type and price of hotel was not met and you are therefore in breach of contract. Therefore I am entitled to compensation from you.

[*You can either leave the amount open or work out what you think is a reasonable amount such as comparing the standard with similar accommodation and including the following statement:*] I believe [*£xxxx*] to be a reasonable total. This has been calculated by detail.

I look forward to hearing from you within seven days. Should I not be fully satisfied with your response I will not hesitate in taking the matter further. This will include, but not be limited to, informing Trading Standards. I will be sharing my experiences on review sites also.

Yours [*sincerely/faithfully*]

Timeshare

Timeshare entitles you to a set amount of time per year in certain accommodation. There is a one off payment plus yearly charges for maintenance and management.

You may need to complain about a variety of things such as poor maintenance/repair, missing equipment, or services which you are paying for as part of your contract not being fulfilled.

In the first instance contact the owner's committee (if there is one) and explain the issue(s). Often the committee oversees the management and is able to sort out the problems and/ or change the management company if appropriate. If there is no committee you will need to contact the timeshare company or management company directly.

Check your timeshare agreement for what is covered, if the company is in breach of contract and if so what for. If you signed your agreement in a European Economic Area (EAA) country on or after 23rd February 2011, your agreement should tell you about all the services and facilities for your timeshare. If your agreement is covered by the regulations, this gives you more protection and rights to cancel your agreement. Lithuania, Norway and Slovenia haven't put the Timeshare Regulations into force though, so if you signed an agreement in one of these countries you should obtain legal advice about what your rights are.

If you think you have been mis-sold your timeshare contact the UK European Consumer Centre (ECC) which should be able to advise you and also help on what to do if your timeshare is not in the EU. The Consumer Protection from Unfair Trading Regulations 2008 protects you from being misled into buying something that you may not have bought if you had been given all the facts. Report the matter to Trading Standards.

For timeshare outside of the Europe you can also contact the American Resort Development Association (ARDA).

Unless you can sort the matter out directly you will very likely need to take legal advice and action.

See chapter 7 *Finance* for details on how you may also get your money back if paid for on credit card.

Luggage

If your luggage is lost or damaged you should be able to claim from the airline. Different airlines have different rules, but as a general rule of thumb, the CAA says airlines often don't automatically consider themselves liable for consequential losses and so the only way you could enforce a request, if the airline initially refuses to comply, is in court. A consequential loss may be missing a connecting flight because you were waiting for your luggage. Airlines will usually deal with these issues on a case by case basis. They should pay out for essentials and you will have to follow the airline's specific procedures for complaints, noting the time within which you need to complain. You may get more on your travel insurance but this will depend on the cover taken out and, of course, the excess.

Luggage is considered lost after 21 days. You must report the fact that your luggage has been lost, delayed or damaged at the airport and keep a copy of the Property Irregularity Report which staff of the airline will complete. To make a claim you must then contact the airline in writing:

- Lost/stolen/damaged luggage - within 7 days
- Delayed bags from receiving the delayed bag –within 21 days

If the airline accept your claim, they may pay for your baggage to be repaired, or may provide replacement baggage.

TEMPLATE: **Lost luggage**

Dear [*xxx*]

Re: Lost Luggage [*flight number*]

I flew with your airline on [*xxx*] between [*departure airport*] and [*arrival airport*].

My checked in luggage did not arrive at my destination and has now been missing for 21 days.

Under the Montreal Convention I would like to claim [*£xx*] compensation for my lost luggage.

I [*enclose/attach*] copies of my receipts for the replacement items.

Yours [*sincerely/faithfully*]

Car hire

Before hiring a car, shop around and check what is included in the contract. Some quotes may appear cheap but there may be hidden add ons, such as different insurance levels. Theft protection may be extra (it is mandatory in Italy). This is one of the times it is probably better to deal with one of the larger companies based in the UK. They are more likely to have roadside coverage, better models and quality of cars. It will be easier to complain if things go wrong too! Pre-book in the UK for ease of comparing prices and for what is likely to be a cheaper deal.

When you take the vehicle check tyres, fuel tank and bodywork. Take photographs with the date on them if possible. This is your evidence should there be any dispute. Take photos again when returning the vehicle if necessary.

If you have a complaint, write to the company. If not satisfied with their response then you can take further. For UK rentals, the British Vehicle Rental and Leasing Association (BVRLA), can help you with complaints about its members. It has a code of conduct which members must abide by and it will investigate if a member has breached this. It aims to resolve disputes within 30 days.

The European Car Rental Conciliation Service (ECRCS) is the dispute resolution scheme for a number of car rental companies throughout the EU. So check this list before hiring so you know that you can take a complaint to an independent body if you have a complaint. This works in the same way as any other ADR scheme but for across the whole of Europe. In order to use ECRCS you must have booked with the company direct and not through a travel agent/broker.

There is also the European Consumer Centres Network, which has a free service to help resolve disputes and help you get your money back.

Holiday Insurance

See chapter 11, *Insurance*.

Rail travel in Europe

See chapter 15, *Public Transport*.

13 **EBAY**

The complaints procedures are all on eBay but most of us know at least one person who has been stung either as a seller or a buyer, or both. I was caught out as a buyer a few years back when I forgot about an item I had purchased. Although I had contacted the seller within the 3 month time limit set by eBay I had not raised the complaint in the resolution centre in that time. So if I can be caught (albeit a few years ago) and be unable to get my money back from a personal seller then anyone can! This is why I decided to include eBay as a separate chapter in this book.

Most people will say that the complaints procedure is stacked against the seller. I have bought and sold hundreds of items on eBay over the years and would probably agree that this is so, but there are ways you can protect yourself both as a seller and a buyer.

On the eBay site there is a section "Reporting members who are breaking the rules". This is quite a long list of reasons for which you can report both sellers and buyers.

The "eBay community" is a forum where you can ask questions. Some years ago I used it, found people really helpful and got a speedy response. However, this forum certainly shows eBay as appearing to favour the buyers. Sellers have many a story to tell about buyers giving bad feedback for their competition to use – saying items didn't arrive and many other tales of woe. The community forum is full of people warning eBay that sellers are leaving eBay to sell on Facebook and Gumtree for free. So do be careful when selling and remember it isn't the only place you can sell now.

If you have bought a counterfeit/fake item, also see chapter 6 *Buying Goods*.

Seller

Protect yourself from complaints. Decide prior to listing what your refund policy is. I tend to state "No Refunds". Whilst eBay advises that you are less likely to sell your items, or sell them for less, I have done just fine. I now don't offer refunds because I think it is too easy for a buyer to be dishonest. A few years ago I sold a baby sling. Used but perfectly clean. I advertised it as such and showed a photo. The buyer said that it had a discoloured patch. I don't believe that this was true. I think she may have sent a photo which showed a stain which was not there when I posted it. I said that if she wanted a refund she would have to post it at her cost. She refused to do this and said she would just throw it away. Because of this she did not get her refund from me or PayPal. I believe she had every intention of keeping it for free.

To show that I am a good seller, I state that buyers can view items before purchase and also pay cash on collection however small or light the item. That way even if buyers live too far away they still know that I'm selling items in the knowledge that if someone came to my house they could refuse to purchase. I would advise you do this. Should a buyer then lie, you have said no refunds and therefore PayPal should, in theory, support you. (Unless you are a business which is slightly different).

Always get proof of posting making sure that the full address and postcode is listed on the receipt. This of course is not proof of delivery but it does cover you for claiming against Royal Mail should the item get lost. You can send "signed for" delivery but then things start getting more expensive, people pay less for your item and you make less profit. You can offer more than one alternative for posting but then if you are selling a few items it takes a lot of time to work out all the various different postage costs! When I started selling a few years ago I offered various postage options which was time consuming and pointless. Everyone went for the cheapest, second class. As a buyer I go for second class and it annoys me when sellers only offer first class postage. Sellers lessen the number of bids they receive as people usually set themselves a limit including postage, so only to offer first class postage is giving your profit straight to Royal Mail! That said of course you do have more protection if you offer proof of delivery.

Never post anything until it is paid for! Also, provide a deadline for when payment must be made or the item will be relisted. This stops the time wasters and reduces likelihood of having to complain about a non-payment.

Good feedback is obviously a bonus. If you get a bad one make sure you respond to the feedback, the buyer gets the last word but at least anyone really going through your feedback will see your response. Don't worry about the one bad feedback in many. I used to and it annoyed me intently when one dishonest buyer ruined my 100% positive feedback, but as all the other buyers clearly gave excellent feedback no-one else took any notice and it only lasts for 6 months.

It's not been possible to give buyers negative feedback for a while now, but you can block them. You can also stop certain buyers from bidding on your items. You can set your listing to stop those who:

- don't have a PayPal account
- have unpaid items recorded on their account
- have a primary delivery address in countries you don't post to
- have breached eBay policies
- have a feedback score lower than the number you specify
- are currently winning or have bought 1-100 of your items in the last 10 days (you can specify the number).

Ensure you only post to an address listed on the transaction page to ensure PayPal protection. Make sure that your item is clearly as described – it's fine if an item is being sold for parts and doesn't work but that must be clearly stated. Your main address must be in the UK or Ireland and you should follow all postage requirements.

Contact a buyer first before opening up a dispute on eBay. Try to come to an agreement. If you are able to do this then on the eBay site go to the help section and open a case to "Cancel the transaction". eBay will automatically cancel everything with the buyer not owing money and you free to relist the item. If you can't agree anything then "Open an unpaid item case". You can also "follow up on a case you've already opened" and you can report the buyer if you suspect fraud for example.

The seller can open an unpaid item case in the Resolution Centre from 2 days or up to 32 days after the listing ended. If the buyer doesn't pay, manually close the case in the Resolution Centre. The buyer has 4 days to pay so you can do this from 4 days after you opened the case, and up to 36 days after the listing ended. If you don't close the case, it expires on the 37th day after the listing has ended and you won't receive a final value fee credit.

Buyer

Your consumer rights cover you for buying from business sellers but not private sellers. However, the eBay Money Back Guarantee (formerly eBay Buyer Protection) covers your purchase price plus original postage for almost everything. It guarantees you will get the item you ordered or your money back. For more details read the eBay guidance.

If you have a complaint about a seller check the description for the returns policy. It is rare to find a seller who accepts returns and then refunds the return postage. However, if the item is bought from a business seller then you are covered by the Consumer Rights Act 2015 (Sale and Supply of Goods Act 1994 for purchases made before 1st October 2015) and if the item is faulty/misdescribed/not satisfactory then you are entitled to a full refund. If you have simply changed your mind then the seller's policies regarding postage costs apply.

In the first instance you should contact the seller through the eBay email system to ensure that eBay has all records should there be a need to investigate.

TEMPLATE: **Contacting eBay business seller**

The following template is actually quite strong and whenever I have complained to a business seller I don't actually quote the law at the first contact as usually just a note explaining the problem resolves the issue. However, if the seller refuses then I would suggest the following:

For purchases prior to 1st October 2015 quote "Sale and Supply of Goods Act 1994"

> Dear [***xxx***]
>
> On the [***date***] I purchased this item from you [***when going through the system it automatically picks up the transaction so you do not need to detail the purchase***]. It is [***faulty/misdescribed/not received***] [***describe***].
>
> Under the Consumer Rights Act 2015 I am entitled to items of satisfactory quality, fit for purpose and which are as described. Therefore you are in breach of contract and I am requesting a full refund including postage costs/ that you send a replacement at no further cost to me. I am willing to return the item if you agree to pay postage.
>
> Please ensure that you respond within 3 days. Should you not do so I will enter the eBay Buyer Protection dispute resolution process and if necessary pursue the matter in the Small Claims Court.

TEMPLATE: **Contacting a private seller**

For purchases prior to 1st October 2015 quote "Sale and Supply of Goods Act 1994"

> Dear [***xxx***]
>
> On the [***date***] I purchased this item from you [***when going through the system it automatically picks up the transaction so you do not need to detail the purchase***]. It is [***faulty/misdescribed/not received***] [***describe***].
>
> Please ensure that you respond within 3 days regarding how you would suggest resolving the problem. (*8 days for item not received*). Should you not do so I will enter the eBay Buyer Protection dispute resolution process.

A buyer can report in "My eBay" that they didn't receive an item once the item's latest estimated delivery date has passed and for 30 days (previously 45) after the latest estimated delivery date. The seller has 8 days from the report to respond to the buyer or offer a solution. If the seller does not respond or offer a solution, the buyer should open a case with eBay in the resolution centre.

If you don't gain any success within 20 days of raising the claim in the resolution centre and you paid through PayPal you will be able to use their Buyer Protection Scheme. See chapter 7 *Finance* for details.

Fake items

A seller may or may not know that the item that they sold is fake. In the first instance contact the seller who should refund all costs. If the seller won't do this then follow the guidance above. You can also "Report item" on the listing. eBay should take action. For other suggestions of what you can do to report the seller see chapter 6 *Buying Goods*.

14 POST OFFICE/ROYAL MAIL

Post Office Ltd and Royal Mail Group are part of the same group of companies and are run as separate businesses. Post Office Ltd offers customers access to Royal Mail's service, acting as an agent of Royal Mail. Royal Mail is regulated by Ofcom and the Post Office Ltd is not. Post Office staff act as advisors regarding Royal Mail services.

Post Office

Postal service complaints should be addressed to Royal Mail. However, if your complaint is about staff conduct or non postal services such as the passport "check and send" service, financial products or the Parcelforce courier service then complain to Post Office Counters Ltd either in writing or through the online form.

Royal Mail

If not satisfied with Royal Mail's response, one can then escalate the complaint within Royal Mail by contacting them again requesting the complaint be referred to the Royal Mail Escalated Customer Resolution Team. If still unhappy with the response provided by the Escalated Customer Resolution Team the Postal Review Panel will re-examine the case and issue a final response from Royal Mail. If the complaint cannot be resolved to your satisfaction, the panel will issue a deadlock letter that will allow you to ask the independent Postal Redress Scheme to investigate your case. If you do not feel your complaint is being properly and promptly dealt with you should request the deadlock letter. Then, if all else fails, issue a claim in the Small Claims Court but I'd think carefully about that, this is the Royal Mail and I can't find any cases online where anyone won a case against it. That said of course, yes I would go to court if I wasn't happy!

Junk mail

You can opt out of receiving unaddressed mail by requesting and filling out an "Optout" form. Some of the items that it delivers may contain information issued by local and central Government departments, (e.g. materials relating to elections). Because Royal Mail cannot legally separate these items from the others it delivers – such as advertising offers or leaflets – you will not receive these if you choose to opt out. You will stop getting these after 6 weeks and will need to register again after 2 years.

Real example of lost item prohibited from posting

Some time ago I helped someone with her Royal Mail problem. She had bought a bottle of perfume from a private seller on eBay. The contents turned out to be fake. The seller agreed a full refund including postage. Not surprising given the considerable trouble she could have got into had Sarah simply reported her to certain authorities....!

Now, the Royal Mail lost the item. Sarah wrote to Royal Mail and explained what had happened. Someone from Royal Mail wrote back and said that she wouldn't be getting a refund because she had posted a prohibited item. There is a list of prohibited items on the Royal Mail website. Call me cynical but apart from some obvious stuff this list includes other toiletries which you may well send as gifts, so check this list before you post liquid gifts. After shaves, perfumes and nail varnishes are allowed but there are restrictions on size etc.

Sarah told me that no-one in the Post Office had asked her what was in the parcel and no reference was made to what wasn't allowed. There is no information on the walls or in leaflets regarding this in the Post Office, so I thought this was pretty unfair. I believe that the Post Office has a duty of care to ensure that the public knows Royal Mail policies. So I wrote Sarah's letter for her, telling them exactly that and that I expected a full refund due to their failing to undertake reasonable skill and care in ensuring the public knew their rules. Matthew at Royal Mail agreed and Sarah got her full refund.

Real example of complaining about "insufficient postage"

A few years ago I sent some hand-made cards (made by my son!) to various people at Christmas using A5 envelopes. Despite all of them being the same size and weight some people were charged £1 to go and collect theirs. I complained to Royal Mail because clearly this was not fair. Either they were all wrong or all right! I enclosed one example and demanded a refund. It wasn't given. I went to the next stage and the complaint was found in my favour and I received 30 first class stamps.

15 PUBLIC TRANSPORT

Trains

Cancellations

If your train is cancelled you are due a full refund of the ticket price paid. If you still wish to travel you should be able to get on the next train then claim as for a delayed journey (see below). If you have a date and time restricted ticket you may not be able to get on a later train. You should check with the station staff before travelling who will be able to advise. If you don't travel due to the cancellation you are entitled to a full refund of the ticket price paid.

Delays

If you don't want to travel because of the delay then you should be able to get a full refund of the ticket price paid. It is the time of arrival not the time of departure that is considered. Under the National Rail Conditions of Travel you are entitled to 50% refund for a delay of over 60 minutes. However, most companies now operate a "Delay Repay" scheme, providing compensation for these delays regardless of cause. For most of the companies operating this scheme you will get at least 50% refund current threshold is a delay of 30+ minutes, but a threshold of 15 minutes is being introduced between now and 2020 and at the point of going to print 9 companies have signed up to this.

Not travelling out of choice

If you choose not to take the train journey for which you booked you should be refunded. It could be, for example, that an event to which you were travelling was cancelled so you didn't want to travel. Or any reason! So long as it wasn't an advance ticket you should be able to get a refund minus an administration fee. The maximum administration fee that the companies can charge is £10.

Season tickets
Different train companies operate different policies. You will need to check with the relevant company. You will need to submit a claim for each journey rather than a discount at renewal. The amount paid will depend on the specific company's Passenger Charter.

Consequential loss
The National Rail Conditions of Travel (NRCT) state that companies are not liable for consequential losses. For example, If you couldn't make use of a hotel stay or theatre tickets. However, they do state that companies will consider exceptional cases. Since October 1st 2016 the Consumer Rights Act 2015 (CRA) now applies to travel, including trains. Under this act you are entitled to services to be carried out with reasonable skill and care. It would certainly be worth trying to claim using both the CRA and the exceptional circumstances of the NRCT.

On 10 March 2016 the National Rail Conditions of Travel finally removed the warning that operators will not accept liability for a "consequential loss" after delays or cancellations.

In September 2013, The Court of Justice of the European Union ruled that rail passengers are entitled to a partial refund of the price of their train ticket even in poor weather circumstances.

How to claim
If you don't use your ticket to make all or part of your journey, take the unused ticket to any train company's ticket office and receive an immediate refund.

For most train companies you can also apply online via the company's website.

Alternatively you can send the claim to the train company by postal mail. Before you do, take a photo of the tickets just in case they get "lost in the post"!

Make sure you claim within 28 days of the date of travel.

Find your company on the National Rail Enquiries page which will take you to the relevant page.

Missed connection
If you have missed a connecting train due to the cancellation or delay, you can claim a refund for the unused part of the journey should you not go on a later train or have to use an alternative form of transport. You could consider claiming for consequential losses, as above.

Emergency timetables
Some train companies run what they describe as an "emergency timetable". In these instances it is possible that this may affect what you can claim. If you bought your ticket before the new timetable was put in place and decide not to travel then you can claim a full refund, as above. However, should you travel and be delayed then the level of compensation will be based on the timings of trains according to the new timetable.

Not satisfied with response?
If you think that the response from a train company is unsatisfactory, read the NRCT and the train company's Passenger Charter which will have the details of the procedure you should follow. If you are still not happy and your journey was outside of London contact Transport Focus. For London (including under and overground) contact London Travel Watch. If after this you are still not happy you can take the matter to the CEO of Transport Focus or of London Travel Watch.

The Rail Ombudsman
The Rail Ombudsman was launched 26 November 2018. It is funded by the train companies which have all signed up to the service and are obliged to abide by the decisions it makes. You must have reached the end of the provider's complaints procedure before taking the matter to the Rail Ombudsman.

The Rail Ombudsman can accept claims from England, Scotland and Wales.

Although rail companies are bound by the decision of the Rail Ombudsman, you are not. So, if you are not happy with the outcome and believe you have enough evidence to support a claim, you can go to the Small Claims Court.

Eurostar

The European Regulation on Rail Passenger Rights and Obligations 2010 entitles passengers to meals and refreshments appropriate to the delay, once delayed more than an hour.

If delayed overnight, transport to and from overnight accommodation should be provided.

After 60 minutes you become entitled to compensation. You will be able to change your ticket for another date, refund or claim compensation via e-voucher or cash, all offered at different rates and dependent on how long you have been delayed.

Length of delay	E-voucher	Cash refund
60 - 119 minutes	25% of value of affected ticket	25% of value of affected ticket
120 - 179 minutes	50% of value of affected ticket	n/a
120 minutes or more	n/a	50% of value of affected ticket
120-179 minutes	75% of value of affected ticket	

If your train is cancelled or if it seems likely that you'll be delayed over an hour you can exchange your ticket for another day for free or request a full refund. The refund can be requested from wherever you bought the ticket up to two months after the original date of travel.

Brexit
The Government has said that should there be a no-deal these rights will remain unchanged. Passengers on cross-border rail services will continue to be protected by the EU regulation on rail passengers' rights, which will be brought into UK law.

Rail in Europe

The European Regulation on Rail Passenger Rights and Obligations and the Convention Concerning International Carriage by Rail (COTIF) set out your rights for international European rail travel.

If your train is delayed or cancelled, meaning you miss a connection and can't continue your journey on the same day, the train operator must provide assistance, which includes the reasonable costs of overnight accommodation and the cost of notifying anyone expecting you at your destination. If the train is delayed or cancelled and it's not reasonable to expect passengers to continue with the journey on the same day, the train operator is liable for the same costs.

Ferries/cruises

The Consumer Rights Act 2015 was applied to ferries from 1st October 2016. You are now entitled to services carried out with reasonable skill and care. If they are not then you should be able to gain redress.

If your ferry service is cancelled or departure is delayed for more than 90 minutes, you are entitled to either an alternative sailing at the earliest opportunity at no additional cost or reimbursement of the ticket price which should be paid within seven days. If you choose an alternative crossing, you're still entitled to claim compensation for the delay to your original journey.

While you wait (when delayed for more than 90 minutes or it is expected to be cancelled) you are entitled to meals and refreshments if they can be reasonably supplied even if the reason is bad weather.

If an overnight stay is required due to the delay/cancellation then the ferry or cruise operator must offer you accommodation free of charge, if possible. This can be on board or ashore.

Your ferry company can offer alternatives such as permitting you to make your own separate plans to travel and reimburse your expenses. No overnight accommodation has to be offered or costs reimbursed if the delay is caused by weather conditions endangering the safe operation of the ship.

Brexit
The Government has said that should there be a no-deal passengers on ferry services will continue to be protected by the EU regulation on passengers' rights, which will be brought into UK law.

The Government has also said cruise operations will continue on the same basis as today. Passengers who embark on a cruise at a UK port will continue to be protected by the EU regulation on maritime passengers' rights, which will be brought into UK law.

Buses

The Consumer Rights Act 2015 was applied to all travel from 1st October 2016. You are now entitled to services carried out with reasonable skill and care. If they are not then you should be able to gain redress.

When you complain, ensure you give as much detail as you can – times, dates, registration number of the bus, route number etc. Send copies of receipts/tickets etc. If the company insist that you send the original retain a copy.

London
Transport for London and bus companies do not have a standard compensation policy for compensation for bus delays and won't compensate for delays out of its control such as weather and traffic jams.

If you have any complaint about buses/bus drivers in London contact Transport for London. If you are dissatisfied with the response contact TravelWatch detailing why you remain unhappy. If you are still not satisfied contact the Local Government Ombudsman.

Non London
Outside London complain directly to the bus company. If not happy with the response you can contact the Bus Appeals Body. You can also contact the Traffic Commissioner for the area in which the company is based. (There are 7 Traffic Commissioners who are appointed by the Secretary of State for Transport). Their responsibility includes the licensing of the operators of heavy goods vehicles (HGVs) and of buses and coaches (public service vehicles or PSVs) and the registration of local bus services.

The Traffic Commissioner for Scotland deals with both appeals against decisions by Scottish local authorities on taxi fares and with appeals against charging and removing improperly parked vehicles in Edinburgh and Glasgow.

Other useful information
Bus companies must adhere to regulations laid by the Traffic Commissioner and the 3 rules of the CPC (Certificate of Professional Competence) holder's licence, these are:
1. Professional Conduct
2. Good Repute
3. Financial Standing (for alternative transport arrangements)

If companies fail in any of the above you can write to the Commissioner. If you feel that a bus/coach/limo is unsafe you can write to the Driver and Vehicle Standards Agency (Until April 2014, The Vehicle and Operator Services Agency (VOSA)) or any of the bodies named above.

Under The Freedom of Information Act 2000 (for public transport) you can ask for a certified copy of the vehicle's MOT, COIF (Certificate of Initial Fitness), Insurance documentation, Driver Daily Check sheet, with name redacted, and public liability certificate. You may not get these but adds strength to your case.

Real example of complaint to Stagecoach

A colleague had problems with Stagecoach which operates the buses in Cambridge. One late evening Ed's bus was prevented from following his route because a car had been abandoned on the busway. The driver did not contact the office and nothing was done to help the passengers. So I wrote an email to the CEO outlining the issue and saying that he had had to pay £20 for the taxi fare. The CEO said that they had staff on site at all times while vehicles were out, in case of emergencies and breakdowns. He said they had a 24 hour contact number for drivers who for some reason could not contact the depot which would then in turn contact the next level of management. He reimbursed the £20 taxi fare. I wanted Ed to email again and point out that as the driver did try to ring the office and got no answer it would appear that their "Tried and tested" processes have not been tested well enough but he didn't!

You can download a Passenger Rights App for your mobile from the Europa website (see chapter 27, *Useful Contacts*) which will give you your travel rights wherever you are in Europe.

16 TELECOMS

I think that this is one of the most, if not the most, complained about sector. Although the energy sector is in the news all the time for being at the top of the tree for complaints I see more complaints about communication companies than any other. People often say that they are going to swop from one company to another but frankly, in my opinion they are all appalling. The irony is not lost on me that that they are communication companies but their own internal and external communications are dreadful. Twice I have used a telephone ombudsman service.

BROADBAND

Router

If the router is faulty complain within a few weeks and request a refund. You could accept a repair but I always go for full refunds on items. Strictly speaking after a few weeks you are seen as accepting the goods and the company can offer you replacement or repair. See chapter 6 *Buying Goods* for details on how to complain about products.

Speed and interruption to service

This can be quite a problem of which people are not really aware. Check your broadband speed by using a search engine to find many sites that will do this. Look at the speed that you are paying for and complain if necessary! Usually this is via the company's complaint form, you can use the template below to fill out the form of course. From

23 May 2018, the Advertising Standards Authority brought in changes to Broadband advertising rules. Download speeds must be available to 50% of customers at peak times and described as "average" in adverts.

The service must meet what was promised to you before you signed up though, otherwise the supplier could be in breach of contract - so you can complain if the service is frequently not meeting the speed. Check the terms and conditions of your contract. Maximum speeds may not be guaranteed and other factors such as where you live, how many people are on a website at one time etc. come into play.

Ofcom's voluntary code of practice which signed-up telecoms providers should follow, states that they must give a detailed quote for speeds on your line so ask for this. Also under these rules you can break the contract or take an alternative package without penalties if the speed is not per the original estimate.

Log your speeds over a few weeks and provide this information when informing your supplier that it is in breach of contract.

From 31 October 2016, the Advertising Standards Authority recommended that in order for broadband providers to ensure they stay within the new rules, (regarding advertised fixed broadband price claims to avoid customers being misled) that future broadband ads which include price claims should:

- show all-inclusive up-front and monthly costs; no more separating out line rental
- give greater prominence for the contract length and any post-discount pricing
- give greater prominence for up-front costs.

From 1 March 2019 providers must abide by Ofcom's new guidelines. These are:

- provide realistic estimates of speeds at peak times at the point of sale of contract
- provide a guaranteed minimum speed at the point of sale of the contract
- if speed levels fall below the guaranteed minimum level, time is limited for the provider to fix the issue before offering right to exit a contract early

TEMPLATE: **Broadband speed**

Dear [*xxx*]

Re: [*Account number*]

On [*date*] I contracted with you to order [*detail package*]. Since installation I have been extremely disappointed with the speed of broadband I have received. I have undertaken regular speed checks over the last month and these are the results:

[*Date – speeds (provide list).*]

Therefore you are in breach of contract.

I trust that you will investigate this matter and provide me with your findings and a way forward such as an alternative package, reduction in charges or termination of the contract with no fee. In addition to this, I expect appropriate redress in relation to the speed for which I have paid and not received.

I look forward to hearing from you within 14 days. Should I not be fully satisfied with your response I will refer the matter to [*CISAS/ Ombudsman Services (delete as appropriate)*].

Yours [*faithfully/sincerely*]

TEMPLATE: **Interruption to service**

You should log all interruptions to the service, with dates of interruption along with the duration. How long you should do this for depends on how often you are getting interruptions. For example if it is happening several times a day for a week that is enough for you to complain. However, if it is only once or twice a week you might want to log for a couple of months to show that it is an ongoing problem.

Dear [*xxx*]

Re: [*Account number*]

On the [*date*] I contracted with you for [*detail package*]. I have been extremely disappointed with the service I have received. I [*enclose/attach*] a log of interruptions.

Therefore you are in breach of contract.

I trust that you will investigate this matter and provide me with your findings and a way forward. In addition to this, I expect appropriate redress in relation to the service for which I have paid and not received.

I look forward to hearing from you within 14 days. Should I not be fully satisfied with your response I will refer the matter to [*CISAS/ Ombudsman Services (delete as appropriate)*].

Yours [*faithfully/sincerely*]

Real example of complaining about poor communication

Years ago I contacted Virgin regarding an ignored query. Someone 'phoned me from Virgin and oddly I took the call. I think I was shopping and didn't realise what I was doing as I really don't like dealing with complaints on the 'phone. He was very apologetic and helpful and I asked for some redress for the inconvenience and he said "I am a believer in if you don't ask you don't get" and he credited my account with £10.

Mobile 'phones

Your consumer rights are the same for when your mobile 'phone develops a fault as any other product, but in my experience people are frequently getting fobbed off with lines such as "Send it back for repair" and "Contact manufacturer".

If your 'phone forms part of your mobile 'phone contract, your claim would be against your mobile 'phone service provider and you may be entitled to a free repair or replacement as part of your contract. Check the terms and conditions in your contract for your entitlements. However, regardless of the contract you retain your right under the Consumer Rights Act 2015 (Sale and Supply of Goods Act 1994 for purchases made before 1st October 2015) to goods that are satisfactory, fit for purpose and as described.

I would always say, for at least the first 6 months you are entitled to a replacement 'phone if it develops a fault.

There are currently no rules regarding poor network coverage. Even if you move house, you are unlikely to be successful in cancelling a contract because of poor network coverage if the provider's terms and conditions allows for breaks in coverage. However under the Consumer Rights Act 2015 (Supply of Goods and Services Act 1982 prior to 1st

October 2015), a service provider must provide the contracted service with reasonable care and skill.

If you are receiving regular interruptions to service use the template above for Broadband and change accordingly.

If you bought your 'phone without any contract then your complaint is always against the retailer and not the manufacturer. You may have a guarantee with the 'phone and after 6 months you might want to claim on this with the manufacturer, but go to the retailer first who might also contact the manufacturer directly for you.

CISAS and Ombudsmen Services – Communications only cover mobile 'phone services and not issues with the actual 'phones.

TEMPLATE: **Faulty mobile 'phone**
For purchases prior to 1st October 2015 quote "Sale and Supply of Goods Act 1994"

Dear [*xxx*]

Re: [*make/model of 'phone*]

On the [*date*] I bought [*detail 'phone*] from you. It has developed *a* fault(*s*) [*detail*]. Under the Consumer Rights Act 2015 I am entitled to goods that are satisfactory and fit for purpose. This is clearly not the case and you are in breach of contract. Therefore I am requesting a [*full refund/repair/replacement (delete as appropriate)*].

I look forward to hearing from you regarding whether you will be collecting the 'phone or providing returns packaging/labels or reimbursing my recorded delivery. Should I not be fully satisfied with your response I will not hesitate in taking the matter further. This will include, but not be limited to, reporting the matter to Trading Standards and pursuing the matter through the Small Claims Court.

Yours [*faithfully/sincerely*]

Mis-sold contracts

So many times I am hearing of people who believe that they have been mis-sold a contract. It is extremely difficult to successfully complain about it. That doesn't mean you should not do it however! It is just that in my experience mis-selling of a contract is one of the most annoying and tedious complaints to deal with. The fob offs come thick and fast and I'm sure put many people off.

Keep records of everything. If the company rings you around the time of the end of your contract make sure anything that they offer for a new one they also put in writing. Although you can request transcript of conversations, (under the General Data Protection Regulations 2018) they will charge for this and again it is time consuming. Be ahead of the game. If you agree a contract over the 'phone remember that you have the 14 day cooling off period (Consumer Contracts (Information, Cancellation and Additional Charges) Regulations 2013) in which you can cancel.

Real example of complaining about a mis-sold contract

This was tedious and hard work but perseverance won through in the end. Ben bought a 'phone with a Vodafone contract from Phones 4u. He was told that after one year the monthly fee would reduce by £5.00 a month but this didn't happen. Ben wrote to complain to Phones 4u and was offered £60 as a goodwill gesture. (i.e. the difference). Ben's letter stated that he actually wanted to terminate the contract but both Phones 4u and Vodafone refused to do this. We emailed CEOs, heads of operations, refusing to pay for transcriptions of 'phone calls when Vodafone refused to deal with anything in writing and quoting the Misrepresentation Act and the false statement made by the sales person which convinced Ben to enter into the contract. As stated on the Advice Guide "If the statement made by the sales person is false and it influenced your decision to buy the service, this is called misrepresentation. If this is the case, you can cancel your contract without charges and may be able to take legal action for compensation. A false statement which influenced your decision to enter into a contract is also an example of an unfair commercial practice. This is a criminal offence." We got a further £90 from Vodafone.

TEMPLATE: **Mis-selling mobile 'phones**

Dear [*xxx*]

Re: [*Mobile 'phone number*]

On the [*date*] I was sold a contract with your service for my mobile 'phone. I was told that [*bullet point the details of what you believe you were sold*].

However, I have since discovered that this is not the contract I am on. [*Bullet point details of differences*].

I believe that this is a clear breach of the Consumer Protection from Unfair Contract Terms 2008 as this has harmed my economic interests as an average consumer. I made this purchasing decision based on the information I was given, had this been accurate I would not have taken out this contract.

As you are in breach of contract I am terminating it with no penalties. Please confirm within 7 days that you agree. Should I not be fully satisfied with your response I will not hesitate in taking the matter further. This will include, but not be limited to, reporting the matter to Trading Standards and taking the matter through [*CISAS/ Ombudsman Services (delete as appropriate)*].

Yours [*faithfully/sincerely*]

Mobile 'phone price hikes

From 23 January 2014, if mobile 'phone providers hike prices on new fixed contracts, you can cancel without paying any fee. Price rises for existing customers and new customers are permitted as long as you're told about this at the point of sale. Your mobile 'phone provider may be able to hike the price of your fixed contract by the rate of RPI (Retail Price Index). RPI is based on the cost of a theoretical basket of everyday goods and services.

Roaming Charges

Roaming charges are put in place when the mobile phone network detects that you are abroad and adds extra costs on top of what you normally pay on your national network. Charges are incurred for making calls, receiving a voicemail, picking it up, sending and receiving SMS text messages and pictures and, of course, using the Internet and downloading or streaming.

In 2007 the European Commission started to tackle reducing roaming tariffs when travelling in the EU. It has been progressively capping the maximum amount a mobile 'phone provider can charge for services in Europe. The costs were capped in July 2014 and again from 30th April 2016 (excluding VAT for calls, texts and downloading data). On the 15th June 2017 they ended completely. This is only for countries in the EU. The new regulation, called "Roam Like at Home", means that you will pay the same in 28 EU countries as if you were at home as part of your contract allowance.

Keep an eye on your provider's free use policy. Some providers add a charge for using all data allowance (although still free for calls and texts). All mobile operators have to apply a cut-off limit once you have used €50 (excluding VAT) – (around £44 as at June 2017) – of data per month, wherever you travel in the world unless you choose another limit.

The provider must send an alert to your phone when you reach 80% and then 100% of the agreed data roaming limit. Operators must stop charging for data at the 100% point, unless you explicitly agree to continue to use data.

Under the Consumer Protection from Unfair Trading Regulations 2008, the retailer must ensure the customer understands what goods and services are being provided and ensure that there are no hidden costs. If the paperwork does not comply with these requirements you may not have to pay. When retailers send you an email confirmation of the purchase this must now include a full description of the goods and services purchased, including their characteristics, and the full price including tax and any additional charges or delivery prices.

Under the Consumer Rights Act 2015 traders must also provide services with reasonable skill and care.

Brexit
If there is a deal the Government has said that free roaming will remain guaranteed for the implementation period. (This should apply until the end of December 2020 at least. This may be extended until December 2022 for a variety of reasons, but both sides need to agree). Future arrangements after this date will depend on the details of the deal.

If there is a no-deal Brexit, at the point of going to print the Government has proposed a statutory instrument to prepare for changes to mobile roaming arrangements. If it is approved, it will remove the obligation for mobile providers to offer free roaming in the EU. The proposed new law retains the current global data cap on mobile roaming of £45 per monthly billing period and would also legislate to ensure the current alerts issued at 80% and 100% data usage continue.

Ombudsman Services/CISAS

The ombudsman covers; bills, the quality of customer service received and communication services provided to customers. You will need to check with which ombudsman your provider is registered with and use that one. Request a deadlock letter from the company if you remain unsatisfied. If the company does not provide this or 8 weeks has passed you can then take the matter to the ombudsman.

Ombudsman Services runs one of the ombudsman services for the communications sector. It will work to resolve the matter and, if simple, can offer to try and resolve it over the'phone or email with the company in under 5 days and the resolution can be agreed by both the company and you. If the ombudsman decides that the decision will take more than 5 days, the company will be asked for more information. The ombudsman will prepare an investigation plan and propose a resolution to you and the company. Both of you can offer more information at this stage before the ombudsman makes the final decision. Decisions are legally binding in court and the company has 28 days to comply. It can award you up to £10,000 to return you to the position you would be in had the mistake not occurred and can reflect the trouble to which you have been put.

It should take 6-8 weeks to resolve.

CISAS runs the other ombudsman service. You will need to fill out a form which is easily done online or by post. Online the site states that evidence must be sent within 5 days, but note my warning about sending evidence in the example below.

CISAS sends the company which you are complaining about the details of your complaint within 10 days and sends you the response. You have 5 days in which to respond to this. Within 3 weeks the adjudicator will make the decision. You can also be awarded up to £10,000 to return you to the position you would be in had the mistake not occurred and the award can reflect the trouble to which you have been put. The company must provide the remedy within 20 days (or what has been agreed in the settlement).

Real example of using CISAS

I used CISAS for Virgin many years ago. I can't remember what it was for but I won. After judgement Virgin apologised and gave me another month's credit on top of the approximate £200 award.

This year I used CISAS for Virgin. My partner's email wasn't working. He couldn't log on to find out bill information and despite many efforts to get Virgin to sort it out nothing happened.

I sent a complaint via the form (I had actually tried to ring but couldn't get through) and received a standard email asking me to ring! Various emails went back and forth with the Executive Team (at one point with an "assigned specialist agent" – if that means one person has been assigned to your case to resolve it then the title was incorrect). Emails went unanswered, Virgin changed passwords without being asked to do so and my letter requesting a letter of deadlock, so that I could take the matter to CISAS, was opened and returned. Bizarre.

I found CISAS a very simple and easy process last time. However this latest experience allows me to give you some words of warning. The administrative processes are dire in my opinion. No one person handles your case and if you send more details or queries different people will respond at different times which can be very unhelpful and muddled as you don't always know what they have seen. For example I sent a scan of a letter I had received to add to the case and got an email back days later telling me that I needed to submit a claim to CISAS. No continuity at all and because of the delays between getting a response and (despite an immediate response by me) the delay in them dealing with it again when it was received, it was not submitted. However, when you submit your form the details are sent to the company for their response. You can then respond to that. Note that this was 2014 so things may have improved.

The process was incredibly slow. In the time that I was waiting for a date more information came to light and I forwarded this but the administrators would not allow it to be included. I had attached emails with the original form. I had to update the form with the account holder details and this is where I urge you to be careful. I had (wrongly) assumed that all the appendices that I had sent would be kept on file and used. When I received the adjudicator's decision (eventually, as that was delayed a further two weeks) she agreed that the service had been poor and ruled that Virgin pay £100 (a slightly lower sum than requested). However, in the ruling she found that my evidence referred to emails but did not include them. I followed this up and was told that my form copied and pasted parts but there was no evidence of the emails. Very annoying as they had been sent and in the CISAS guidelines it says that the adjudicator can ask for more information. A simple request for actual emails could have been made in my opinion. So, should you need to resubmit your form, make sure you resubmit everything.

Nuisance calls

Sign up for TPS. The Telephone Preference Service. You can register both your landline and mobile numbers. It doesn't stop them all but it certainly reduces it. As for the ones it doesn't stop, report them. It is the law that companies must check names and numbers against the TPS register so they are breaking the law if you are registered and they contact you. Allow 28 days for it to be all registered. TPS is not able to enforce the law or fine, but does pass the information onto the Information Commissioner's Office (ICO).

If you have consented to receive marketing calls then you will still get these even if you are registered with TPS. Watch out for comparison and other sites and make sure that box is unchecked for wanting marketing emails.

For silent and abandoned calls, (frequently caused by automated systems dropping calls as soon as one is answered) contact Ofcom. Abandoned calls are where you hear a recorded message and there is a standard form online to report these calls. Ofcom won't take action on individual complaints, however, once it gets a large number regarding the same company it will take action. In 2013 it fined Talk Talk £750,000 for an excessive number of silent and abandoned calls. So report these kinds of calls. The form is simple and quick to fill out.

For unwanted marketing calls, contact the Information Commissioner's Office (ICO). In May 2011 it was given powers to impose a fine up to £500,000 on companies who break the rules on unsolicited texts and phone calls.

Spam emails/texts

The Privacy and Electronic Communications Regulations 2003 cover the sending of email marketing. Texts are defined as "electronic mail" in the regulations. Signing up with the TPS will not stop spam texts because companies do not have to screen against TPS because they should already have prior consent to send you texts. Organisations can only send marketing emails to you if you have agreed to receive them, except where there is a clearly defined customer relationship.

The Information Commissioner's Office (ICO) can only investigate complaints about marketing emails from identifiable UK senders. However, the ICO has an agreement with a number of overseas bodies to cooperate and exchange information to try and stop spam emails that are sent from non UK addresses.

You can report spam texts to your mobile 'phone provider (All operators use 7726, which is free of charge, as the short code to report spam texts) as well as the ICO. Don't respond to spam texts or emails it just lets the company know that you are live and it will send more.

Do not pay any company that offers to stop/reduce unwanted calls and texts as they can only do what you can do for free.

You can also opt out of marketing emails in a similar way to mailings. (See chapter 27 *Useful Contacts*)

17 **HOME IMPROVEMENTS**

Builders

Try to prevent many of the problems which arise with builders before using one. Get 3 quotes and describe the job you need in detail. Discuss the length of time the job will take. A rough price is an estimate and a fixed price a quote. If you don't agree a price then the Consumer Rights Act 2015 (Supply of Goods and Sales Act 1982 prior to 1st October 2015) dictates that you are entitled to a "reasonable price". That of course depends on the job and could be difficult to quantify, so always get a price agreed. If it's a large job get a contract drawn up. The Defective Premises Act 1972 provides a claimant with 6 years from the completion of the building work to make a claim if they consider the building to be defective. It relates to work undertaken by builders, developers, surveyors, architects etc. "Defective" is limited to work causing the property to be unfit for human habitation as a result of design, workmanship or materials. Improvement, small jobs and refurbishments are not covered by the Act but you are covered by the Consumer Rights Act 2015/Supply of Goods and Services Act 1982 which entitle you to work undertaken with reasonable skill and care and within a reasonable length of time.

If you have a complaint, try to resolve the matter in person or over the 'phone before formally writing. Give the trader an opportunity to remedy the work. If they refuse to do this or they fail to do it satisfactorily then you can take the matter further. When you write to complain ensure that that you state that you retain your legal rights under the Consumer Rights Act 2015/ Supply of Goods and Services Act 1982 so that you are still able to claim if necessary afterwards when you write to complain. A template for this is below. Should the trader not respond or not remedy the work, proceed with getting an independent report and 3 quotes. Get the work done and write to the trader requesting this amount attaching the paperwork. You could attach a quote before the work is done to give the trader one last chance if you wish.

If the trader is a member of a trade association you can contact it and see if you are able to use a resolution scheme.

Painters/decorators

Painting and Decorating Association members either hold formal qualifications in painting and decorating (City & Guilds, NVQs etc.) or have a minimum of five years' experience in the industry. They comply with the Association's Code of Practice. The Association has a searchable database of members and operates an internal complaints and arbitration scheme to deal with all complaints against members.

In Scotland Scottish Decorators Federation members must comply with their Code of Conduct. The SDF operates an internal complaints and arbitration scheme to deal with complaints against members.

Architects

All architects must belong to the Architects Registration Board (ARB) and follow the 'Architects Code'. Most architects belong to the Royal Institute of British Architects (RIBA) and are bound by the RIBA Code of Professional Conduct. There is an internal conciliation and arbitration scheme to deal with complaints against members. Most working in Scotland belong to the Royal Incorporation of Architects in Scotland (RIAS), and follow 'The Charter' and 'Byelaws'. There is a conciliation and arbitration scheme to deal with complaints against members. Architects in Scotland can join the Royal Institute of British Architects instead of, or as well as, RIAS. The Royal Society of Ulster Architects (RSUA) is the professional body for chartered architects in Northern Ireland. RSUA can provide advice on matters relating to architecture.

These organisations will help you deal with complaints against an architect.

Surveyors

The Royal Institution of Chartered Surveyors (RICS) is one of the professional bodies for chartered surveyors and is international. Members of RICS must comply with rules of professional conduct. Breaches of these rules can be investigated by RICS. It operates an indemnity scheme to protect clients' money against fraud or dishonesty by RICS members. The indemnity scheme covers any money held by RICS members for clients.

Surveyors are insured against negligence and you should contact a solicitor regarding taking legal action.

See also surveyors in the chapter 18, *Property*.

Glaziers

If the glazier is a member of the Glass and Glazing Federation (GGF) or FENSA you can also use The Glazing Arbitration Scheme (TGAS). Where the glazier is a member of both, contact the GGF. However TGAS costs consumers £100 + VAT to take their complaint to arbitration. This is for a so-called "documents only" arbitration. If the appointed Arbitrator decides a site visit is necessary, then a reasonable additional fee will apply. You would be asked to pay 20% of this additional fee.

Ombudsman Services considers complaints regarding domestic installations undertaken by traders that belong to The Double Glazing & Conservatory Quality Assurance Ombudsman Scheme (DGCOS), who are contractors or installers of windows, doors, conservatories and associated products.

Home Insulation & Energy Systems

Ombudsman Services considers complaints regarding domestic installations undertaken by traders that belong to The Home Insulation & Energy Systems Quality Assured Contractors Scheme (HIES), who are contractors or installers of home insulation, energy saving and energy producing products.

The Dispute Resolution Ombudsman

Operated by the same people as The Furniture Ombudsman, this scheme helps to resolve disputes across a range of other sectors including retail and where tradesmen and tradeswomen are involved. This Ombudsman covers every trader within the Which? Trusted Traders scheme, such as electricians, plumbers and builders.

TEMPLATE: **Rejecting increase in price over quote**

Dear [*xxx*]

Re: [*quote number*]

On the [*date*] I discussed the work in my property I wished to be undertaken for a quote of [£*xxxx*] which was the basis for agreeing the work. However you have invoiced me for [£*xxxx*] a difference of [£*xxxx*].

You have explained that was due to [*detail*]. However this was not discussed at any point and has no bearing on the contract.

I have therefore enclosed a cheque for the agreed amount as full and final settlement.

Yours [*faithfully/sincerely*]

TEMPLATE: **Poor workmanship**
For purchases prior to 1st October 2015 quote "Supply of Goods and Services Act 1982"

Dear [*xxx*]

On the [*date*] you undertook [*detail work*] at my property. However, this work is defective. [*Bullet point defect(s).*]

Under the Consumer Rights Act 2015 I am entitled to work to be undertaken with reasonable skill and care and that uses materials of a reasonable quality. The above defect(s) show(s) that you are in breach of contract.

Whilst I reserve my rights under the aforementioned Act I am willing to provide you with an opportunity to remedy the defect(s) within a reasonable and agreed length of time at no further charge to me.

I look forward to hearing from you within seven days. Should I not be fully satisfied with your response I will not hesitate in taking the matter further. This will include, but not be limited to, obtaining an independent report on the work, using another contractor to complete the work and looking to you to bear this cost. If this is not forthcoming I will pursue the costs through the Small Claims Court.

Yours [*faithfully/sincerely*]

TEMPLATE: **Delays in work**

For purchases prior to 1st October 2015 quote "Supply of Goods and Services Act 1982"

Dear [*xxx*]

Re: [*quote number*]

On the [*date*] we agreed for you to undertake [*list job(s)*]. You assured me that the work would be completed by date. However [*detail*] is still to be undertaken.

It was part of the contract that you would finish the job by [*date*] and you assured me that this would be the case. However it is now [*date*], [*xx*] days later and the work is not completed.

I am therefore making time of the essence and expect the work to be completed by [*date*]. If this work is not completed within this time, I will consider the contract between us ended (as I am legally entitled to do under the Consumer Rights Act 2015 which entitles me to work to be completed within a reasonable time and/or by an agreed date). I shall then instruct another company to finish the work and will deduct the cost of this from your final invoice.

Yours [*faithfully/sincerely*]

Real example of not paying for repairs and being taken to the Small Claims Court

About twenty years ago, I let my flat out. (No, I am not a rich landlord I let it out while I rented with a friend – surprising given my anti-social tendencies!) An estate agent managed the property. There was a burglary and the front door was seriously damaged. The estate agent did not contact me and instructed their property maintenance man to repair the door. However, on inspection with a builder we saw that the work was far from satisfactory. The door did not close properly, and nearly all of the glass inserts had been put in back to front. Clearly the work had not been undertaken with reasonable skill and care.

I refused to pay the bill and he took me to court. I enjoy going to the Small Claims Court and this would be my second visit. It apparently was possible to put in a counter claim against the estate agents but I was only in my twenties then and it was complicated but I'd do it now! I refused to pay and we sat before the judge and discussed the matter. The independent report I had clearly showed that the work had not been carried out with reasonable skill and care under the Supply of Goods and Services Act 1982 and the judge quickly and easily saw in my favour.

So don't be afraid of being taken to court to pay up for faulty work it is not really any different to taking the trader to court for the refund.

18 PROPERTY

Estate agents

The Consumer Protection from Unfair Trading Regulations 2008 (CPRs) cover estate agents and other businesses involved in property sales and lettings.

The CPRs prohibit all traders from using unfair commercial practices in their dealings with individual consumers, (see chapter 5, *Consumer Rights*). Estate agents are prohibited from engaging in commercial practices that are unfair to sellers, buyers, potential sellers or potential buyers of residential property.

Those agents found to have breached either the CPRs or BPRs could be at risk of prosecution by their local authority trading standards services who are responsible for enforcement by bringing criminal prosecutions. On conviction, agents can face substantial fines or in more serious cases imprisonment. Those classic descriptions of "Stunning" and "Highly sought after" now have to have evidence to back them up!

As a seller you have rights under the Consumer Rights Act 2015 (Supply of Goods and Services Act 1982 prior to 1st October 2015), to services carried out with reasonable care and skill, but there are no legal regulations about what estate agents have to do to find you a buyer. So do your research to find the best estate agent for you depending on the services that they provide and their costs.

The Consumers, Estate Agents and Redress Act, 2007 requires all estate agents in the UK to register with an Estate Agents Redress Scheme which can investigate complaints from members of the public. From the 1st October 2014 all letting agents in England have also been obliged to join a scheme under the Enterprise and Regulatory Reform Act 2013.

If you believe that an estate agent has not been acting in your best interests, has not been contacting buyers, provides inaccurate information or is discriminating against you etc., complain first to the manager or owner of the agency. If a chain you can then write to the head office. You can of course take your business elsewhere or withhold some of the agent's fee. If you do the latter take legal advice first – you may be sued by the estate agent so you need to be very clear on your position.

If you cannot agree the fee with an estate agent for any reason, such as finding your own buyer, seek legal advice.

The Property Ombudsman Code of Practice for Residential Estate Agents is voluntarily followed by many estate agents. Estate agents who follow the Code of Practice are required to provide additional consumer protection that goes beyond that required by law. They can be recognised by the blue TPO logo which they will display on their literature, websites and office windows.

TEMPLATE: **Rejecting estate agent's claim to commission not agreed**

Dear [*xxx*]

Re: [*Property address*]

On the [*date*] I instructed you to put my property on the market. It was an express term of our contract that you would only be paid commission if you introduced a buyer who proceeded with purchasing the property.

On the [*date*] I received an invoice from you for [*detail reason e.g. introducing new fees, charging for introducing a buyer who didn't purchase the property*].

The Estate Agents Act 1979 requires details of fees and charges including any addition to agency fees to have been supplied in writing which you failed to do. Therefore you are in breach of contract and I will not be paying this charge.

I will be contacting Trading Standards and trust that I will hear from you within seven days to confirm that I do not need to pay this charge.

Yours [*faithfully/sincerely*]

Surveyors

When carrying out the inspection of a property a surveyor must deliver services with reasonable skill and care. If the surveyor does not and you suffer loss and damage as a direct result you have a claim for compensation. Surveyors' reports may include phrases relating to not being able to access certain areas but they must make reasonable attempts to access all areas or risk breaching the Unfair Contract Terms Act 1977 and the Unfair Terms in Consumer Contracts Regulations 1999 prior to 1st October 2015 and the Consumer Rights Act 2015 thereafter. If you believe that your surveyor has been negligent then you may need to take legal action which can be very costly so you should take legal advice.

For more information regarding professional bodies and ombudsmen see chapter 17, *Home Improvements*.

TEMPLATE: **Unsatisfactory surveyor's report**
For services prior to 1st October 2015 quote "Supply of Goods and Services Act 1982"

Dear [*xxx*]

Re: [*Address of property*]

On the [*date*] I instructed your company to provide a survey on the above address. As a result of this survey I proceeded with the purchase of the property. However after taking possession of the property I discovered [*bullet point problem(s)*]. [*This/these*] issues require remedial work and should have been identified and noted in the report.

Under the Consumer Rights Act 2015 I am entitled to services carried out with reasonable skill and care and to a reasonable level of competence. You are therefore in breach of contract and I am legally entitled to compensation from you in relation to the costs incurred to undertake the remedial work.

I [*attach/enclose*] 3 quotes for the work. You may inspect the issue(s) for yourself.

I look forward to hearing from you within seven days. I expect you to arrange a day when you can inspect the issue(s) and confirmation that you will be paying the compensation due. Should I not be fully satisfied with your response I will not hesitate in taking the matter further which will include, but not be limited to, either contacting the Ombudsman or progress the matter through the Small Claims Court.

Yours [*faithfully/sincerely*]

New houses

The Consumer Code for Homebuilders is an industry-led code of conduct for builders, which was developed to make the home buying process fairer and more transparent for purchasers and is adopted by the main warranty providers. The Code consists of 19 requirements and principles that home builders must meet in their marketing and selling of homes and their after-sales customer service. As part of this code warranty providers must provide a complaint procedure. There is a dispute resolution scheme to deal with complaints within two years of buying a home, if builders don't comply with the code. The scheme can award up to £15,000.

Renting

The list of problems that tenants can have with landlords and landlords with tenants is long. It really would be another book. Generally they all break down into the fact that if you have a complaint then you should make attempts to try and sort it out amicably between you. Ensure that the contract is fair and read all the conditions before making a complaint.

The local authority can help you as a tenant even if you are in a private let, if, for example, the property is in such disrepair that it is breaching environmental health laws. The Citizen's Advice website and Shelter provide lots of information for tenants

Should you not be happy with the response you can take the matter to the Housing Ombudsman so long as the landlord is a member. From April 2013 the Housing Ombudsman now considers complaints about a local authority's relationship as landlord to its tenants or leaseholders, rather than the Local Government Ombudsman, although the Local Government Ombudsman can look at complaints against councils about homelessness, some housing allocations, housing improvement grants and housing benefit. As a tenant you can fill out a form detailing the issue(s) and giving the ombudsman permission to contact the landlord.

From the 27th May 2015 under the Consumer Rights Act 2015, lettings agents are required to include a description of each fee which explains the service that is covered by the cost or the purpose for which it is imposed. So you will be able to see clearly where an estate agent is charging both tenant and landlord. From 01 June 2019 The Tenancy Act came into force in England. This bans estate agents from charging tenants for looking round a property, setting up a tenancy, such as references and checks or for checking out of a property.

The Citizens Advice website and Shelter provide lots of information for tenants.

19 **OTHER SERVICES**

Hairdressers and beauty therapists

Consumers are covered by the Consumer Rights Act 2015 (Supply of Goods and Services Act 1982 for services carried out prior to 1st October 2015). Services should be undertaken with reasonable skill and care. So good hairdressers will undertake a patch test for colour dye for example. There is however no trade body or ombudsman if you have a complaint. The Hairdressers Registration Act was passed by parliament in 1964, with the aim of endorsing hairdressers and reassuring consumers. The Hairdressing Council was created to establish and maintain a register of qualified hairdressers. However, registration is voluntary so very few 'State Registered Hairdressers' exist as being officially recognised as qualified to practise hairdressing on the public.

If you have a complaint, complain at the time and if necessary follow up in writing. A complaint may develop later, such as a reaction to a perm. You can either write to the Hairdressing Council (if the salon is a member) which will take up your complaint for you and possibly deregister the salon. Or, (and if the salon is not a member of the Council) you will need to write in the normal way and threaten legal action.

Beauticians are not regulated by any independent body. The Consumer Rights Act 2015/ Supply of Goods and Services Act 1982 principle of 'providing services with reasonable skill and care using products of a satisfactory quality' applies however.

TEMPLATE: **Hairdresser**

For purchases prior to 1st October 2015 quote "Supply of Goods and Services Act 1982"

Dear [*xxx*]

Re: [*treatment*]

On the [*date*] I attended your salon for a [*treatment*]. On the [*date*] I noticed that [*description of damage e.g. burning of your scalp*]. I *attach/enclose* photos of the damage.

Under the Consumer Rights Act 2015 I am entitled to services to be carried out with reasonable skill and care using products of a satisfactory quality. You are clearly in breach of this Law.

As a result of the damage caused I have suffered [*time off work, medical expenses etc.*] and expect to receive redress for this.

I believe [*£xxx*] to be a fair amount to reflect your not meeting your legal obligations.

I look forward to hearing from you within seven days. Should I not be fully satisfied with your response I will not hesitate in taking the matter further which will include, but not be limited to, seeking redress through the Small Claims Court.

Yours [*sincerely/faithfully*]

Real example of a complaint about therapists

A friend and I enjoy spa days in Colchester where we often go. Once we went and I was given a male therapist for a body massage. I didn't want this and nor did my friend so we complained and the therapist was changed. However, when I came out of my treatment my friend had been given the male therapist and she had missed 15 minutes of her treatment because she and the therapist had gone back to reception to find that someone else had taken her appointment. (The stupidity of not using surnames when calling out people's names!) At the end of the treatment which she had, she was given a voucher equivalent to the amount had the massage been paid for separately.

We said that we would be unlikely to use the voucher as we only came for whole days. My friend was told that she could have the equivalent cost in products.

Another time we went, I complained only at a later date about the facials. Two face masks had been applied instead of one and a very short scalp massage whilst one mask was on. I also complained about the body massage being short. I received a quarter of the cost of the facials had the facials been separate and nothing for the body massage. I think this was very poor customer service as my complaints were certainly genuine. We had been to the spa many times and knew how to compare the treatments. However, their main objection was that we had not complained at the time. Having had experience of much better complaint handling previously, these examples do show the importance of complaining at the time.

Service bookings

If for example you have booked a venue or transport for an event such as a wedding or celebratory party and they cancel you are entitled to a full refund and redress. Same with a photographer or caterer.

Supply/delivery and fitting of items

For goods and services prior to 1st October 2015 the consumer is protected by the Sale and Supply of Goods Act 1994 when having items delivered and the Supply of Goods and Services Act 1982 for any services attached such as the fitting of a new washing machine. You can expect the items to be of a satisfactory quality and be fitted in an agreed and/or reasonable time. If a supplier does not meet its obligations and misses appointments you are entitled to redress for this.

From 1st October 2015 you are covered by the Consumer Rights Act 2015 which also covers your entitlement to items be installed correctly, where installation has been agreed as part of the contract.

TEMPLATE: **Booking cancellation**

For purchases prior to 1st October 2015 quote "Supply of Goods and Services Act 1982"

Dear [*xxx*]

Re: [*booking*]

On the [*date*] I booked you to provide [*detail service e.g. photographer/catering etc.*] on the [*date(s)*]. You have since cancelled this booking at very short notice. I have now had to book an alternative. The difference of cost is [£*xxxx*].

You are in breach of the Supply of Goods and Services Act 1982 and I am legally entitled to a full refund and difference in having to organise an alternative supplier.

I look forward to hearing from you within seven days. Should I not be fully satisfied with your response I will not hesitate in taking the matter further. This will include, but not be limited to, pursuing the matter through the Small Claims Court.

Yours [*faithfully/sincerely*]

Real example of non-fitting of bedroom furniture

A friend of mine was having problems getting the bedroom furniture she had paid for from Sharps delivered and fitted and so I wrote the following:

Dear Mr Smith

RE: Drawing No: 101513

I am writing to you to express my disgust at the atrocious service we have received from Sharps.

We recently purchased a made to measure set of bedroom wardrobes and units from your company which were delivered to our address on 05/11/2013. Until this point we had received excellent service from your company. The designer and the surveyor were both very professional and left us feeling confident that the work would be completed to a high standard and in a reasonable time frame. In order for the work to be completed as scheduled we employed our own builders at our personal expense to carry out the necessary preparation e.g. moving electrical sockets and redecorating to accommodate the wardrobes and units. Our bedroom was cleared of all furniture as instructed by the surveyor, including our bed, on the 05/11/13. However since the units were delivered on the 5/11/13 there has been no progress.

After initially being told the installation would take place a few days after the delivery date we were then informed that installation would take place on the 12/11/2013. This was not ideal for us but we were satisfied that at least we had a confirmed date and arranged to take annual leave from work as we were informed installation would take 3 days. However things went from bad to worse.

12/11/13 – No one attended our property to install the wardrobes. A breach of the Supply of Goods and Services Act 1982. We did not receive any notification that installation was not going ahead. We telephoned customer services and spoke with Ms C. who informed us that a colleague had called and left us a message on Saturday (9/11/13) informing us that installation would be delayed until the 13th November. We did not receive any such 'phone call or message and I am appalled that I was told this. We were informed a fitter would be with us on the 13th between 8 – 9am. As I had taken annual leave from work I had to re-negotiate a change in it at short notice, again.

12/11/13 At 7:30 pm – I received a call from customer services informing us that a fitter was not available to attend on the 13th but we would be contacted the following morning when they could find a fitter for the 14/11/13. – At such short notice it was obviously hard for me to re-negotiate my annual leave again.

13/11/13 (am) – I received a call from Ms C. informing us that she was trying to find a fitter for the next day and she would call us back. Later that day it was left to me to follow up this 'phone call. We called the customer service department to find out if a fitter had been arranged and were told "No, as it was a very busy time of the year" (wholly irrelevant and this should be planned for especially as we had already been dreadfully treated) and they would contact us the following day for a fitter to attend Friday (15/11/13) and Saturday (16/11/13).

14/11/13 (pm) - I received a call from Ms C. informing us that she had not been able to arrange for a fitter for the Friday & Saturday but guaranteed a fitter would be with us on the 20/11/2013 between 8 -9am. Again I had to arrange more annual leave for the following week.

19/11/2013 (pm) - I rang customer services to confirm someone would be attending on the 20/11/2013 and was told it was on the system and a fitter would definitely be there between 8am-9am.

20/11/13 @10am – No-one arrived. We rang and spoke to Ms C again only to be told that no-one would be available today and we should never have been told someone would be (even though she had guaranteed it the previous week). The earliest date would be Friday 22/11/13; however she would try and find someone for 21/11/2013.

20/11/13 (pm) – I called again to ascertain if a fitter had indeed been found for 21/11/13 and was told by Ms C that it would be Friday 22/11/13.

21/11/13 (pm) - I called customer services again to ascertain if a fitter would be attending on Friday 22/11/13 and was told a fitter by the name of John would be with us between 8-9am on Friday 22/11/13.

21/11/13 (9.00am) – A 'phone call received from Ms C. asking whether the fitter had arrived. No-one had arrived up to this point. She promised to contact the fitter and then call us back with an update. I had to call back at 09:50am to find out what was going on, unfortunately Ms C. was unavailable. She returned our call at 10:06 when we were informed that the filter was unobtainable and his manager was unaware where he was.

To date we are no closer to an installation date and are left not knowing when our units will be installed. We are appalled at the service we have received. You are in breach of the Supply of Goods and Services Act 1982; you have not provided services of a reasonable standard to which we are entitled. I found Ms C's attitude dismissive and not at all sympathetic to the stress of the constant inexcusable delays, the repeated broken promises, the poor communication, the inconvenience of having to change and re book leave from my work place at very short notice to accommodate a date for a fitter and of course not having a bed to sleep in for two weeks.

I trust that you will be as appalled as we are with the outrageous service we have received. Sharps is clearly in breach of the aforementioned Act. I am legally entitled to services of a satisfactory standard which should be completed within a reasonable length of time with no inconvenience to us and obviously we have not received this.

I expect to receive redress for the stress and inconvenience caused in addition to the out of pocket costs I have incurred. I have now used up all my leave as I was not able to change all the days I had previously booked. I expect redress for the loss of my annual leave. I earn £xxx a day and lost 5 days due to the errors made by Sharps. I expect this to be reimbursed in addition to an appropriate amount for the inconvenience and stress of the continued delays and being without the furniture. I expect the furniture to be fitted by Saturday of this week and this is non-negotiable.

If I am not fully satisfied with your response I will not hesitate in taking the matter further which will include, but not be limited to, Trading Standards, social media and The Small Claims Court. I will be seeking a full refund, costs as above plus court costs and further costs incurred.

Yours sincerely

She got £250 in redress and the bedroom was fitted by the Saturday.

Removal services

When you have instructed a removal firm to move your possessions from one place to another you are covered by the Consumer Rights Act 2015 (Supply of Goods and Services Act 1982 for services prior to the 1st October 2015). You can expect to receive services undertaken with reasonable skill and care. That means no damage and arrival at an agreed time. Should this not be the case then you have grounds to complain.

The British Association of Removers is the relevant trade organisation. It has a Trading Standards Institute Code of Practice and an independent Alternative Dispute Resolution (ADR) scheme. So, should you encounter problems and your removal firm is a member then you are able to use an arbitration scheme. You may like to check their website before deciding on a removal firm to give you peace of mind.

The National Guild of Removers and Storers ensures its members are regulated and quality checked through the Removal Industrial Services Ombudsman Scheme. You submit a form and any relevant evidence and the company is given 10 days to respond. The ombudsman then makes a decision which is final and binding but the option of the Small Claims Court is still open to you.

TEMPLATE: **Items damaged in transit**
For purchases prior to 1st October 2015 quote "Supply of Goods and Services Act 1982"

Dear [*xxx*]

Re: [*Removal number*]

On the [*date*] your firm moved my possessions from [*address*] to [*address*]. The following item(s) [*was/were*] damaged. The damaged caused was as follows [*describe item or bullet point list of damaged items and the damage caused*]. I pointed this out to your staff on that date. [*Or you state that I found this damage after unpacking the item which appeared to have been dropped (or similar).*] I [*enclose/attach*] pictures of the damage caused.

Under the Supply of Goods and Services Act 1982 I am entitled to services to be undertaken with reasonable skill and care. You are clearly in breach of contract for not meeting your legal requirements.

I am willing to offer you an opportunity to undertake remedial work to put the damage right whilst retaining my rights under the aforementioned Act. [*Or leave out that last sentence and say*] Due to this breach I am entitled to compensation for the damaged goods and I calculate this to be a total of [*£xxx*] [*bullet point list of items and costs.*]

I look forward to hearing from you within seven days. Should I not be fully satisfied with your response I will use the arbitration service at the British Association of Removers in the first instance. [*If not members say:*] I will start Small Claims Court proceedings*).*

Yours [*sincerely/faithfully*]

TEMPLATE: **Not keeping appointment**

For purchases prior to 1st October 2015 quote "Supply of Goods and Services Act 1982"

Dear [*xxx*]

On the [*date*] we arranged for your firm to move my possessions from [*address*] to *address*]. No-one turned up and no 'phone calls were received.

Your failure to arrive is a breach of contract and under the Consumer Rights Act 2015 I am entitled to compensation from you for my out of pocket expenses. [*Bullet point them.*]

I believe [*£xxxx*] a fair sum to reflect the inconvenience, stress and out of pocket expense I incurred and look forward to receiving this within seven days. Should I not be fully satisfied with your response I will use the arbitration service at the British Association of Removers in the first instance. [*If not members say:*] I will start Small Claims Court proceedings.

Yours [*sincerely/faithfully*]

Dry cleaners and launderettes

The Consumer Rights Act 2015 (Supply of Goods and Services Act 1982 prior to 1st October 2015) covers again. If services are not undertaken with reasonable skill and care and your items get damaged or lost then you have the right to claim compensation. This can be the cost of replacing the damaged or lost item although there may be a reduction for wear and tear of the original item.

You should inspect the item(s) at the premises and bring damages to the attention of staff. However, you can still complain once you get home to follow up if you are unsuccessful complaining at the time or if you discover the damage once at home.

Membership of the Textile Services Association is available to Laundries, Dry Cleaners, Textile Renters and their suppliers. If the company you are using are members then it offers a conciliation service. You may be asked to prove your claim and, on a loser pays basis, use the association's testing service. It also offers an arbitration service if the matter still cannot be resolved.

If the firm is not a member of the TSA, then you have the option of taking the matter through the Small Claims Court.

If the dry cleaner tries to blame the manufacturer saying that the item was incorrectly labelled you should put your complaint in writing. Follow the tips in the link above as you will need this claim in writing to take the matter further. Your contract when you bought the item was with the retailer not the manufacturer so you should write to the retailer outlining the issue and enclosing a photograph of the damage.

The retailer will probably want to undertake tests with the supplier or manufacturer. If the retailer finds that the label was incorrect you should claim from the retailer for a full refund of the item.

If the retailer denies responsibility you will need to take this evidence to the dry cleaner and state that it is responsible for not carrying out the service with reasonable skill and care. You have a choice if the dry cleaner is a member of the TSA of going through arbitration and/or threatening the Small Claims Court.

TEMPLATE: **Dry cleaning a suit**
For purchases prior to 1st October 2015 quote "Supply of Goods and Services Act 1982"

Dear [*xxx*]

Re: Dry cleaning suit

On the [*date*] I brought my suit to you for dry cleaning. On the [*date*] I collected it. I have discovered [*describe damage(s)*]. [*If applicable add that you are following up the complaint you made at the time of collection.*] Under the Consumer Rights Act 2015 I am entitled to services to be carried out with reasonable skill and care. The suit is suitable for dry cleaning and therefore you are in breach of contract.

To replace the suit will cost [£*xxxx*]. I expect you to reimburse me this cost.

I look forward to hearing from you within 7 days. Should I not be fully satisfied with your response I will not hesitate in taking the matter further. This will include, but not be limited to, reporting you to Trading Standards and issuing a summons against you in the county court with no further reference to you.

Yours [*faithfully/sincerely*]

Real example of a dry cleaning complaint

Earlier this year, I took a suit to a local dry cleaners and picked it up two days later. Luckily I noticed there and then that the mark on the jacket was still there. I complained and said it looked as though the jacket hadn't been done or, at the very least, the mark hadn't come out and I had expected it to do so. The owner was very apologetic and asked me to come back the next day. Apparently the jacket had not been done! I didn't even need to complain and assert my legal rights and I got the jacket cleaned for free. So either my reputation goes before me or my face must have said it all. Perhaps it was a good dry cleaners? Or at least had a good manager who had words with his son who only cleaned the trousers!

Another time I took in curtains to a different dry cleaner. Condensation had ruined the bottom of them. This did not come out. I complained and received a full refund. They did tell me afterwards that those sort of stains do not come out. (So please let me know if you know different and you can get a mould stain out!) Also, lesson here, check with the dry cleaner if they think the stain will come out before they waste their and your time.

Florists

As with any service you are covered by the Consumer Rights Act 2015 (Supply of Goods and Services Act 1982 prior to 1st October 2015). So you should expect flowers to last a reasonable length of time whatever the weather and whatever the occasion.

There isn't a regulatory body or code of practice for florists. However, most independent florists rely on word of mouth recommendation and would want to rectify any complaints. Larger companies run the risk of poor reviews. Should you not gain any redress from a florist then your only option would be the Small Claims Court. Whilst the amount you paid for the flowers may be not much more than the court fee, it is of course the principle of the thing and if you can easily evidence a breach in contract (such as not delivering) or the flowers turning up dead then there is no reason why you should not be successful. Remember to take photographic evidence if they did arrive.

TEMPLATE: **Quality of flowers delivered**

For purchases prior to 1st October 2015 quote "Supply of Goods and Services Act 1982"

Dear [*xxx*]

Re flower delivery

On the date I paid [£*xxxx*] for a bouquet of flowers to be delivered to [*address*]. This cost [£*xxxx*]. However, the flowers were not of satisfactory quality and I [*enclose/ attach*] a photograph of the flowers. As you can see, they [*were not as described on the website/are not in good condition with wilting leaves (delete/change as appropriate)*].

Under the Consumer Rights Act 2015 I am entitled to goods of a satisfactory standard and services to be undertaken with reasonable skill and care. You are in breach of contract.

I was very disappointed with the flowers and trust that you will refund the cost and provide redress accordingly.

I look forward to hearing from you within 7 days. Should I not be fully satisfied with your response I will not hesitate in taking the matter further. This will include, but not be limited to, sharing my experiences on review and social media websites, informing Trading Standards and starting Small Claims Court proceedings.

Yours [*faithfully/sincerely*]

Real example of florist complaint

I ordered a bouquet of flowers from Flowers Direct for a friend. Luckily I asked if she liked the flowers and she said she hadn't received them. I emailed Flowers Direct on the 30th April to say that they hadn't been delivered. I got a stunning email in return; a confirmation on the 1st May that the delivery on the 30th April would be made. I emailed again and got a response to say that they were looking into it. Days later I emailed again but heard nothing. So on the 11th May I emailed the CEO quoting the Supply of Goods and Service Act 1982. I drafted a letter to the credit card company as Flowers Direct had not delivered anything for the money. I sent them a copy of it and then received a reply.

The amount was under £100 so it was not protected by Section 75 of the Consumer Credit Card Act. However it is fraud if a company takes money and doesn't provide anything for it!

Flowers Direct was involved in one business buying out another and so emails were getting lost I was told. So often it's poor internal communication that results in the non-delivery of goods/service. The Customer Services Representative gave a full refund and asked if I would like a bouquet sent to the recipient or myself. I told her both (and got them!)

20 PARKING TICKETS

One of the most annoying things known to drivers everywhere. You approach your car or motorbike and you see that ticket. If you are human your heart sinks and you probably swear, at least under your breath. Then, it is quite possible that you get angry. Either because it's your own fault and you are berating yourself or you don't think the ticket is fair. In this second instance, appeal.

Council Parking Tickets

You can only appeal if you think that the fine has been placed unfairly, not if you have just been unlucky and caught out. So, for example, reasons for appeal may be that the sign giving times was obscured, bay markings not clear, or you may dispute where the car was parked. As soon as you see that you have the ticket, take photographic evidence. Pictures of your car, the signage, the markings, the meter time or anything else that you dispute all help your appeal. As do witness statements and other evidence, such as crime numbers proving that your car was stolen, DVLA documents showing change of ownership etc.

Unfortunately one can now get tickets through the post, so getting photographic evidence might be more difficult. However, under new rules from 6th April 2015, English councils may only use cameras to enforce parking outside school entrances, and on bus stop clearways. This follows concerns that the use of the 'spy' camera-cars were being abused, for what critics said, bordered on 'entrapment' on high streets.

For tickets from 6th April 2015 local authorities in England must give 10 minutes grace for motorists overstaying in parking bays in council run car-parks and on the street. The rules do not apply to parking on single or double yellow lines, in front of dropped kerbs or in permit bays. Nor does the 10 minute 'grace' period apply if a driver has yet to buy a ticket and fix a ticket on the windscreen but has instead left the car and gone off to a shop to find change.

You have 28 days in which to pay but this is halved if paid within 14 days (21 for tickets issued using CCTV). So if you are going to pay, pay within this time. However, if you appeal within this time and your appeal is not upheld you should be able to pay the lower rate. Make sure that you ask for the fine to be put on hold when you appeal.

Refer to all the tips earlier in the book. Don't be rude and do be factual and assertive. Those are the key factors here. Remember that this isn't strictly a complaint, you can't threaten any further action such as Trading Standards or an ombudsman!

Check the council's website for more information and you may be able to appeal online. If not, do it by letter.

Reasons for appealing a council parking ticket

The contravention did not occur – where signage was blocked, faded or tampered with. You were on your way to get a ticket (although this is normally only a few minutes leeway) or it was an eager beaver warden giving you a ticket before the time ran out.

The penalty exceeded the amount applicable in the circumstances of the case – this is unlikely through a council issued ticket as prices are standard and you can check these against the council website.

The traffic order is invalid – you believe the parking restriction in question is invalid or illegal. For example, if the council has not followed the correct procedure for passing the traffic order.

The civil enforcement officer (CEO) was not prevented from issuing the Penalty Charge Notice (PCN) – you disagree that the CEO was prevented from issuing the PCN.

You were not the owner/keeper of the vehicle at the time of the contravention – you did not own the vehicle when the PCN was issued.

The vehicle was taken without your consent – the vehicle had been stolen when the PCN was issued.

You are a hire firm and have supplied the name of the hirer – you are a hire company and the hirer has signed a formal agreement accepting liability for the PCN. You must enclose the name and address of the hirer and a copy of the statement they signed

The notice to owner (NtO) was served out of time – you feel that there has been an unreasonable delay (or at least 6 months) in issuing the NtO.

There has been a procedural impropriety by the council – the council must provide the following detail in the NtO; the date it is served; name of the enforcement authority; registration of the vehicle; date and the time the alleged contravention occurred; why the ticket has been issued; amount of the penalty charge; that the penalty charge must be paid within 28 days; that if the penalty charge is paid within 14 days the fine will be reduced and how to pay the charge; if the charge is not paid within 28 days, a 'Notice to Owner' form will be sent to the vehicle owner; that you can appeal within the first 28 days and how you need to make the appeal, including the address (and email and fax if appropriate) that appeals should be sent to; the grounds under which you can make an appeal, and that if your formal appeal is made on time but is rejected that you can appeal to an adjudicator. For posted tickets the rules are broadly similar but must include why the PCN has been posted and the date of the notice which must be the date it is posted.

TEMPLATE: **Appealing wrongly issued ticket**

Dear Sir/Madam

Re: [**Parking ticket number/vehicle registration number**]

On the [*date*] I received a parking ticket for the reason of [*insert offence code and reason on PCN*] which I believe was wrongly issued. I would therefore like to submit an appeal and request that the fine is put on hold while I do so. I believe that the ticket was wrongly issued because [*give details*].

I enclose evidence to support this appeal. [*Bullet point evidence (delete sentence if none available).*]

Yours faithfully

Real example of complaint about process

I got a parking ticket. I don't like getting them. I caught the parking warden writing the ticket and told him that I had had to queue for a ticket in the shop and look it was in my hand. The warden took a photo and told me that he would make a note of it and I should appeal. So I did.

I appealed using "The contravention did not occur" reason and got no response. I emailed the borough department and asked why I hadn't heard anything and that it was past the time they should have responded by. Three days later I received a letter telling me that because I hadn't paid the fine it was going up to £60. So, I wrote again telling them to have the courtesy of responding and to look through the correspondence!

I received an auto response. So I emailed again and emailed the CEO. Always a good one – speeds things up somewhat! Threatened to tell portfolio holders in the council. Immediate write off of payment.

Even if it is possible that it has been issued correctly, it is quite possible that the powers that be won't process your appeal properly, which is what happened here. The appeal may or may not have been upheld, but they were out of time for responding to my appeal and therefore in breach of process so they had no option but to throw out the charge.

Reasons for appealing a parking ticket using mitigating circumstances

You can also appeal using mitigating circumstances. You are admitting to parking illegally but providing reasons for doing so. For example, you were on holiday when a bay you were permitted to park in was suspended. So send evidence of flights, or death certificates if a bereavement, or doctor's letter if you were sick. Some councils may allow your appeal if you are in financial hardship but you will need to provide evidence for this and you will be relying on someone's good nature

TEMPLATE: **Appealing parking ticket citing mitigating circumstances**

Dear Sir/Madam

Re: [*Parking ticket number/vehicle registration number*]

On the [*date*] I received a parking ticket for the [*reason of insert offence code and reason on PCN*]. However I believe that there are mitigating circumstances for parking at that spot. I would therefore like to submit an appeal and request that the fine is put on hold while I do so.

[*Describe mitigating circumstance.*] I provide [*detail evidence*] to support this. [*Delete sentence if none available.*]

Yours faithfully

When your appeal is not upheld

If your letter at the informal stage has failed you do have the option of carrying onto the formal second stage. Whilst 50% of appeals are upheld at this stage, strongly consider if you want to proceed as you risk higher costs.

So, if the appeal was not upheld or you didn't appeal within the 28 days you will be sent a request for payment and an appeal form. You have another 28 days to pay or appeal bearing in mind that the fine could go up another 50%. When you receive the Notice to Owner letter, it must be accurate and include: the date of the notice, which must be the date on which the notice is posted; the name of the enforcement authority; the amount of the penalty charge; the date on which the Penalty Charge Notice was served; why the ticket has been issued; that the charge must be paid within 28 days; that if the charge is not paid in that time it can be increased and the amount of the increased charge. The NtO must be sent within six months of the ticket to be valid.

Councils must respond within 56 days of receiving your formal appeal otherwise the penalty is unenforceable.

If your appeal is not upheld then you can go to tribunal. It is independent and you don't even have to attend. You can request a telephone or personal hearing but usually a letter with all the evidence is fine. It isn't like the Small Claims Court, it is free to attend. The adjudicator will not have seen anything of the case so ensure that you fully fill out the form that you will be sent and re send all the evidence.

Clamped or towed

Even worse than the ticket. Returning to your vehicle only to find it has been clamped or even that it isn't there and you don't know if it has been stolen. It is pure bad luck if your vehicle is towed or clamped. The offence doesn't have to be any worse than if you are given a ticket, it just depends on the patrolling wardens at the time. If you have been clamped, pay as quickly as possible as your vehicle could be towed and you will incur more charges.

Don't try and remove the clamp because as well as probably damaging your vehicle you may also be charged for criminal damage.

Pay the fines and then appeal. Paying the fine is not an admission that you accept it. But if you don't pay costs just escalate.

Private Land

In 2012, clamping on private land was banned under the Protection of Freedom Act. (Northern Ireland is not covered and it has been banned in Scotland also since 2012). Landowners can claim charges from the keeper of the vehicle, as well as the driver.

There is an independent appeals service funded by the British Parking Association (BPA). This allows motorists to appeal against a parking charge issued on private land by a company that is a member of the BPA's approved operator scheme. Appeal through POPLA (contact details in chapter 27, *Useful Contacts*).

21 NEIGHBOURS

If you are having problems with your neighbours you should try your best to sort it out amicably and in person. Once you start a more formal route things can get messy and what could have been sorted with a chat over a coffee or glass of wine gets expensive and/or the problem gets worse. For example, if you are complaining about noise, your neighbours may increase this just to annoy you.

Noisy neighbours

This is probably the most common complaint people have about their neighbours. A few years ago, when our neighbours were teenagers and their parents were out, they had their music really loud if they had a few friends with them. I went round and complained and they turned it down. The father the following day came round to apologise, I think the kids got into trouble but I still thought it was better to warn him that I had complained. I wasn't even The Complaining Cow at this point! We never had trouble with noise again. Obviously I appreciate that other neighbour disputes are not as easily dealt with and I would have preferred to write but sometimes it does just take a little bit of effort.

If, after asking your neighbours to reduce the noise, it continues and they are tenants contact the landlord if you know their details. Otherwise contact the Environmental Health Department which is able to measure the noise levels. Keep a diary of the noise and use it as evidence to show Environmental Health the extent of the problem. You will need to convince them that the noise is disturbing your sleep and/or preventing you from enjoying your property. Witness statements from neighbours and/or letters from your doctor saying how it is affecting your health all help. Environmental Health Officers are able to give an expert opinion on how it rates a noise nuisance. Local authorities have powers to seize noise-making equipment.

If the Environmental Health Officer (EHO) considers there is a noise nuisance and has been unable to resolve the matter by discussion, the authority can then serve a notice on the person causing the noise, or on the owner or occupier of the property. If the person causing the noise does not comply with the notice, the local authority can prosecute them. The local authority can also apply for an injunction.

Alternatively you can go to court yourself and get an injunction but get legal advice as this can become costly.

TEMPLATE: **Noisy neighbour**

Dear [*xxx*]

On the [*date*] I was seriously disturbed by the noise coming from your property. I asked you to turn it down which you refused do. I have been disturbed by this noise on [*xx*] occasions [*provide log*] and you refuse to desist.

I am unable to tolerate these disturbances any longer. It is affecting my health for which I can provide evidence. I am writing to inform you that should I be disturbed again by this noise I will be contacting the Environmental Health Department and asking them to investigate. An officer will measure the levels to determine whether they are producing a noise nuisance. The local authority has the power under the Noise Act 1996 which was amended by the Clean Neighbourhoods and Environment Act 2005 to serve you a notice. If you do not comply with this the authority can prosecute you. The authority also has the power to seize equipment and apply for an injunction against you.

Should the authority not take action I will apply for an injunction restraining you from making this noise in the future and also sue you for compensation.

I do hope that this action won't be necessary and that we are able to come to an agreement regarding this issue. I would consider mediation if this were agreeable to you also.

Yours [*faithfully/sincerely*]

Neighbourhood noise

A friend of mine has young children and the ice-cream van that comes round her estate had the chimes on going past her house where her children were sleeping, so I looked up what we could do.

Loudspeakers (emergency service vehicles are exempt) must not be used in streets between 9.00pm and 8.00am. It is illegal to use loudspeakers in the street at any hour for advertising, entertainment, trade or business. Vehicles which sell food (such as ice cream) are exempt, but loudspeakers or chimes on these vehicles may only be used between the hours of noon and 7.00pm in such a way as not to annoy people nearby. Under Section 62 within the Control of Pollution Act, 1974 action may be taken if ice-cream van chimes are sounding after 7pm, or before midday, or if they are sounded at any time which causes an annoyance. There is a Code of Practice on Noise from Ice Cream Van Chimes (2013) which states that it's an offence to sound chimes 'so as to cause annoyance'.

The Noise Act 1996 was amended by the Clean Neighbourhoods and Environment Act 2005. Whereas, prior to the amendments made by the Clean Neighbourhoods and Environment Act 2005, the Noise Act only applied to night noise from dwellings, a complaint may now be made by someone within a dwelling concerning noise emitted from 'any premises in respect of which a premises licence or a temporary event notice has effect'. Local authorities have additional powers to deal with loud noise coming from domestic premises between the hours of 11.00pm and 7.00am.

The Antisocial Behaviour etc (Scotland) Act 2004 is applicable in Scotland.

Overhanging branches

You are legally entitled to cut off any branches overhanging your property at the point where they cross the boundary. Technically they belong to your neighbour and you should offer them back. Or if you are feeling lazy and don't like them very much just throw them over the fence! Check that there isn't any tree preservation order associated with anything before you start cutting as in that case you need permission from the appropriate authority before doing it. Our neighbours hang a washing line from a branch of a tree that we have in the garden. We are often tempted to cut the branch…

If anything overhanging causes damage or injury to you, your neighbour could be sued for compensation if you make a claim for damages.

Dangerous trees

Local authorities in England and Wales can intervene where a tree on private land is at risk of causing damage. It can make it safe on behalf of the owner of the land where the tree sits and reclaim the costs from the owner. It can also do this at your request where you don't know who owns the land. You can also ask the local authority to inspect the condition of the tree. Departments responsible for this vary. They will only take action if they believe that the tree is on the point of causing damage.

In Northern Ireland, local councils only have powers to make a dangerous tree on private property safe if it is overhanging a public footpath or road. If a dangerous tree is overhanging from a neighbour's property, you will have to try to resolve the matter with the owner of the tree or consider legal action.

Roots

If the roots of your neighbour's tree have spread into your property they can be removed using the least damaging method available, unless there is a tree preservation order on it – see below. If you have to enter the tree owner's property to do this, you must give reasonable notice.

Your neighbour could also consult their insurers if there is a possibility that your property may be damaged by the roots. If the roots have already caused damage, the tree owner is liable to pay compensation but it must be shown that the tree owner knew, or ought to have known, of the danger. Our neighbour's tree was shown to have caused damage to their neighbour's property and their insurance paid up. It's easier to get an insurer to pay up than sue your neighbour.

Hedges

If your neighbour's evergreen or semi-evergreen hedge is more than two metres high and is blocking out light you can complain to the local authority. You can prune but you can't cut down. The local authority will expect you to have discussed the matter with your neighbour and may charge you a large fee to consider the matter and both you and your neighbour can appeal. You will need to take advice from a solicitor if you cannot find a resolution with your neighbour and don't want to pay the authority.

Children

If your neighbours' kids throw a ball over the fence give it back or let them collect it. There just really is no good reason to keep it. You have my full permission to do what we do though and refuse unless we hear a "Please" and "Thank you". If something they have thrown over the fence causes damage you are entitled to financial compensation.

If you have bought a house where there are clearly going to be children around as neighbours, then you need to live with their noise. If it is incredibly bad and stopping you from going out in your garden then speak to your neighbours and perhaps use a mediation service. Children being children do not break any laws.

If a child has caused damage to your property and they were old enough to know what they were doing the child can be sued! But no court would look favourably at that and how would a child pay anyway?! But if a parent or carer is shown to be negligent by allowing their child to play with something that was not suitable for their age and likely to cause damage, like an air pistol, then the parent/carer could be liable for damages.

Parking

You do not have automatic rights to any particular parking space unless you have residents' parking. You do have a right of access to your drive and if it is shared with your neighbour(s) then all of you have a right to access and none of you should block access. Both the local authority and the police have the right to remove vehicles that are illegally parked, causing an obstruction on the highway, or which are abandoned, so you can contact either and ask them to deal with the matter.

22 FREEDOM OF INFORMATION REQUESTS

This could perhaps have gone in the tips section of the book, but I thought it deserved a chapter on its own as it can be used to help any complaint you may have. Freedom of Information Requests can be made of any public body:

- government departments, and other public bodies and committees
- local councils
- schools, colleges and universities
- health trusts, hospitals and doctors' surgeries
- publicly owned companies
- publicly funded museums
- the police

For example, you may want to contact your college regarding any complaints it has received about one of its courses in the previous year to back up a complaint about non improvement. The Parliamentary expenses scandal of 2010 broke because of Freedom of Information requests – used well they can be powerful.

Public bodies must respond within 20 working days. There are exceptions to providing information. Some sensitive information isn't available to members of the public. If this applies, the organisation must tell you why they can't give you some or all of the information you requested or it might ask you to be more specific so they can provide just the information you need.

An organisation can also refuse your Freedom of Information (FOI) request if it will cost more than £450 (£600 for central government) to find and extract the information. That includes administration time. If you have more than one question send them as separate requests.

If the body has not sent you their response within the 20 working days you can report it to the Information Commissioner's Office.

Tips on asking for information

1) Don't ask for qualitative information e.g. why did the organisation make a decision? You would need to ask for copies of minutes of meetings regarding xyz and then see for yourself how the decision was made.

2) Keep a note of the date you asked the FOI. Chase on the 21st working day indicating that you will report the matter to the ICO if you haven't had a reply.

3) When you email an FOI you should receive an email saying that your email has been received, if you do not receive this, follow up to ensure that it has been received and get a reference number.

4) When you receive your confirmation, keep their reference number – should you need to follow up if you haven't had a response then you will need this.

5) Check the public body's website for the information, if the information is available and online the public body will send you a link. It is not obliged to answer detailed questions or post you the information if it is readily available.

6) Follow the complaint procedure if you do not agree with a decision not to provide you with the information. This will mean using the internal complaints procedure explaining clearly your arguments for why you don't agree. If you remain dissatisfied you can take the matter to the ICO.

Real examples of FOIs I have made

CCTV parking offences. A couple of years ago I asked how much money was generated from the car in our borough which sits at the end of a road and "catches" people turning left. (Which in my humble opinion is utterly pointless – if they turn right they can turn right again instantly and turn round in the short in/out road to a car park causing more disturbance to pedestrians than turning left). I was given piles of information! Some I wasn't given because the work was up for tender and therefore deemed as "sensitive". It was an incredibly high amount which more than paid for the staff and vehicles. Unfortunately this was before discussions and rulings about CCTV being income generating…

Police. Last year someone was putting stickers on keyholes giving the number of a locksmith. This number was unobtainable. Stories about this happening in other boroughs had been in the media over the previous year or so. The story went that burglars were putting on these stickers and if in the following one or two days they were still up then the house was empty and could be burgled. The local paper ran this story, Facebook posts were shared all over the place and a head teacher of at least one school sent this warning home. People were very worried about a rise in crime and violence with these robberies.

I emailed our local police. Firstly I asked if there was truth in this story and if so what they were doing about it and why they weren't warning residents. I was told that actually there was no truth in the story whatsoever. A neighbourhood police officer had actually caught someone putting the stickers on doors and confiscated the roll to prompt that person's boss to 'phone the police officer. He duly did so. This was a new company who thought that this was a good idea to drum up business… before their 'phone lines were in use. I don't suppose I need to state my opinion on that!

However, people seemed certain that they were hearing of far more burglaries than the previous year so I asked some FOIs regarding the number of burglaries in the previous 8 weeks and for the same period in the previous year, how many were with violence and roughly day or night. There was no increase. Only one case involved violence and that case had other complicating factors. The media and people's perception (perhaps with so much social media activity) was unfounded. I was therefore able to share all the facts on Facebook local area group pages, on my page etc., and alleviate some fears. The local paper never printed the correct story despite requests by the police. So an answer to an FOI can also stop you sending in a complaint if it gives you different/more information.

Department of Work and Pensions. I am unfortunate enough to have Iain Duncan Smith as my MP. Luckily I have never had to meet him to ask him to help me with anything. However, I took it upon myself to challenge him regarding food banks, cost of living and ATOS. I went twice and recorded the events. The write ups can be found on my blog www.thecomplainingcow.co.uk and the clips on my YouTube channel Helen Dewdney. I asked various questions of the DWP, some I forwarded to activists, and others I shared on my Facebook page, such as the number of verbal and physical threats made to staff.

Council. I asked for details regarding the number of complaints about refuse collection.

This supported my own complaint that the contract was not being managed properly and so when the contract officer was utterly useless in responding to me about my complaint and did not get my refuse collected when she said she would, twice, I escalated the complaint with the added information. I hope that this helped the changes I was told were going to be made to the contract.

23 LOCAL AUTHORITIES

You cannot just withhold some of your council tax. You can complain though!

Look online for the department to which you want to complain. (Or phone the switchboard or look in the library). Write to the person who you believe will be dealing with your complaint or simply address it to the Director of the department, which should at least ensure it goes to the right person.

If you are not satisfied with a service you have received from a local authority department request (or access from the authority website) a copy of their Citizen's Charter covering the local authority or the department you are complaining about. Generally these cover the authority's commitment to quality standards covering such things as how many rings before a telephone is answered, response times for emails, performance indicators etc. Refer to these statements and how they have been broken if necessary.

See also chapter 27 *Freedom of Information* for how these requests can assist you in a complaint.

Ask for the complaints procedure for the department/council and follow it if you remain unhappy with the service you are receiving.

You can also write to the CEO. When I worked in a local authority complaints sent to the CEO were known as "perils" and had to be dealt with within a quicker timescale than complaints to departments. Not having worked in every local authority in the country I do not know if this will always work but it's worth a try!

You can also contact your local councillor or portfolio holder for the service. E.g. the portfolio holder for Education. See chapter 20 *Council Parking Tickets* for example of mentioning a portfolio holder.

You can also contact your MP. How good your MP is of course will determine how effective this is. I know of people who have found their MP to be very helpful in getting an issue moving and resolved and others whose MP is utterly useless. This doesn't depend on what political persuasion they are either, it is simply pot luck. You can contact your MP by correspondence and/or book a surgery. Have a look at my YouTube channel and blog to see what luck I have with my MP!

You can also contact the Local Government Ombudsman. (LGO). It looks at complaints about councils and some other authorities and organisations, such as education admissions, appeal panels and adult social care providers (such as care homes and home care providers). It is free to use and covers the following:

- Housing (but only some topics as some are dealt with by the Housing or Property Ombudsman)
- Planning
- Education
- Social care
- Housing benefit
- Council tax
- Transport and highways
- Environment and waste
- Neighbour nuisance and antisocial behaviour
- Privately arranged adult social care

It can carry out joint investigations with the Parliamentary and Health Service Ombudsman (e.g. complaints about councils' social services departments and the NHS) and with the Housing Ombudsman Service.

The LGO can decide that you should receive an apology; be provided with a service you should have had; force an authority to take action or make a decision that it should have done before; reconsider a decision that it did not take properly in the first place; improve its procedures so that similar problems do not happen again to you or anyone else; make a payment, including reimbursing costs or losses you may have been caused.

When complaining to any department be clear about the issues and how you want the matter resolved and warn them that you will take the matter to the ombudsman.

24 HEALTH

I am a strong advocate of the NHS, however sometimes things can and do go wrong. Sometimes this is due to cuts in services and not enough staff available, however, this is not always the case and I strongly believe that the need to complain is greatest when it comes to our own or loved ones medical care. People don't always know what they don't know. Complaining about the services received often means that unknown issues can be dealt with and most importantly, at the very least, you will get an apology and people in the future should be prevented from receiving similar treatment.

Generally people are just so pleased to be out of hospital that they simply can't face complaining – they don't see what it will achieve and/or they themselves are recuperating and don't have the energy. The trouble with this though, is that the staff who would be only too happy to try and improve services don't get to know what some of the problems are.

Three years ago when my father was in hospital for 6 weeks his care was, in parts, appalling. He died in hospital and whilst it was obviously a traumatic time for the family I felt I had to do something. I would be a hypocrite if I of all people didn't try to effect some changes in the hospital and I know he of all people would have expected it of me. I sent a 7 page log of failings and a covering two page letter to Patient Advice and Liaison Services (PALS). Whilst I praised the nursing care of some individual staff I pointed out some failings in processes, procedures and care. It is not necessary or appropriate to detail them here, but the family received a 6 page very comprehensive letter from the Divisional Director. All the matters had clearly been investigated and the apologies and condolences from staff we felt were genuine. Most importantly our complaints led to the Director concluding that 8 different issues had or would be addressed. These included sharing the complaints with the ward, reviewing how pain control is managed (including training and reviewing documentation), other specific training, ensuring staff know the procedure on escalation if patient dependency is higher than staffing levels can manage and improving communication on the ward. That must have improved at least some care for future patients.

The NHS Constitution was created to protect the NHS. The Constitution sets out your rights as an NHS patient. These rights cover how patients access health services, the quality of care you'll receive, the treatments and programmes available to you, confidentiality, information and your right to complain if things go wrong. The Constitution is 16 pages and the guidance handbook 146. There are arrangements allowing patients to complain if they are dissatisfied with the services they receive. You have the choice of making a complaint to either the service provider or the body that arranged for that service to be provided. This could be the local Clinical Commissioning Group (CCG) or the NHS Commissioning Board (NHS CB) for primary care services e.g. GP services. If the CCG runs one you can go to the PALS. If you remain unhappy with the local resolution of your complaint, you can ask the Parliamentary and Health Service Ombudsman to look into your case.

The NHS Constitution explains your rights when it comes to making a complaint. You have the right to:
● have your complaint dealt with efficiently, and properly investigated
● know the outcome of any investigation into your complaint
● take your complaint to the independent Parliamentary and Health Service Ombudsman if you're not satisfied with the way the NHS has dealt with your complaint
● make a claim for judicial review if you think you've been directly affected by an unlawful act or decision of an NHS body
● receive compensation if you've been harmed

Firstly try to resolve the complaint informally, discussing the matter with your health care professional or the organisation or the body which buys or commissions the service. For hospital treatment, this is a clinical commissioning group and in the case of GP services it is NHS England. If it's another service, you can find out who commissions it by contacting NHS Choices. This is called a local resolution.

You should complain within 12 months and your complaint should be acknowledged within 3 days. In this acknowledgement they should tell you how the complaint will be investigated and likely timescales (for which there are no limits) for the response. Your local Healthwatch and NHS Complaints advocacy can help you make your complaint. PALS can provide help and guidance and help resolve some less serious complaints.

If your complaint crosses more than one organisation or department you should only need to write to one which should work with the other to resolve your complaint.

Parliamentary and Health Service Ombudsman

If you are not satisfied with the response to your complaint you can take the matter to the Parliamentary and Health Service Ombudsman. If your complaint is upheld the organisation can be asked to apologise and provide an explanation of what went wrong. It can also call for changes to prevent the same issue(s) happening again or for a review of procedures.

It can also order financial compensation although this is usually lower than a court could award. Therefore, if the amount of financial compensation you're looking for is high, you might have to take legal action.

If you remain unhappy with the decision you can refer the matter to a special team which will investigate complaints about the Parliamentary and Health Service Ombudsman. You will need to contact the office.

Organisations which can help with complaints

Action against Medical Accidents (AvMA) is a charity works for patient safety and justice. Its team of medically and legally trained caseworkers provides free and confidential advice following a medical accident.

The Patients Association is a national healthcare charity that highlights patients' concerns and needs. They give advice to help people get the best out of their healthcare and advise on where to get more information and advice.

Action on Elder Abuse (AEA) is a specialist charity which works to protect, and prevent the abuse of, vulnerable older adults.

Age UK provides guidance about your NHS rights and what should happen when you're discharged from hospital. It also provides advice if you're being discriminated against because of your age.

Mind provides advice and support to empower anyone experiencing a mental health problem and can advise on complaining about NHS services. (Northern Ireland Association for Mental Health and Scottish Association for Mental Health).

Young Minds provides information and advice for anyone concerned about the mental health of a child or young person.

Carers UK supports carers, including those caring for people with mental health issues, through providing information, advice and support and by campaigning for change.

Patient Opinion is an independent organisation which you can contact to share your experiences both good and bad about services you have received. After filling out a form, Patient Opinion will publish it if you wish on the website and will contact the relevant people to respond to you. I have had a look round this site and seen a mixture of praise and complaint. There is also a mix of kinds of response. Some PALS respond to every complaint with details on how to contact them. Others give details of the changes they have made thanks to the suggestions made.

Care Quality Commission

(CQC) is the independent regulator for health and social care services. They are responsible for monitoring and inspecting all hospitals both NHS and private, GP practices, dentists, community health services, care homes and agencies that provide care to people in their own homes. The CQC doesn't investigate complaints but does want to know about people's experiences which helps build a picture of what and when to inspect.

Dentists

In the first instance you should complain to the dentist or practice manager or if you prefer you can contact the NHS in your region. An NHS dentist will follow the NHS complaints procedures and private dentists will follow their own procedures. If you are unhappy with this you can contact the Dental Complaints Service which is made up of a team of trained advisors who aim to help private dental patients and dental professionals settle complaints about private dental care fairly and efficiently. It provides a free and impartial service funded by the General Dental Council (GDC), the organisation that regulates dental professionals in the UK.

Dentists are covered by the Consumer Rights Act 2015 (Supply of Goods and Services Act 1982 prior to 1st October 2015) so you should expect services to be carried out with reasonable skill and care. See chapter 19, *Other Services*.

The GDC will act if a dental professional's ability, behaviour or health means it's not suitable for them to continue working. If you are not satisfied with the response you can contact the Parliamentary and Health Service Ombudsman.

Opticians

Opticians are covered by the Consumer Rights Act 2015 (Supply of Goods and Services Act 1982 prior to 1st October 2015) so you should expect services to be carried out with reasonable skill and care. See chapter 19, *Other Services* for more help about complaining about services.

In the first instance you should complain to the optician or practice manager and give them a chance to put the matter right, such as providing replacement glasses.

The Optical Consumer Complaints Service (OCCS) is an independent and free mediation service for consumers (patients) of optical care and the professionals providing that care. The service is funded by the General Optical Council (GOC) who regulate opticians, optometrists and dispensing opticians.

You can report the optician to the GOC if you are not satisfied with the optician's response. The GOC will investigate your complaint and provide a solution through its mediation services. This may be a refund, replacement or repeat procedure, an apology or explanation of what has happened and why.

25 SMALL CLAIMS COURT

You may consider using an alternative dispute resolution service before taking someone to the Small Claims Court. See the section on *Alternative Dispute Resolution* in chapter 4 *Ensuring Your Complaints Are Effective.*

If you cannot resolve the matter with the trader and no trade association, ombudsman or mediation has helped – then when all else fails and you can't get the money you are owed you may choose to go to the Small Claims Court. You have up to 6 years from purchase to do this. There isn't actually a Small Claims Court. It is the County Court through which a simple shorter process is available. Usually hearings last less than a day.

There are different processes in Scotland (where you can claim for up to £3,000 or up to £5,000 depending on case) and Northern Ireland £3,000.

You must try and resolve the matter before applying to the court. The court will expect you to have done this and given the defendant warning about going to court if a satisfactory response is not received within a set time. This is called a "Letter before action" which needs to state the facts – that there is money owed, why it is owed and how much is owed. The demand, with a reasonable period (usually 14 days is sufficient for the debt to be repaid), needs to state that if acknowledgment or reply is not received within 14 days, then proceedings will be prepared and issued.

If you purchase an item or service within the EU and you have tried the advice already given in this book without success, you can go to court. If for example you want to take a retailer in Italy to court you will need to follow Italy's small claims court procedure. Go to the Justice Europa site (see chapter 27 *Useful Contacts*) for advice and procedure for each state.

TEMPLATE: **Letter before action**

Dear [***xxx***]

Letter before action

On the [***date***] I wrote to you regarding [***detail issue(s)***]. I informed you of what I would accept as a satisfactory resolution and you have failed to provide this.

Should I not receive the payment within 14 days I will issue a summons against you in the County Court with no further reference to you.

Yours [***sincerely/faithfully***]

What to consider before using the Small Claims Court

1) It takes ages. From start to court hearing is usually about 6 months. The process is relatively simple but not always completely clear, and changes, so don't be caught out if you have been through the process before and read through all the information about all the stages and possible outcomes. It takes 6 months because there is time between all the stages of different paperwork

2) If you are thinking of taking a large organisation like Tesco to court as I did, the chances of you being paid when you win are of course high. I really wanted to not be paid in time so I could send the bailiffs in and I didn't get paid but it was just the usual poor internal communication. But seriously, if you take a rip off builder to court for example, consider the chances of being paid, the potential further costs of enforcing the judgement, and the builder going bankrupt.

3) Whether you can take on further stress knowing that the whole process will take 6 months and a fair bit of your time putting evidence together and undertaking the court paperwork. (I did not find the court paperwork cumbersome but putting evidence together can be).

4) The likelihood of winning.

Fees

You can go through the small claims track process for amounts up to £10,000. Over £10,000 the case can still go through the small claims process but if you as a claimant lose you may have to pay the defendant's costs. Claims for personal injury must be under £1,000. It also needs to be less than £1,000 when a tenant is claiming against their landlord because they want repairs or other work undertaken on the property and those works are less than £1,000. In Scotland and Northern Ireland, the Small Claims Court cannot be used to claim personal injury compensation at all. If you're filing a personal injury claim in Scotland or Northern Ireland, contact a solicitor for advice on how to begin proceedings.

You may be exempt from paying fees if you are on a low income but there is a long form to fill out to discover if you are eligible.

Using Money Claim Online (MCOL) is cheaper and I would recommend you use it. You can still 'phone the court for advice (administrative) and when I have done so I have found them really helpful.

Claim amount	Sending form to court centre	Using Money Claim Online
Up to £300	£35	£25
£300.01 to £500	£50	£35
£500.01 to £1,000	£70	£60
£1,000.01 to £1,500	£80	£70
£1,500.01 to £3,000	£115	£105
£3,000.01 to £5,000	£205	£185
£5,000.01 to £10,000	£455	£410
£10,000.01 to £100,000	5% of the value of the claim	4.5% of value of the claim
£100,000.01 to £200,000	5% of the value of the claim	N/a
More than £200,000	£10,000	N/a

If you don't know the claim amount choose the range for the amount you're claiming.

Claim amount	Fee
Up to £10,000	£500
£10,000 to £25,000	£1,250
More than £25,000	£10,000

Fees correct as of August 2017

Process

When you apply online all the details you need are on the website, but these are the very basics. You fill out a form from your local court but ideally online. Here you fill out all the details of the claim and contact details. One you keep and one is sent to the defendant. If it is complicated seek legal advice (Citizens Advice is free). You can also claim interest at 8%. The court sends a copy to the defendant.

The defendant can accept the claim and pay you, or they can make an offer of how to pay. You can accept this offer and if the defendant doesn't pay you can take further legal action to enforce payment. If you do not accept the offer you will need to give your reasons and a court official will decide what is reasonable and will send both of you an order for payment ('judgment for claimant after determination'). If you are not happy with this decision you can write to the court giving your reasons. A judge will make a final decision and if the defendant does not keep to this arrangement you can take enforcement action.

If the defendant chooses to defend the case, they must respond within 14 days. A questionnaire is then sent to both parties. The parties will at this stage indicate whether they wish to try small claims mediation. Once all Direction Questionnaires are received the file is then referred to the District Judge for allocation. If parties have indicated that they wish to try mediation the District Judge will list the case for hearing for a date in the future and refer to mediation. If mediation is successful then the hearing will be cancelled, if not then the Claimant would pay the hearing fee 14 days before the hearing and the hearing will take place.

If mediation is successful then the Claimant would not get the issue fee back as this is for the issue of the claim and allocation, The fees that have been paid by the Claimant should be taken into account when accepting a settlement sum from the Defendant.

A date and time is set for the hearing. Evidence is exchanged between the parties at least 14 days before the court hearing date.

Sometimes the court will not set a final hearing date at the allocation stage (when both parties are sent questionnaires). It could instead propose that the claim is dealt with without a hearing. If agreed by both parties it could be decided on papers only. The judge could hold a preliminary hearing if the claim requires special directions or where the judge feels that one party has no real prospect of succeeding and wants to sort out the claim as soon as possible to save everyone time and expense – or if the papers do not show any reasonable grounds for bringing the claim. A preliminary hearing, therefore, could become a final hearing where the matter is decided.

If the defendant doesn't respond within the 14 days the judge can decide the case.

If the judge finds in your favour the judge will provide reasons for the decision. You will win your court costs.

If the defendant does not pay you can enforce the judgement. You have four choices:

Bailiffs for which you will pay another fee and fill out a "Warrant of control form". The bailiff will attend the defendant's property within 7 days and see if there are goods that can be sold. The defendant can make an offer to pay in instalments which you can agree or reject. If you reject you will return to court for the judge to determine repayment. You can add further costs for attending this hearing from the defendant.

Get money deducted from wages for which you will need to fill out a form to request that the defendant's employer takes money from their wages to pay the debt – an "Attachment of earnings order".

Freeze assets or money in an account for which you will need to fill out a "Third party debt order" so that assets in the defendant's bank or building society are frozen and the court will decide if the money can be used to pay the debt.

Charge the person's land or property. You can ask the court to charge the defendant's or company's land or property for which you will need to fill out a "Charging order". If the land or property is sold, the defendant must pay this charge before they get their money.

At the court and on the Government website you will find all the necessary forms and details of the process and details of the various possible outcomes and charges for different enforcements.

Tips for preparing and being in court

1) Sue the right person, check you have the registered not just the trading name for example
2) Read everything the court sends you carefully
3) When using appendices (I had numerous in the Tesco case) number them and refer to each piece by the number in the explanation in order. Make it easy for the judge.
4) Clearly demonstrate how the law has been broken e.g. "The photo of item in appendix x shows described fault."
5) Use good English and get someone to check it if you are unsure.
6) Check deadlines for court processes.
7) Check and double check your paperwork and, unless you are absolutely sure it makes perfect sense, get someone to check through for you.
8) Be objective don't use any emotive language.
9) Be polite and precise.
10) When at court be respectful and allow for them running late.
11) Don't forget to claim for court fees and any out of pocket expenses for going to court and to provide receipts for these.

I have been through the Small Claims Court process 3 times.

Real example of taking an employer through the Small Claims Court

About 25 years ago I was a sales representative for about 2 months. Hated it and not being money motivated wasn't that interested in hard selling to make commission. We agreed that I would leave! However, this was the day before pay day. I was paid a weekly salary plus commission. One company had not paid up on the sale I had made. I was not paid anything because the contract stated that I would not be paid anything if a company with which I had made a sale owed money. I believed that this broke the Unfair Contract Terms Act 1977 and took them to court.

The date was set and a representative from the sales company tried to negotiate with me just before the hearing. I was owed about £250 and he offered about half of this. I refused and I won the full amount. On the last date they had to pay me they still hadn't so I sent in the bailiffs and I got the payment plus the bailiff costs.

Real example of taking Tesco to Small Claims Court

Tesco provide reward vouchers for spending in their shop. More if you use their credit card. Every so often it is double up rewards time. So when toys were in this promotion it was very popular in November!

So, I start my sorry tale back on the 20th November 2012. The system said my required items were in stock, and when I reached the checkout they were not. I emailed and said this was failure of their site. I had cashed in vouchers that if not spent by the 13th December would be lost.

So I spent them. Later I tried numerous times to process my vouchers on £80 worth of items. I got this message "Sorry, we cannot place your order at the moment. We're trying to fix the problem as soon as possible. Please try again later." So fed up was I that I telephoned. That's how annoyed I was. The automated answering message informed me that they had had problems on the site and they were resolved. They were not and as was quite clear from the @Tesco Twitter timeline, problems remained. Whilst waiting to try again on the line the line was cut off. I wasn't even speaking so it wasn't me being rude! So I emailed. I got a response to say that the technical team were looking into it. I emailed back saying there was still a problem and I expected redress as the time spent on the matter amounted to more than any savings from using the vouchers.

I got an email back saying that I would receive a goodwill gesture. Charlotte told me that if I couldn't use the vouchers then I should pay and she would refund on receipt of the voucher codes. So I duly tried again leaving the system for 24 hours. This time it was a different error. It accepted some of the codes. So I just paid for the full amount and emailed Charlotte. This was the 26th November.

Now Tesco had my money. Actually it had the £80 plus £40 of vouchers which doubled up were £80 and those couldn't be used. So I told Charlotte this and the email went unanswered. I forwarded it 2 days later stating that I would go to Trading Standards for breach of the Consumer Protection from Unfair Contract Terms 2008 and the amended Sale of Goods Act 1979 for not honouring a contract. I emailed the following day saying that papers were ready to go the Small Claims Court.

So I wrote to the CEO. He never responded to customers but I thought that there was a slight chance that someone in the Executive Office might see it and save me the time and trouble of going to Trading Standards and the Small Claims Court. But there was no response. So I took to Twitter. @UKTesco offered to help. I just got standard responses, delay tactics and no actual resolution. To cut a long story short, @UKTesco said Charlotte was waiting for the voucher codes. It appeared that she didn't think it appropriate to respond to 3 emails to her to ask me for them. At first I refused, demanding the courtesy of a response. That tweet went ignored. So I said I would do it their way and sent Charlotte the codes. But still no response. I tweeted @UKTesco, the last tweet they sent me said they would get back to me. They didn't.

So for £25 I took Tesco to court. Their defence was non existent. I quote Tesco. "That the claimant has been unable to use the vouchers is neither accepted nor denied""The Defendant has no knowledge of any problems with these vouchers, as long as the claimant was using the correct process..." Copies of 3 emails saying there were problems, an automated error message on their website and an automated telephone message saying that there was a problem conflicted with this.

A week before the 6th June Tesco attempted to negotiate. At first, they didn't even offer me the court fee! Asked for more and got the court fee and a few quid extra and I thought, it's the principle of the thing, I'm going to court.

Tesco didn't turn up, understandably as that would have cost them more than the money they owed me. The Judge told me that he couldn't see how I was owed any more than the £80 and court fee. "I thought it was important that a single person should make a stand against a big company like Tesco and make people realise that they can stand up to organisations treating customers with contempt" I tried. The judge gave me a big big smile nodded and said "Well done". "I can deem Tesco as being unreasonable and therefore award you £80 refund, £11 for expenses, and £50 for time. Total of £166.

Tesco's cheque didn't arrive, even after 14 days from receiving the letter. It was tempting to send in the bailiffs! I so wanted to do that! But I was worried that the cheque may cross and that I would still have to pay for the bailiffs!! I wrote to the woman at Tesco who said that the cheque would be with me within 14 days. She apologised and said that the cheque had been requested from the accounts department. No evidence or explanation for why it wasn't raised though! But it was requested "again" and I got it 2 days later.

When the court fees went up in April 2014 the Observer covered the story (you can see the details on *www.thecomplainingcow.co.uk*) and I appeared on BBC Breakfast commenting on the court fees rises, the clip of which can be seen on my YouTube channel.

See also *Real example of not paying for repairs and being taken to the Small Claims Court* in chapter 17 *Home Improvements*.

Real example of taking an individual to the Small Claims Court

Jabeen bought a cat from a cat breeder for £300. It didn't work out. Sadly the cat didn't settle and for various valid reasons Jabeen wanted to return the cat. The breeder took the cat back but would not give the money back. I got involved and wrote a couple of emails quoting the Sale and Supply of Goods Act 1994 and we got no response. So we threatened to take her to court and still nothing. So we did it.

Using the Moneyonline service we started the process. We sent the breeder the particulars of the claim:

"I bought a kitten from Mrs M in September 2013. I had been in a lot of contact with her regarding a kitten that would be suitable for my family as I have young children. The kitten she sold to me was not suitable and did not settle with my family. I contacted Mrs M almost immediately and kept her informed as I saw the kitten wasn't settling. I did everything I was advised to do, however the kitten did not settle. She was pooping everywhere and was extremely frightened of my children and would not leave the bathroom. I asked Mrs M for advice and she decided to come and take the kitten back on the tenth day. She offered me a full refund, verbally, when she collected the kitten subject to her rehoming. The kitten was rehomed and when I asked for my refund Mrs M said she would not give me a refund. I will provide the defendant with separate detailed particulars within 14 days after service of the claim form.

Details of claim
Amount claimed
£500.00
Court fee
£35.00
Total amount
£535.00"

(It was £35 as it was prior to the fee rise in April 2014). The £500 included the £300 for the kitten plus £200 for expenses. We then sent her the evidence and she didn't respond. The judge saw in our favour. Mrs M didn't pay up so we sent in the bailiffs. She offered a monthly payment, we said "No" and awaited the court date for the judge to decide a payment schedule. Jabeen had her court date set for the 1st October 2014 when the judge would decide how Mrs M would pay and when.

We started correspondence threatening legal action in 18th December 2013. The form to start court proceedings was submitted on the 5th February 2014. Judgement was passed on the 7th April 2014. By 24th June bailiffs had visited and the new hearing was set for 1st October 2014. Winning in court does not necessarily mean being paid and can add serious time to the matter. On this occasion Mrs M actually turned up at court and Jabeen said she would like all the amount in one go. Mrs M said she would pay by credit card! The judge said "I am sorry but I don't think the claimant has the ability to take a credit card" and dismissed Mrs M's case. She said she had to pay the amount owed and if the cheque bounced or she didn't pay then Jabeen had the right to go back to court and ask for enforcement. On the way out of the court room Mrs M went to the cash point, withdrew the money and gave it to Jabeen. She didn't ask for a receipt!

So, it took over a year to get the money but we did it eventually.

26 SCOTLAND AND NORTHERN IRELAND

Scotland

In Scotland, laws are broadly similar to England and Wales. Cover for buying goods is the same. Prior to 1st October 2015 service is covered by common law rather than the Supply of Goods and Services Act 1982. EU law obviously covers Scotland.

Consumers have up to 5 years, not 6, to make a claim against a retailer for purchases made prior to 1st October 2015. They have 6 years thereafter under the Consumer Rights Act 2015.

Trading Standards and Citizens Advice Bureaux work in the same way.

Where regulatory bodies are different in Scotland this has been described in the relevant chapter.

The Small Claims procedure is through the Sheriff Court. Forms are available from the local sheriff office or from the Scottish Court website. You can claim for up to £5,000 – over this amount you should seek legal advice.

Northern Ireland

Consumer rights are generally the same as in England and Wales. EU law obviously covers Northern Ireland.

Where regulatory bodies are different in Northern Ireland this has been described in the relevant chapter.

Trading Standards and Citizens Advice Bureaux work in the same way. Small Claims court limit is £3,000.

27 USEFUL CONTACTS

Arbitration/Mediation

Civil Mediation Council
The International Dispute Resolution Centre
70 Fleet Street
London
EC4Y 1EU
0207 353 3227
registrar@civilmediation.org
www.civilmediation.org

Ministry of Justice
www.civilmediation.justice.gov.uk/

Law Works
www.lawworks.org.uk/lw_mediation
01483 216 815

Architects

Architects Registration Board
8 Weymouth Street
London
W1W 5BU
020 7580 5861
info@arb.org.uk
www.arb.org.uk

Royal Incorporation of Architects in Scotland
15 Rutland Square
Edinburgh
EH1 2BE
0131 229 7545
info@rias.org.uk
www.rias.org.uk

Royal Society of Ulster Architects
2 Mount Charles Belfast
BT7 1NZ
028 9032 3760
info@rsua.org.uk
www.rsua.org.uk

Communications

CISAS
International Dispute Resolution Centre
70 Fleet Street
London
EC4Y 1EU
020 7520 3827
info@cisas.org.uk
www.cisas.org.uk

The Email Preference Service
www.ims-dm.com/cgi/offemaillist.php

Information Commissioner's Office
Wycliffe House
Water Lane
Wilmslow
Cheshire
SK9 5AF
0303 123 1113

**The Information Commissioner's Office –
Northern Ireland**
3rd Floor
14 Cromac Place,
Belfast
BT7 2JB
028 9027 8757 / 0303 123 1114
ni@ico.org.uk

Ofcom
Riverside House
2a Southwark Bridge Road
London
SE1 9HA
0300 123 3000
www.ofcom.org.uk

Ombudsman Services: Communications
PO Box 730
Warrington
WA4 6WU
0330 440 1614
www.ombudsman-services.org

Telephone Preference Service
DMA House
70 Margaret Street
London
W1W 8SS
0845 070 0707
tps@dma.org.uk www.tpsonline.org.uk/tps

Comparison websites

Billmonitor
www.billmonitor.com

Broadbanchoices
www.broadbandchoices.co.uk

Cableco
www.cable.co.uk/compare/broadband

Energy Helpline
energyhelpline.com

Energylinx
energylinx.co.uk

GoCompare
www.gocompare.com

MoneySupermarket
www.moneysupermarket.com

My Utility Genius
myutilitygenius.co.uk

Runpath
runpathdigital.com

Simplifydigital
www.simplifydigital.co.uk

Simply Switch
simplyswitch.com

Switch Gas and Electric
switchgasandelectric.com

The Energy Shop
TheEnergyShop.com

Unravel It
Unravelit.com

UK Power
UKPower.co.uk

uSwitch
uSwitch Limited
Notcutt House
36 Southwark Bridge Road
London
SE1 9EU
0800 093 06 07
customerservices@uswitch.com
www.uswitch.com

Consumer Advice/Reporting

Brand Information Limited
1 Sylvan Court
Sylvan Way
Basildon
Essex
SS15 6TH
info@brand-i.org
www.brand-i.org

CEO contact details
www.ceoemail.com

Citizens Advice Consumer Service
PO Box 833
Moulten Park
Northampton
NN3 0AN
0208 185 0710
www.adviceguide.org.uk

Northern Ireland
No 'phone or email
www.adviceguide.org.uk/nireland

Scotland
No 'phone or email
www.adviceguide.org.uk/scotland

Wales
03454 04 05 06
Online form for email
www.adviceguide.org.uk/wales

Competition and Markets Authority
Victoria House
37 Southampton Row
London
WC1B 4AD
020 3738 6000
general.enquiries@cma.gsi.gov.uk
www.gov.uk/government/organisations/
competition-and-markets-authority
Sheila.Scobie@cma.gsi.gov.uk (Scotland)
Simon.Harris@cma.gsi.gov.uk (Wales)
Marian.Cree@cma.gsi.gov.uk (Northern Ireland)

Consumer Council (Northern Ireland)
The Consumer Council
116 Holywood Road
Belfast
BT4 1NY
028 9067 2488
info@consumercouncil.org.uk
www.consumercouncil.org.uk

Legal Beagles
www.legalbeagles.info/forums

Money Saving Expert
(Martin Lewis website)
www.moneysavingexpert.com

Resolver
support@resolver.co.uk
www.resolver.co.uk

UK European Consumer Centre
Trading Standards Institute
1 Sylvan Court,
Sylvan Way
Southfields Business Park
Basildon,
Essex
SS15 6TH
01268 886 690
ecc@tsi.org.uk
www.ukecc.net/contact/index.cfm

Which?
www.which.co.uk

Dentists

Dental Complaints Service
Stephenson House
2 Cherry Orchard Road
Croydon
CR0 6BA
020 8253 0800
info@dentalcomplaints.org.uk
www.gdc-uk.org

General Dental Council
37 Wimpole Street
London
W1G 8DQ
020 7167 6000
information@gdc-uk.org
www.gdc-uk.org

Energy

Consumer Council (Northern Ireland)
See Consumer Advice

National Grid
National Grid
Brick Kiln Street
Hinckley
Leicestershire
LE10 0NA
0345 070 0203
www2.nationalgrid.com/uk

Ofgem
London
9 Millbank,
London,
SW1P 3GE
Tel: 020 7901 7000

Glasgow
3rd Floor,
Cornerstone,
107 West Regent Street,
Glasgow,
G2 2BA
0141 331 2678

Cardiff
1 Caspian Point,
Caspian Way,
Cardiff Bay
CF10 4DQ

www.ofgem.gov.uk

Ombudsman Services: Energy
PO Box 730
Warrington
WA4 6WU
0330 440 1624
www.ombudsman-services.org

EU
European Justice
(Information on law in the EU)
e-justice.europa.eu/home.do

EC. Europa
(Passenger Rights in the EU for your mobile device)
ec.europa.eu/transport/passenger-rights/en/index.html

UK European Consumer Centre
See Consumer advice

Finance

Financial Conduct Authority
25 The North Colonnade
Canary Wharf
London
E14 5HS
0800 111 6768
consumer.queries@fca.org.uk

Financial Ombudsman Service
Exchange Tower
London
E14 9SR
0800 023 4 567
0300 123 9 123
www.financial-ombudsman.org.uk

Independent Case Examiner
PO Box 209
Bootle
L20 7WA
0345 606 0777
ice@dwp.gsi.gov.uk
www.gov.uk/government/organisations/independent-case-examiner

Money Advisory Service
enquiries@moneyadviceservice.org.uk
England – 0333 321 3434
Wales – 0300 330 0520
moneyadviser@citizensadvice.org.uk
Scotland – 0808 800 0118
Northern Ireland – 0333 321 2424
www.moneyadviceservice.org.uk

Paypal
Whittaker Ave (Whittaker House)
Richmond upon Thames
London
TW9 1EH
0800 358 7911

Pensions Advisory Service
11 Belgrave Road
London
SW1V 1RB
0300 123 1047
www.pensionsadvisoryservice.org.uk

Pensions Ombudsman
Office of the Pensions Ombudsman
11 Belgrave Road
London
SW1V 1RB
020 7630 2200
enquiries@pensions-ombudsman.org.uk
www.pensions-ombudsman.org.uk

Pensions Regulator
www.thepensionsregulator.gov.uk

TaxAid
304 Linton House
164-180 Union Street
London
SE1 0LH
0345 120 3779
taxaid.org.uk

Tax Help for Older People
Unit 10, Pineapple Business Park
Salway Ash
Bridport
Dorset
DT6 5DB
01308 488066
taxvol@taxvol.org.uk
www.taxvol.org.uk

Tax Office Helplines
Child Benefit 0300 200 3100
Employer 0300 200 3200
Income Tax 0300 200 3300
National Insurance 0300 200 3500
Self Assessment 0300 200 3310
Tax Credit 0345 300 3900
VAT, Excise & Customs 0300 200 3700

Freedom of Information

FOIMan
07799 654509
paul@foiman.com
www.foiman.com

ICO – see Communications

Tribunal Appeal Against ICO Decision
General Regulatory Chamber
PO Box 9300
Leicester
LE1 8DJ
0300 123 4504
grc@hmcts.gsi.gov.uk

Goods

Dispute Resolution Ombudsman
Premier House
1-5 Argyle Way
Stevenage
SG1 2AD
0845 653 2064
info@disputeresolutionombudsman.org
www.disputeresolutionombudsman.org

The Furniture Ombudsman
Premier House
1-5 Argyle Way
Stevenage
SG1 2AD
0845 653 2064
info@thefurnitureombudsman.org
www.thefurnitureombudsman.org

Health

Action against Medical Accidents
Freedman House
Christopher Wren Yard
117 High Street
Croydon
CR0 1QG
0845 123 23 52
www.avma.org.uk

Action on Elder Abuse
PO Box 60001
Streatham
SW16 9BY
080 8808 8141
www.elderabuse.org.uk

Age UK
Tavis House
1-6 Tavistock Square
London
WC1H 9NA
0800 169 6565
www.ageuk.org.uk

Care Quality Commission
CQC National Customer Service Centre
Citygate
Gallowgate
Newcastle upon Tyne
NE1 4PA
03000 616161
www.cqc.org.uk

Carers UK
20 Great Dover Street
London
SE1 4LX
020 7378 4999

Carers Wales
River House
Ynys Bridge Court
Cardiff
CF15 9SS
029 2081 1370

Carers Scotland
The Cottage
21 Pearce Street
Glasgow
G51 3UT
0141 445 3070

Carers Northern Ireland
58 Howard Street
Belfast
BT1 6JP
02890 439 843

advice@carersuk.org
www.carersuk.org/about-us

General Medical Council
3 Hardman Street
Manchester
M3 3AW
www.gmc-uk.org

Mind
15-19 Broadway
Stratford
London
E15 4BQ
020 8519 2122
contact@mind.org.uk
www.mind.org.uk

Mind Cymru
3rd Floor
Quebec House
Castlebridge
5-19 Cowbridge Road East
Cardiff
CF11 9AB
029 2039 5123
contactwales@mind.org.uk

The Patients Association (England/Wales)
PO Box 935
Harrow
Middlesex
HA1 3YJ
020 8423 9111
helpline@patients-association.com
www.patients-association.com

Scotland Patients Association
PO BOX 2817
Glasgow.
G61 9AY
0141 942 0376
contact@scotlandpatients.com
www.scotlandpatients.com

NHS Complaints Advocacy
0300 330 5454
nhscomplaintsadvocacy.org

Northern Ireland Association for Mental Health
info@patientopinion.org.uk
www.patientopinion.org.uk

Patient Opinion (Scotland)
Scion House
Stirling University Innovation Park
Stirling
FK9 4NF
0131 208 1206

Scottish Association for Mental Health
Brunswick House
51 Wilson Street
Glasgow
G1 1UZ
0141 530 1000
enquire@samh.org.uk

Young Minds
Suite 11
Baden Place
Crosby Row
London
SE1 1YW
020 7089 5050
ymenquiries@youngminds.org.uk www.
youngminds.org.uk

Holidays/Flights

ABTA Ltd
30 Park Street
London
SE1 9EQ
020 3117 0599
abta.com

ATOL
Civil Aviation Authority
Gatwick Airport South
West Sussex
RH6 0YR
020 7453 6700
claims@caa.co.uk
www.caa.co.uk

Civil Aviation Authority
CAA House,
45-59 Kingsway
London
WC2B 6TE
01293 567171
infoservices@caa.co.uk
www.caa.co.uk/home

Timeshare Consumers Association Ltd
8-10 Bk Church St
Blackpool
Lancashire
England
FY1 1HP
01253 299753
www.timeshareconsumerassociation.org.uk

Home Improvements

Dispute Resolution Ombudsman
Premier House
1-5 Argyle Way
Stevenage
SG1 2AD
0845 653 2064
info@disputeresolutionombudsman.org
www.disputeresolutionombudsman.org

The Glazing Arbitration Scheme
GGF Consumer Office
54 Ayres Street
London
SE1 1EU
020 7939 9103
conciliation@ggf.org.uk
www.ggf.org.uk

The Glazing Arbitration Scheme
FENSA Consumer Office
54 Ayres Street
London
SE1 1EU
020 7645 3713
complaints@fensa.org.uk
www.fensa.co.uk

Ombudsman Services: Home Insulation & Energy Systems
PO Box 730
Warrington
WA4 6WU
0330 440 1614
www.ombudsman-services.org

Painting and Decorating Association
32 Coton Road
Nuneaton
Warwickshire
CV11 5TW
024 7635 3776
info@paintingdecoratingassociation.co.uk
www.paintingdecoratingassociation.co.uk

Scottish Decorators Federation
Castlecraig Business Park
Players Road
Stirling
FK7 7SH
01786 448838
01786 450541
info@scottishdecorators.co.uk
www.scottishdecorators.co.uk

Mail Order

SHOPS
22–24 King Street
Maidenhead
Berkshire
SL6 1EF
01628 641930
www.shopspromise.com

Opticians

General Optical Council
41 Harley Street
London
W1G 8DJ
020 7580 3898
goc@optical.org
www.optical.org

Optical Consumers Complaints Service
6 Market Square
Bishop's Stortford
Hertfordshire
CM23 3UZ
0844 800 5071
enquiries@opticalcomplaints.co.uk

Post Office

Post Office Customer Care
Freepost
PO Box 740
Barnsley
S73 0ZJ

Property

Federation of Master Builders
David Croft House
25 Ely Place
London
EC1N 6TD
020 7025 2900
www.fmb.org.uk

Housing Ombudsman Service
81 Aldwych
London
WC2B 4HN
0300 111 3000
info@housing-ombudsman.org.uk
www.housing-ombudsman.org.uk

National Association of Estate Agents (NAEA) and ARLA
Arbon House
6 Tournament Court
Edgehill Drive
Warwick
CV34 6LG
0845 250 6009
www.naea.co.uk

National House Building Council
NHBC House Davy Avenue Milton Keynes, Bucks
MK5 8FP
0800 035 6422
www.nhbc.co.uk

Property Ombudsman
Milford House
43-55 Milford Street Wiltshire
SP1 2BP 01722 333306
www.tpos.co.uk

Public Sector

Local Government Ombudsman
PO Box 4771
Coventry
CV4 0EH
0300 061 0614

Ombudsman Northern Ireland
Freepost BEL 1478
Belfast
BT1 6BR
02890 233821
www.ni-ombudsman.org.uk

Parliamentary & Health Ombudsman
Millbank Tower
Millbank
London
SW1P 4QP
0345 015 4033
phso.enquiries@ombudsman.org.uk
www.ombudsman.org.uk

Public Services Ombudsman for Wales
1 Ffordd yr Hen Gae
Pencoed
CF35 5LJ
0300 790 0203
www.ombudsman-wales.org.uk

Scottish Public Services Ombudsman
FREEPOST EH641
Edinburgh
EH3 0BR
0800 377 7330
www.spso.org.uk

Public Transport

Bus Appeals Body (England & Wales)
Terminal House
Shepperton
TW17 8AS
0300 111 0001
enquiries@bususers.org
www.bususers.org

Bus Appeals Body (Scotland)
Hopetoun Gate
8b McDonald Road
Edinburgh
EH7 4LZ
0300 111 0001
enquiries@bususers.org
www.bususers.org/scotland

The Rail Ombudsman
1st Floor
Premier House
Argyle Way
Stevenage
Hertfordshire
SG1 2AD
0330 094 0362
info@railombudsman.org
www.railombudsman.org

Transport Focus
Fleetbank House
2-6 Salisbury Square
London
EC4Y 8JX
0300 123 0860
www.transportfocus.org.uk

Transport for London
0343 222 1234
www.tfl.gov.uk

Removals

The British Association of Removers
Tangent House
62 Exchange Road
Watford
Hertfordshire
WD18 0TG
01923 699 480
www.bar.co.uk

National Guild Of Removers and Storers Limited
PO Box 690
Chesham
Bucks
HP5 1WR
01494 792279
info@ngrs.co.uk
www.ngrs.co.uk/contact-us

Removals Ombudsman
Chess Chambers
2 Broadway Court
Chesham
Bucks
HP5 1EG
01525 850054
ombudsman@removalsombudsman.co.uk
removalsombudsman.co.uk/

Small Claims Court

Money Claim Online
www.moneyclaim.gov.uk

Northern Ireland Courts & Tribunals Service
www.courtsni.gov.uk

Scotland Small Claims
www.scotcourts.gov.uk

Small Court Genie
www.smallclaimscourtgenie.co.uk

Surveyors

Royal Institution of Chartered Surveyors
12 Great George Street (Parliament Square)
London
SW1P 3AD
024 7686 8555
contactrics@rics.org
www.rics.org/uk

Vehicles

BVRLA
River Lodge
Badminton Court
Amersham
HP7 0DD
complaint@bvrla.co.uk
www.bvrla.co.uk

Institute of Automotive Engineer Assessors
High Street
Whitchurch
Buckinghamshire
HP22 4JU
01296 642895
sally@theiaea.org
www.iaea-online.org

The Motor Ombudsman
71 Great Peter Street,
London,
SW1P 2BN
0843 910 9000
www.themotorombudsman.org

Scottish Motor Trade Association Ltd
Palmerston House
10 The Loan
South Queensferry
EH30 9NS
0131 331 5510
www.smta.co.uk

Water

Consumer Council for Water
1st Floor Victoria Square House
Victoria Square
Birmingham
B2 4AJ
0121 345 1000
enquiries@ccwater.org.uk

INDEX

CONSUMER RIGHTS

LIST OF TEMPLATES

LIST OF REAL EXAMPLES

ACKNOWLEDGEMENTS

Sue Blake. My mentor when I was a Programme Manager in a local authority. Often editing my emails to colleagues she once remarked whilst rewriting an email of mine "You are absolutely right in what you are saying about them and the work that they are doing but if you ever want to work in the authority again you better rewrite it like this..." Now, having written this book I wasn't so worried about tact this time! But not even my emails were ever this long, complicated or in need of so much editing and proof reading. Fantastic job as always by someone I'm proud to call a dear friend to whom I am eternally grateful always. Thank you for doing so much editing and proofing especially helping whilst moving house for one edition! Always a star.

Nigel Dewdney for being such a good geek and helping with my website so much and forever sorting me out when I am stupid forgetting simple stuff!

Marcus Williamson for just being a fabulous friend and colleague, editing, proofing, mentoring, advising, putting up with me being ridiculous and never appearing to lose patience! And for still doing this and dealing with billions of my emails several years on! General Saint! ☺

My Mum, Jane (and The Calmer Cat to my Complaining Cow), **Laura**, **Lynn & Pete**, **Catherine**, **Adam & Mel**, **Andrea**, **Joanne**, **Ed**, **John & Mel**, **Jenni & Andy**, **Ben**, **Jabeen**, **Debbie**, **Elaine** and cousin **Tricia** for letting me share our stories. Some names were changed in the making of this book to protect the names of the innocent...not that the others are guilty...!

Marty Dee Donovan for giving me my first and favourite live radio experience at All Hallows Community Radio.

Simon for designing the first covers. Cheers!

Dave at Citizen's Advice Bureau for providing some much needed clarity on the CRA at the time.

Paul at Extrabold (*www.extraboldbooks.com*) for doing such a great job with the typesetting even when he discovered what the "Dewdney" factor involved!

Tesco because if the service was not so utterly diabolical I wouldn't have such good endless material for my blog or gone to court, ultimately gaining enough interest in what I do that encouraged me to write this book.

Wally because he did a lot of helpful stuff!

All those who are always liking, engaging with and sharing my posts on Facebook and who tweet my links to my blog on Twitter and have supported and encouraged me. Far too many to mention and if I started I'd be bound to miss someone.

ABOUT THE AUTHOR

Helen Dewdney is The Complaining Cow. She champions consumer rights through a blog at *www.thecomplainingcow.co.uk*. She has gained recognition for her knowhow in complaining effectively, and appears on BBC Radios 2, 4 and 5 as an Expert, various BBC local radio and community stations, BBC Breakfast, ITV News, The One Show, Rip Off Britain and in national and local press. Helen's background is in children's services and she has no legal training whatsoever, but provides advice through her blog, YouTube channel and social media demonstrating that one does not need to be a legal expert to assert your legal rights. Due to the popularity of the blog and the increased call on her time to help people having difficulty with companies, she has written this book.

To keep up to date with consumer news and free updates to this book please go to **www.thecomplainingcow.co.uk** and sign up to the newsletter.